WINNING TENNIS WITH THE TACTICAL POINT CONTROL SYSTEM

How to Win Tennis Points against Any Opponent

JOHN RUDER

Head Men and Women's Tennis Coach Tabor College. USPTA, WTCA, ITA

WINNING TENNIS WITH THE TACTICAL POINT CONTROL SYSTEM
HOW TO WIN TENNIS POINTS AGAINST ANY OPPONENT

iUniverse books may be ordered through booksellers or by contacting:

iUniverse
1663 Liberty Drive
Bloomington, IN 47403
www.iuniverse.com
1-800-Authors (1-800-288-4677)

ISBN: 978-1-5320-6281-0 (sc)
ISBN: 978-1-5320-6280-3 (e)

Library of Congress Control Number: 2018914507

Print information available on the last page.

iUniverse rev. date: 03/30/2019

Contents

Dedication

To Sandra Faye Ruder, my beautiful and loving wife. She has saved my life from many missteps and poor decisions. I owe her a greater debt than I can ever repay. This book would never have come about without her influence on my life. She is my best friend, my confidant, my sounding board, and most of all, the love of my life.

To Brooke Brantley and her loving husband Daniel and Lance Ruder and his lovely wife Angel, they are my children of whom I am so proud. They have taught me so much. Tennis was a big part of their lives. Brooke was a state champion and earned a tennis scholarship to Southern Nazarene University. Lance was a state quarterfinalist and received a tennis scholarship to Oklahoma Baptist University. Today they have moved on to other pursuits, Brooke as an RN and Lance as a combat medic in the United States Army. Of all my accomplishments, they are my best.

To my darling grandchildren, Harrison Brantley and Natalie Brantley. They both are so full of energy and enthusiasm. Truly, they are the joy of my life. Grandpa could not be prouder.

To my father, Richard Ruder and my late mother, Marie Ruder, who guided me through the early stages of my life. Their prayers have followed me down every road for which I am eternally grateful.

To all my coaches, without whom none of this would have been possible.

To all my players, who have taught me more than all the matches I have ever played and all the books I have ever read. Those lessons are contained in the following pages.

Finally, to my Lord and Savior Jesus Christ, to Father God, and to the Holy Spirit who has guided me on every step of this journey called life. Nothing I have ever done or will ever do could have been possible without them.

Galatians 2:20 (NLT) "My old self has been crucified with Christ. It is no longer I who live, but Christ lives in me. So I live in this earthly body by trusting in the Son of God, who loved me and gave himself for me."

Proverbs 3:6 (NLT) "Seek His will in all you do, and he will show you which path to take."

Foreword

"After 21 years of coaching and ten years of athletic administration, I have discovered that the best coaches possess the ability to teach the details of their sport while at the same time motivating athletes to achieve above and beyond what they believed they were capable. This combination can only be achieved through study, innovation, and creativity. Tabor College Head Tennis Coach John Ruder is one of the best I have been around when it comes to teaching and motivating. This is what sets him apart, and the reason the word excellence is associated with his name." **Rusty Allen - Tabor College Vice-President for Athletics/Athletic Director**

"One of the reasons I was drawn to Tabor College to play tennis was because of Coach Ruder; not only did he convey a depth of knowledge in tennis tactics, but I could also tell that he genuinely cared about each of his players. Coach Ruder's understanding of tennis and care for his players has undoubtedly improved my game as well as the abilities of each of my fellow teammates. It has been an honor to be coached by such a caring and dedicated coach." **Jessica Emoto – Tabor College Tennis Player; 4-time ITA All-American, 4-Time NAIA All-American, 3-Time NAIA Academic All-American; 4-Time Unanimous KCAC First-team All-Conference; 3-Time KCAC Player of the Year; 2017 Tabor College Outstanding Women Athlete; ITA National Arthur Ashe Jr. Sportsmanship and Leadership award winner for NAIA women's tennis.**

As a veteran college tennis coach, I am always looking for ways to give my team a competitive edge. Having coached against Coach Ruder in the same conference, I have seen firsthand the vast improvement his players have made in the areas of mental toughness and tactical point building. Coach Ruder has the great ability to recognize the needs of his players in these areas and take them to the next level, and his unique insight makes this a must read for any coach or player wanting to take the next step towards becoming a champion.

Lonnie Isaac – Sterling College (KS) Head Tennis Coach;17th year of collegiate coaching; 6-time KCAC Coach of the Year

Introduction

Key Thought: *Tennis, not a game for the faint of heart.*

Tennis is the ultimate individual sport and one of the few high school, collegiate, and amateur sports where you must not only keep score but also act as both umpire and referee. At the competitive levels, it is a game of both tension and pressure. It has no time clock, no halftime, no timeouts, and no substitutions. A tennis match can last anywhere from 30 minutes to 4 hours. During that time, you can run over 5 miles and hit well over 1,000 shots. It is just you and your opponent battling it out one-on-one from the first serve until the last point of the match. In the end, both the thrill of victory and the agony of defeat will rest solely upon your shoulders.

Chapter 1
Tactical Point Control

Key Thought: *"It is our choices, that show what we truly are, far more than our abilities."* – J.K. Rowling, British author of the Harry Potter series

The game of tennis is relatively easy to learn but quite challenging to master. To the casual observer, tennis may seem like a simple game where the winner is the player who hits the most balls over the net. Although there is much truth in this assumption, it is but the tip of the tactical iceberg. My goal in the Tactical Point Control System is to delve below the tactical waterline giving you a system of play that can help you make the most of your tennis abilities.

Make Your Brain Your Biggest Weapon
To win tennis matches, you must have an advantage. If your shots are better than your opponent's shots, then shot-making is your advantage. If you are more athletic than your opponent, then athleticism is your advantage. If you can control your emotions and outthink your opponent, then mental toughness is your advantage. If physically you can outlast your opponent, then fitness is your advantage. In every match, the first tactical objective is to discover where you hold an edge over your opponent. However, before you can find this tactical edge, you must first understand your strengths and weaknesses.

This personal awareness of your strengths and weaknesses is precisely what the Tactical Point Control System is all about. It is designed to help you develop a tactical game plan that takes advantage of your strengths while minimizing your weaknesses. When you embrace the TPC System, you will stop playing 'hit and hope' tennis. Instead of just sending ball after ball back over the net hoping your opponent makes a mistake, you will learn to hit every shot with a purpose. The TPC System gives you a game plan that both forces errors from your opponent and sets up more opportunities to hit winners. It teaches you to use your brain as your biggest weapon.

Mastering the Tactical Point Control System will give you the ability to win every time you step on the court. Instead of dwelling on the past or worrying about the future, you will learn to play each point one-shot-at-a-time. Before long, you will start to believe that you can win any point, in any match, against any opponent.

Tactical Key: Talent is important, but how you employ your talent is most important.

Maximizing the Tactical Point Control System
Key Thought: *"When you catch a glimpse of your potential, that's when passion is born."* – Zig Ziglar

Although this book will give you some practical pointers on tennis technique, its primary emphasis is on tennis tactics. There are hundreds of books on the market that can help you improve your shot-making technique, but only a few that will teach you how to build points and win matches. This book is one of those books. However, to get the most from this book, you need to know how to use it. So, as your tennis instructor, let me give you a step-by-step process that will help you to maximize the material presented throughout the rest of this book

Step One: Familiarize yourself with the following fundamental concepts

- The Five Battles found in Chapter 2
- TPC Terminology found in Chapter 3
- The Point-Building Formula found in Chapter 4

Step Two: Take the tennis skill test found in appendix A

The tennis skills test will help you gain an understanding of both the strengths and weaknesses of your tennis game. It will measure the effectiveness of your serve, your groundstrokes, your volleys, and your overheads. To get an accurate measurement, you should take this test on three successive days. Then take your scores from each day of the test and average them together.

Since you want to build points using your strengths, the scores from the skill test will help you determine how you should build tennis points. When you have discovered your strengths, pick out patterns that use combinations of your strongest shots. These patterns should become the primary patterns that you will use approximately eighty percent of the time.

Then, retake the skill test every three to four months to assess your improvement. In practice, experiment with the other patterns as you continually work to strengthen all aspects of your game. As you progress, you will be able to add new point-building patterns to your game plan. Having more patterns will allow you to have both an A and B plan as you enter every match.

Step Three: Learn how to play in each of the four point-building phases.

- First-exchange – Your two-shot patterns for the serve and return *(Chapter 5)*
- Baseline-Rally – Your groundstroke patterns for forcing errors or creating opportunities to attack *(Chapters 7-8-9)*
- Approach-and-Volley – Your plan for finishing points at the net *(Chapter 11)*
- Counterattack-or-defend – Your plan for defending against your opponent's attacks *(Chapter 12)*

Step Four: Use the accompanying drills to practice playing in each of the four point-building phases. *(Chapters 6-10-13)*

The goal of your practice sessions is to advance your game through each of the three learning stages:

- **Cognitive** *(Mental)* **Stage:** In this stage, your focus is on gaining an understanding of how to perform a specific skill. In the cognitive stage, you will use both verbal and visual cues as you guide yourself through the performance. You can also learn by watching other athletes *(in practice or on video)* and yourself *(on video or in a mirror)* as you perform the movements required. The goal of the cognitive stage is to develop a motor program or internal representation of the skill.
- **Associative** *(Practice)* **Stage:** In this stage, your focus moves from simple learning to the performance of the skill with both accuracy and consistency. During the associative stage, the control advances from visual and verbal to proprioceptive control, i.e., the ability to feel the performance of the skill.
- **Autonomous** *(Automatic)* **Stage:** This stage begins when you can perform the skill with a high level of proficiency. In the autonomous stage, performing a skill takes less thought. In this stage, the perfected motor program allows your mind to focus less on the performance of a specific skill and more on the tactics and strategy needed to win points.

Step Five: Develop a playing style.

To develop a solid game plan, you must assess your personality, your physical traits, and your shot-making skills. When you understand your strengths in each of these areas, you can then develop a personal playing style. Once you understand how to play your best tennis, you can begin working on plans for counterattacking the tactics of your opponent. *(Chapter 14)*

Step Six: Develop a game plan for counterattacking each of the four basic playing styles.

Remember, no matter how strong your opponent, they are fully capable of making errors. So, never give up. Throughout the match keep probing to find your opponent's weaknesses. Sometimes you will discover them early, and sometimes you will find them late in the match. *(Chapter 9 and 14)*

Tactical Key: The match is never over until the final point is played. Even if you are down a set or match point, if you can discover a weakness, it is never too late to turn the match around.

Step Seven: Developing a specific game plan for maintaining mental and emotional control throughout an entire tennis match

One of the indescribable joys in tennis is to walk off the court knowing you have defeated a tough opponent by playing at the top of your game. Money cannot buy that feeling of satisfaction. You earn it with your sweat, hard work, and determination. Your technical skills and tactical plan are only two-thirds of the equation. The final third is your mental and emotional toughness. If you fail to train your mind, it will be difficult to play your very best tennis. More importantly, when things are not going your way, it will be impossible to claw your way back into the match. *(Chapter 15)*

Step Eight: Develop an understanding of momentum and how it can be controlled and used to your advantage

Momentum is one of the most potent forces in sport. Unfortunately, young players are rarely taught any method for controlling momentum. Even advanced players often find it difficult if not impossible to manage. If you rely purely on instinct, you might discover a means of control, but all too often the power of momentum is seen as a force over which players have little control.

However, if you understand the six characteristics of momentum, you can find ways to turn momentum into a teammate. When you do, you will have harnessed a skill that has a significant influence on the outcome of every match you will ever play. Do not skip over Chapter 16; it could be the most important chapter in the entire book.

Chapter 1 Summary
Key Thought: *Synergy – the creation of a whole that is greater than the sum of its parts.*

Most players entirely over-rate shot-making. They believe winning is determined solely on a player's ball-striking ability. Players who fall prey to this deception will resort to the 'hit and hope' mentality. They put little thought into their play. Their only strategy is to hit the ball over the net hoping their opponent will make an error.

This kind of thinking is one of the biggest mentality traps in the game. Why do players fall prey to it? Because, for beginning players, this 'hit and hope' tactic actually works. However, as players start to face better competition, their game starts to suffer. Frustration soon sets in as it becomes more difficult to win points by simply keeping shots in play. It seems like no matter how many shots a player can hit over the net; their opponent can always hit one more.

It is my firm conviction that when you master the Tactical Point control System, you will develop a tactical playing style built on a foundation that is much stronger than your shot-making ability. Combining this knowledge with the drills provided throughout this book will give you a system that synergizes your game. The TPC system will make you a strong competitor, possessing both the ability and more importantly the belief that you can win any match against any opponent. And, when you believe you can win, anything is possible!

See you on the court.

Chapter 2
The Five Battles

Key Thought: *"Victorious warriors win first then go to war, while defeated warriors go to war first and then seek to win."* – Sun Tzu

Every opponent you face will bring a different skill set into the tennis match. They will have a preferred playing style and a favorite point-building game plan. If you allow your opponent to impose their game plan upon you, you will lose. Therefore, your primary objective in every match is to impose your game plan upon your opponent. Against a tough opponent, this can be a difficult task. The key is simply this: start out with your primary game plan but as the match progresses and you begin to discover the strengths and weaknesses of your opponent's game be prepared to make adjustments.

You will always know yourself better than you will ever understand any opponent. Thus, you must base your game plan on the strengths of your game. Although you will adjust your tactics, you must never wander too far from your original plan. Straying from your game plan is as dangerous as allowing your opponent to dictate play. Why? For this important reason: it is nearly impossible to defeat a strong opponent by employing your weaker shots or tactics.

It is also important to remember that establishing an advantage is never a one-time event. When facing an intense competitor, you must reestablish your dominance on almost every point. When ahead, you cannot back off or lose your focus. Conversely, when behind, you cannot give up the battle to impose your game plan upon your opponent. At all costs, you must resist the temptation to take wild gambles by turning to low-percentage shots or tactics. Instead, stick with your plan. You give up all hope when you abandon your strengths.

Tactical Key: Going into a match, you must have a tactically sound, well-practiced game plan based on the strengths of your game. As the match unfolds, you must then find a way to impose your strength upon your opponent's weakness. To accomplish this, you need a complete understanding of how you intend to build points during a match.

The Five Battles

Key Thought: *Success never happens by accident. Building your game plan around your strengths is the fundamental goal of the Tactical Point Control System.*

Winning is hard work. You will never succeed unless you are willing to put forth the effort it takes to make winning possible. Part of this hard work is to delve into the essential components of a tennis match. In the Tactical Point Control System, I start by teaching my players that in every match there are five battles. Thus, your first tactical goal is to discover which battles encompass your strengths as well as which battles encompass your weaknesses. When you identify the battles where your greatest strengths lie, you must incorporate them into your strategic game plan. Conversely, you must work hard to improve in the battles in which you are weak. The key is to impose your will or your strengths on your opponent. You cannot win by relying on the battles where you are weak.

Just as importantly, in every match you must also seek out which of the five battles just might represent your opponent's Achilles heel. When you find it, focus your efforts on that battle as it will often hold the key to your victory. This tactic is especially valuable whenever this battle represents one of your strengths.

Of course, your goal is to win as many of the five battles as possible. However, you must remember that you do not have to win them all. The strategic goal is to identify and win the battles where you have the advantage over your opponent. The Tactical Point Control System will help you to identify the battles that can help you turn the tide of the match in your favor.

Battle # 1: The Technical Battle

Key Thought: *What shots have you mastered?*

The first battle is concerned primarily with the fundamentals of shot making. However, I believe that this battle goes far beyond your ability to hit the ball. Most players are quick to blame errors on how they swing the racket. Instead, I believe that most mistakes are a result of three situational mistakes: **1)** Wrong Court Position *(hitting shots that weaken your court position)*; **2)** Wrong Direction *(shot angles that are low percentage or open your court)*, and **3)** Wrong Shot *(being too tentative or too aggressive with your shot selection)*. With these three concepts in mind, I divide the technical aspects of shot-making into four essential components.

- **Anticipation** – Your ability to read the characteristics of the incoming ball *(what you see)*.
- **Shot Direction** – The rally angle on which you will send your shot *(crosscourt, down-the-line, inside-out, inside-in or angle)*.
- **Shot Selection** – The type of shot you will hit *(spin, pace, depth, arc)*
- **Ball Striking** – Your shot-making skills used in sending the ball. *(technical skills)*
- **Recovery** – Your movement back to the correct recovery position after your shot. *(tactical positioning)*

This four-step shot process is a critical aspect of the Tactical Point Control System. I believe that poor shot selection is the explanation for a countless number of missed shots and is an essential ingredient in your understanding of how to manage your errors. Although you cannot eliminate all errors from your game, the shot-selection guidelines and rally patterns found in the Tactical Point Control system can help you achieve an immediate reduction in the number of errors you commit during a match.

Unfortunately, many players base their prospects for winning on the technical battle, and by the time the warm-up is over, they have already calculated their odds of winning or losing the match. Allowing the warm-up to determine your confidence level is a huge mistake. You have probably heard tennis commentators proclaim that a player is an exceptional ball striker. However, you soon realize they are not the player who is winning the match. Why not? The answer is simply this: their opponent's superior tactics are allowing them to use their best shots more effectively.

Tactical Key: Technical skills might make you famous in the warm-up or during practice, but they are not the most crucial battle in a tennis match.

In practice, you must strive to make your game as technically sound as possible. However, you should never base your prospect of winning a match solely on the quality of either your own or your opponent's ball-striking ability. In most matches, it will be the player who understands best how to compete who will win the match.

Battle # 2: The Physical Battle
Key Thought: *How big, how strong, how quick and how fit are you?*

The first component of the physical battle consists of the athleticism you can display during the playing of the point, i.e., your quickness, agility, speed, strength, and power. The second component is your aerobic capacity or fitness. Your aerobic capacity serves two essential functions. First, it is your aerobic capacity that determines how quickly you can recover physically between points. Secondly, your aerobic fitness will determine how well you can execute your shots and game plan during long points, long games, long sets, and long matches. I believe that physical fitness is a key element in the development of mental toughness.

Can the physical battle neutralize a superior opponent? Yes! However, to make the physical battle a determining factor, you must be willing to build your game plan around three key physical components:

- **Body Type:** Are you tall or short, thin or thick? Your physical size can provide you with both advantages and disadvantages. Typically, larger players have more power, but fewer movement skills; whereas, smaller players have less power, but more movement skills.
- **Natural Athleticism:** How strong, quick, and skilled are you? Athleticism is comprised of six key components: agility, coordination, balance, power, flexibility, and strength. Loosely defined it is the ability to execute tennis skills efficiently with both consistency and power.
- **Physical Conditioning:** Of these three, your physical conditioning is of primary importance as it is the only one over which you have almost complete control. Not only that, proper conditioning will allow you to take advantage of your body type, and it can also improve your athleticism. Believe it or not, your conditioning program can help you outplay a more athletically gifted opponent who is less physically conditioned

As you develop a playing style, it must match up with your physical characteristics. For example, if you are a tall, thick player, you will probably have more success playing short first-strike points *(1-4 shots)* than long, consistent points *(5+ shots)*. Conversely, if you are a short, thin player, you will usually have more success developing a playing style that incorporates the long, consistent points of five or more shots. There are many variations, but your playing style must fit with your physical characteristics.

Tactical Key: If you are physically fit and can maintain a never-give-up attitude throughout a point, you can turn any match into a physical contest and by doing so, always give yourself the opportunity to win.

Battle # 3: The Mental/Emotional Battle
Key Thought: *Are you mentally and emotionally stable?*

The third battle occurs between points. This battle is all about how you think. The mental/emotional battle is about imposing your will upon your opponent, while at the same time, resisting every attempt by your opponent to impose their will upon you. Simply put, the mental/emotional battle is about how well you can handle the pressure of the match.

Often this part of the game is referred to as mental toughness. I agree with this assumption; however, to understand mental toughness, you must first dispel the common myth that mental toughness means the absence pressure. If you embrace this fallacy, you are dooming yourself to failure. You may have heard this quote from Dan Rather, "Courage is being afraid, but going on anyhow." This quote describes the truth about pressure. Every player must deal with the pressure to perform. In fact, because of their higher expectations, the top players often face even greater pressure than their opponents.

Going into a match, you have two choices when it comes to pressure: **1)** Believe that no matter how tough the battle, you can find a way forward, or **2)** Reduce your expectations by giving yourself plenty of reasons or excuses to give up. Fighting on will most likely increase the pressure, but it also gives you a chance to succeed. On the other hand, excuse making and giving up will reduce the pressure, making you feel more comfortable. However, it will also cost you the opportunity to play your best tennis. You need pressure to reach your tennis potential. So, instead of trying to eliminate it, you must learn how to allow pressure to push your performance to an even higher level.

Tactical Key: Every player wants to play well under pressure; however, few players are willing to face pressure in practice. You must decide whether success is more important than comfort.

Battle # 4: The Tactical Battle
Key Thought: *Can you execute your game plan?*

The fourth battle is all about what you do to build a tennis point. Your success in the tactical battle is dependent on two components. First, you must find and execute shot patterns that allow you to use one or more of your strengths against one or more of your opponent's weaknesses. Secondly, you must also be able to counter your opponent's attacks with shot patterns that effectively neutralize or even take advantage of your opponent's attack.

Depending on your technical, physical, and mental strengths, there are two ways to win the tactical battle. The first is by playing aggressive, first-strike points that put your opponent immediately on the defensive. You will find that first-strike points are most effective if you are a power player with a big serve or return followed by a second shot attack. For power baseliners, this second shot will be an attacking groundstroke. However, for aggressive net-rushers, this second shot will be a volley.

The second way is a more conservative approach. It is the style of the consistent or counterpunching baseliner who prefer to play longer points that place more emphasis on the baseline rally. This style of point is preferred by players who look first to neutralize an opponent's advantage, and then launching a counterattack into a weakness or an opening in their opponent's attack.

You can be highly successful with either style of play. For beginning players, the conservative approach is often the most effective. However, at the higher levels of tennis, where most matches are very competitive, the match will end in favor of the player who is able to impose their will upon their opponent. No matter which style you prefer, you must always find ways to employ your game plan or playing style against your opponent.

Tactical Key: At the higher levels of tennis, the old 'hit and hope' method described in chapter 1 will almost always lose out to a player who has developed a more advanced game plan.

The Point-Building Blueprint

- **The First-Exchange Phase** which is composed of the first four shots of the tennis point, the serve and service return followed by the second shot by each player.
- **The Baseline-Rally Phase** which is composed of the groundstroke exchange.
- **The Approach-and-Volley Phase** which occurs when you transition forward to the net.
- **The Pass-or-Lob Phase** which occurs when your opponent transitions forward to the net.

You will find a detailed explanation of each of the point-building phases in Chapter 4. However, beware of the temptation to focus too much of your attention on the technical or the tactical battles. As you move up the tennis ladder, you will soon discover that it is often the other three battles which ultimately determines the outcome of the match.

Battle Five: The Momentum Battle
Key Thought: *Are you aware of the match situation?*

Match momentum can be compared to a mental tug-a-war. It is the most awesome and most feared power in sports. Momentum can be your best friend, and it can also be your worst enemy. When momentum is for you, it feels like you can do no wrong. You are dictating the points, the ball seems as big as a volleyball, and your energy level is high. Tennis is fun, and you are in love with the game.

However, when momentum turns against you, it seems like your game just packed up and went on vacation. You have trouble keeping the ball on the court. Every point seems to leave you gasping for breath. Your legs feel like lead, and the ball seems to always be just out of your reach. You are frustrated and uncomfortable. Tennis is no longer fun.

When things are really bad, you want to run away. You are looking for a way out. A way to make the pain stop. It feels like everyone is watching your meltdown and you just want to get off the court and hide.

Tactical Key: The confident player sees themselves as a constant and recognizes their opponent's ups and downs; the player who lacks confidence focuses on their ups and downs and believes that their opponent is the constant.

Most players believe that their technical and tactical skills will determine the outcome of a match. Although these battles are indeed significant, momentum is often the determining factor. I divide momentum control into six critical components: **1)** Maintaining a proper respect for your opponent, **2)** Paying attention to the flow of a match; **3)** Remembering that every point is important, **4)** Avoiding mental lapses or let downs, **5)** Controlling the tempo between points, and **6)** Like a distance runner, developing a finishing kick. Of all the skills you can master, the ability to recognize and control the dynamic of match momentum is one of the most important you will ever acquire.

Chapter 2 Summary
Key Thought: *How hard are you willing to fight? More importantly, how hard are you willing to train?*

In this chapter, I have discussed the five prerequisites to the successful implementation of the Tactical Point Control System.

- Mastery of essential shot-making technique
- A high level of physical fitness
- Total focus and control of the mind and emotions
- A tactical game plan for how you will build tennis points
- An understanding of match momentum and how you can influence it

The goal of the Tactical Point Control System is to prepare you to fight through each of the five battles; thus, equipping you for success even against your toughest opponents. If you fail to prepare for any of the five battles, you will leave an open door for an opponent who knows how to spot your weakness and understands how to use it against you.

This said, no matter how hard you train, you will always encounter opponents who will have an advantage in one or more of these areas. The first key to victory is to identify the battles where you have an advantage over your opponent. The second key is to have a plan to capitalize on this advantage. Against some opponents, you might only be able to win one battle, so make it your focus to win it. Sometimes winning that one pivotal battle is all it will take to upset a superior opponent.

Tactical Key: When facing an equal or superior opponent, the match will often go to the player who first recognizes the critical battle, and then moves forward to dominate it.

See you on the court.

Chapter 3
TPC Terminology

Key Thought: *"The single biggest problem in communication is the illusion that it has taken place."* – George Bernard Shaw

When talking tennis, it is imperative that players and coaches use the same terminology. This common terminology makes communication quicker and more efficient. A shared vocabulary allows coach and player to adjust tactics during the limited time that is available on changeovers or between sets. It also allows for quick and effective communication during practice sessions which leaves more time for the players to hit the ball. In this chapter, I will give you a quick overview of the terminology I use in the Tactical Point Control System.

Tactical Key: *"The ability to simplify means to eliminate the unnecessary so that the necessary may speak."* – Hans Hoffmann, an American abstract expressionist painter.

Term # 1: Shot Accountability
Key Thought: *"Competitive sports are played mainly on a five-and-a-half-inch court, the space between your ears."* – Bobby Jones, American golfer, lawyer, and co-founder of the Masters Tournament.

You are responsible for where your shot lands on the opponent's side of the court. Shot accountability is the most significant key to success in tennis. To win a match against an equally skilled opponent, you must be able to hit the ball into a specific target area. Accuracy is critical to building a tennis point. It allows you to utilize your strengths *(offense)* while neutralizing the strengths of your opponent *(defense)*. Practice is where shot accountability is learned; however, it is when you take responsibility for where you send the ball, that it is mastered. Not just occasionally, but every time you hit the ball.

Tactical Key: To successfully implement the Tactical Point Control System, you must accept responsibility for where you are hitting the ball.

Term # 2: Error Management

Key Thought: *How many shots can you keep in play before you become uncomfortable and either go too big or too tentative?*

To win consistently, you must be able to manage your errors. In tennis, there are two types of errors. Forced errors which occur when your opponent pressures you into a mistake, and unforced errors which happen when you miss shots that you should have made. Of the two types of errors, it is your unforced errors that you must work hard to eliminate. It is difficult to win a tennis match when you are giving away free points to your opponent.

Error management consists of two crucial elements: **1)** Using a targeting system for shot placement, and **2)** Choosing to rely on high-percentage shot selections. I will discuss both of these factors in this chapter. However, in this section, I am going to give you my philosophy as to why shot targets are so important. First, you need to understand the definition of a shot target.

Shot Target: A shot target is an exact spot in the court where you want the tennis ball to land. That said, no player, not even the best in the world, can place the ball precisely on their intended target every time. What happens is this: if you aim twenty or thirty shots at a specific target, those shots will form a circular pattern around the perimeter of the target. Better players will land their shots in a tighter circle, but the pattern of shot placement for every player will be circular in nature.

Tactical Key: You must always give your opponent one more opportunity to make an error.

Aim for the lines, and you will lose.

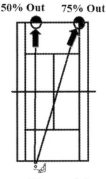

50% Out   75% Out

Diagram 3-1

If you aim for one of the court's boundary lines, whether it be the sideline or the baseline, about fifty percent of your on-target shots will land outside the court. For example, a shot that lands 6-inches inside the line is good, but a shot that lands 6-inches outside the line will be out. However, if your target was the line, both shots landed very close to your intended target which means they were very accurate shots.

If you aim for one of the back corners, your percentages are even worse. Now, seventy-five percent of your accurate shots will land outside the court. If you want to keep more balls in play, you must make sure your target is well inside the boundary lines.

Tactical Key: Aiming consists of two elements: **1)** Choose the target you want to hit, and **2)** Holding the intended target in your mind throughout the hitting motion.

Term # 3: The Three Serving Targets

Key Thought: *You can only win if your serves are in.*

It is essential that you have specific targets for your serve. Getting the serve in the service box is important; however, you will get more serves in play by aiming for smaller and more precise targets inside the service box. Precise targets not only help you get more serves in play, but they also allow you to use your serve as a set-up shot for your next shot.

In the Tactical Point Control System, there are three serving targets in each of the service boxes.

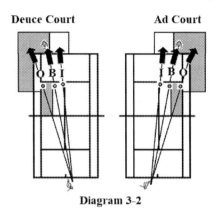

Deuce Court   **Ad Court**

Diagram 3-2

I created the inside and outside targets (**I** *and* **O** *in diagram 3-2*) by drawing an imaginary line down the center of the service box. The third target is the body target (**B** *in diagram 3-2*). The body target is a serve hit through the middle of the service box and aimed directly at the returner's body.

As you can see in *diagram 3-2*, each of the three serves forces the returner into a specific return location. The inside serve will force the returner into the center of the court. The outside serve will force the returner out wide of the singles sideline and the body serve will force the returner into the corner.

Keeping your serves deep in the service box is important, especially on second serves. However, remember to give yourself a safe margin for error. I tell my players to aim their serve so that the ball will land about two feet inside the back, service line. This gives them more room to get their serves into play. The same holds true when aiming your serves into the short corners.

Tactical Key: You should only hit first serves close to the lines. On your second serve, give yourself plenty of margin for error.

Term # 4: The Four Types of Serves
Key Thought: *"There is nothing wrong with change if it is in the right direction."* – Winston Churchill

As a tennis player, you should be working hard to develop four specific types of serves. Why? Because when you can hit multiple types of serves into any of the three serving targets, you can formulate a service attack that will be extremely difficult for your opponent to break.

Serve # 1: The Flat Serve
The flat serve is a serve hit with about eighty-five percent power and only a slight amount of spin. Shorter players often apply additional spin as this helps keep the ball in play. The flat serve should become your reliable first serve; one that you can safely hit into the service box at least seventy-five percent of the time. The key to a successful flat serve is placement and consistency. You should practice placing the flat serve into all three of the service targets. Keep adjusting the pace and spin of your flat serve until you find that perfect mixture of speed and placement which allows you to maintain a success rate of seventy-five to eighty percent. Then use that same combination in your matches.

Tactical Key: Although this is mostly a first-serve option, occasionally you should use the flat serve as your second serve. Using the flat serve as a second serve will make your opponent think twice about moving too far forward to attack your spin serves.

Serve # 2: The Slice Serve

The slice serve is a spin serve hit with side-spin. The side-spin causes a righthanded server's ball to curve to the server's left, the returner's right. A lefthanded server's ball curves to the server's right side and the left side of the returner. Besides curving, the slice serve will also skid off the court with a low bounce that makes for a difficult to return.

A righthanded player uses the slice serve in three ways: **1)** Aimed at the outside target in the deuce court where it will break toward the outside of the court and away from the returner. **2)** Aimed into the body target in the deuce court where the ball will curve into the returner's inside hip, and **3)** Aimed at the inside target in the ad court where it breaks toward the center of the court and away from the returner. The lefthanded server can get the same results by reversing the deuce court and ad court targets.

As your first serve, you should work to get seventy-five to eighty percent of your slice serves in play. On your second serve, the success rate should rise to between eighty to eighty-five percent.

Tactical Key: The lefty advantage is on the ad court side where the lefthanded server can hit their slice serve into a righthanded returner's backhand corner. Righthanded servers have this same advantage against lefthanded returners in the deuce court.

Serve # 3: The Topspin Serve

The topspin serve is a spin serve hit with extreme topspin. You should work to make this serve your most reliable second serve. When used correctly, the topspin will help you keep a high percentage of your second serves in play. The emphasis of the topspin serve is on consistency *(eighty to eighty-five percent)*, depth *(two feet from the back, service line)*, and accurate placement *(into the returner's body or backhand)*. Learn to hit your topspin serve with a high net clearance *(3' to 6')*, trusting the spin to pull the ball down into the service box.

Righthanded servers will aim the topspin serve into the inside target in the deuce court and into the outside target in the ad court. Lefthanded servers will aim it into the outside target in the deuce court and the inside target in the ad court. Both righthanders and lefthanders will also direct the topspin serve into the returner's body.

On second serves, both righthanded and lefthanded servers should direct the ball into their opponent's backhand side where the high topspin bounce makes it a difficult serve to return. In practice, keep track of how you hit your topspin serve until you find the right mixture of spin and pace that allows you to maintain an eighty to eighty-five percent success rate. Then use that same mixture in your matches.

Tactical Key: On your second serve, you should angle your topspin serve into either the returner's body or backhand side. This forces your opponent to use their backhand and will often result in a blocked or sliced return that lands in the center of your court.

Serve # 4: The Power Serve

The power serve is a flat serve hit with heavy pace. Because of its speed, the power serve is difficult to control and is less consistent than the flat serve. To be successful, you must get this serve into play at least seventy percent of the time. Anything under fifty percent is a losing proposition.

When hit with control the pace of the power serve can completely overpower your opponent. If you are a tall player, you have the potential to develop the power serve into a devastating weapon that allows you to pressure your opponent on every first serve. However, for most players, it is best to use the power serve sparingly and as a change-up aimed into the inside or body targets.

In practice, keep track of how often you can get your power serve into play. When you start hitting a percentage that is over fifty percent, you should use it occasionally in matches. If your percentage is above sixty percent, the power serve should become your primary first serve weapon.

Tactical key: Aiming your power serve into the inside target doubles its effectiveness. **1)** Because the distance from the server to the opposite baseline is shorter giving the returner less time to react, and **2)** Because the pace of the power serve further reduces the returner's reaction time.

Term # 5: The Four Target Boxes

Key Thought: *Reducing your number of unforced errors will always be more important than increasing your number of winners.*

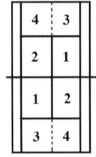

Diagram 3-3

To help my players develop safe or conservative targets, I divide the court into four target boxes. First, I use the two service boxes. We call these our short target boxes. Then I draw an imaginary line from the service T to the baseline hashmark dividing the area behind the service boxes into two additional deep target boxes.

I assign even numbers to the target boxes on the deuce court side and odd numbers to the target boxes on the ad court side. As you can see in *diagram 3-3*, the corresponding numbered boxes will always be diagonal to each other. When employing the target boxes, you will aim most of your groundstrokes into deep targets 3 or 4, and your volleys into short targets 1 or 2.

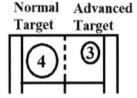

Normal Advanced Target Target

Diagram 3-4

Although I use the lines of the court to outline the target boxes, I teach my players to aim their shots for the exact center of the target box. By aiming for the middle of the target box, you are more likely to keep the ball in play. *(see target-4 in diagram 3-4)*

As you improve or if you need to hit a more aggressive shot, you can move the aim point closer to the sideline. However, I recommend keeping your aim point at least three feet from any of the boundary lines. *(see target 3 in diagram 3-4)* Shots hit closer to the lines must be hit with less power and more control.

Tactical Key: In a match, the temptation to aim for the lines is difficult to resist: First, because you are trying to keep the ball away from your opponent, and second because the lines are always right there in your field of vision. To counter this temptation, you must learn to aim your shots into the center of the target box.

Term # 6: The Four Rally Angles

Key Thought: *Coaches and players must be able to communicate shot direction quickly and effectively during practice and in matches.*

The Four Target Boxes not only give my players a ready-made target for every shot, but they also provide a system for communicating shot patterns to my players. *Diagram 3-5* illustrates the four possible groundstroke rally patterns, and how I would communicate them to my players. You would be the player at the bottom of each diagram.

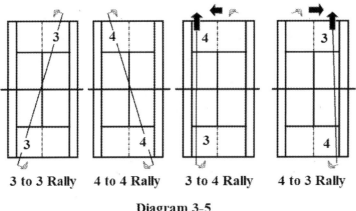

3 to 3 Rally   4 to 4 Rally   3 to 4 Rally   4 to 3 Rally

Diagram 3-5

The Crosscourt Rally Patterns

The **3-to-3** and **4-to-4** rally patterns illustrate a crosscourt-to-crosscourt rally angle. The crosscourt shot is hit over the lowest part of the net and has more room to land in the court making it the highest percentage shot in tennis. Thus, a crosscourt shot is always your safest shot option.

3-to-3 Rally Pattern
The 3-to-3 rally pattern is a crosscourt rally on the ad court side of the court, i.e., shots that are aimed into the center of the 3-Target box. If you are righthanded, this would typically be an outside backhand groundstroke. However, if you choose to run around your backhand, it would be an inside-out forehand.

4-to-4 Rally Pattern
The 4-to-4 rally pattern is also a crosscourt rally, but this time on the deuce court side of the court, i.e., shots are aimed into the center of the 4-Target box. If you are righthanded, this would be an outside forehand groundstroke. Rarely will you run-around your forehand to hit an inside-out backhand, although you might hit an inside-out backhand when the ball is on your backhand side and close to the center of the court.

Tactical Key: Hit most of your shots deep crosscourt or deep through the middle. Keeping the ball deep reduces your chance of making an error and keeps your opponent on the defensive.

The Down-the-Line Switch Patterns
Fundamentally, tennis is a crosscourt game. Switching the direction of the rally from crosscourt to down the line is the lowest percentage shot in tennis. However, when you can contact the ball inside the baseline, it does give you the opportunity to attack your opponent's open court.

Tactical Key: You can multiply the effectiveness of your down-the-line shot by preceding it with a crosscourt angle that forces your opponent outside of their singles sideline.

The down-the-line switch pattern is a high-risk shot. First, you are hitting over the lowest part of the net. Second, the distance to the baseline is shorter than the crosscourt shot giving you less court to land your shot. Finally, changing the angle from crosscourt to down the line will tend to make your shot drift toward the sideline increasing the chances you will hit your shot wide. Thus, the down-the-line switch pattern is your highest-risk option.

3-to-4 Switch Pattern
The 3-to-4 pattern is most often used to switch the rally angle from crosscourt to down-the-line. If you are righthanded, you will usually hit this shot with an outside backhand. If both you and your opponent are righthanded, you will be hitting your backhand into your opponent's forehand side. Although your opponent will have to hit on the move, you will be sending the ball to their stronger groundstroke. Thus, if you are a righty, the 3-to-4 switch pattern will be your highest-risk shot. Occasionally, you might run around your backhand to hit an inside forehand pull-shot down the line. Although you risk opening the court, this can be an effective offensive weapon. If you are a lefty, you will use your outside forehand, which against a righthanded opponent will make the 3-to-4 switch a bit safer.

4-to-3 Switch Pattern
The 4-to-3 pattern is also used to switch the rally angle from crosscourt to down-the-line. If you are righthanded, this will be an outside forehand. Even though the 4-to-3 pattern is a high-risk shot, if both you and your opponent are righthanded, you will be hitting your forehand into your opponent's backhand. Since your opponent's backhand will often be weaker than your forehand, the 4-to-3 switch pattern gives you an offensive advantage. If you are a lefty, you will use your outside backhand. Occasionally, a lefthanded player might run around their backhand to hit an inside forehand pull-shot down the line. Although you risk opening the court, this is a very effective offensive option against a right-handed opponent.

Tactical Key: Since most players will reply to your down-the-line shot by sending their next ball crosscourt, the switch pattern is a great way to change the diagonal rally from one crosscourt angle to the other. Thus, you can use it to set up your strongest groundstroke weapon.

Term # 7: The Tactical Center
Key Thought: *To win you must control the tactical center of the court.*

Controlling the center of the court is the first component of baseline pressure. To accomplish this, you must position yourself at the tactical center of your opponent's next possible shot options. To maintain this court position has two essential requirements.

- You must hit shots that are good for your position. Which means that unless you can put a ball away with a clean winner, you must choose shots that give you time to recover to the tactical center.

- You must be willing to expend the energy necessary to recover after every shot. This factor is a critical element of the physical battle during long rallies and or on points late in the match.

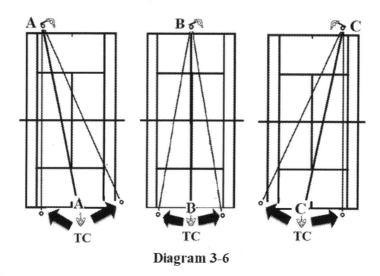

Diagram 3-6

Diagram 3-6 illustrates the appropriate baseline recovery positions based on the location of the ball in your opponent's court.

Position A: When the ball is located at position A, the opponent's deuce court, you will recover to position A on the baseline. This position is approximately two steps to the right of the center hash mark. From position A, any ball hit to your left is an inside shot and any ball hit to your right is an outside shot.

Position B: When the ball is located at position B, the center of your opponent's baseline, you will recover to position B on the baseline. This position is located behind the center hash mark on the baseline. When the ball is in the middle of the court, I consider a ball hit to either side of you as an outside shot.

Position C: When the ball is located at position C, the opponent's ad court side, you will recover to position C on the baseline. This position is approximately two steps to the left of the center hash mark. From position C, any ball hit to your right is an inside shot and any ball hit to your left is an outside shot.

Tactical Key: When you consistently recover to the tactical center, the court appears smaller to your opponent. They see less open court which increases the pressure on their next shot.

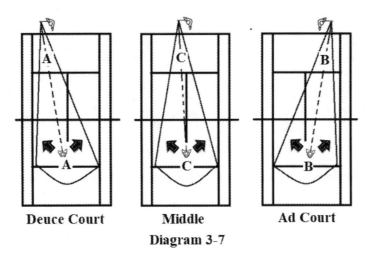

Deuce Court   **Middle**   **Ad Court**

Diagram 3-7

Diagram 3-7 illustrates the appropriate frontcourt recovery positions based on the location of the ball in your opponent's court. When you compare the baseline recovery positions in *diagram 3-6* to the frontcourt recovery positions in *diagram 3-7*, you will see that the tactical center is on the opposite side of the center line.

Position A: When the ball is located at position A, the opponent's deuce court, you will recover to position A. This position is inside the service line and approximately one step to the left of the center service line

Position B: When the ball is located at position B, the center of your opponent's baseline, you will recover to position B. At position B you will be inside the service line and straddling the center service line.

Position C: When the ball is located at position C, the opponent's ad court, you will recover to position C. This position is inside the service line and approximately one step to the right of the center service line.

Tactical Key: In the frontcourt, create pressure with aggressive positioning.

Term # 8: The Three Playing Zones

Key Thought: *The recipe for shot selection is court position.*

In the Tactical Point Control System, I divide each end of the court into three playing zones. As with my four target boxes, I use the permanent lines of the court to mark the boundaries for each zone. It is essential to understand that when referring to a court zone, I am talking about where you strike the ball and not where the ball bounces.

Backcourt Zone: The backcourt zone extends rearward from the baseline to the back fence. This is the building zone where you look to pressure your opponent with your groundstrokes.

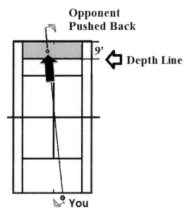

Diagram 3-8

Midcourt Zone: The midcourt zone extends from the baseline forward to the service line. This is the attacking zone where you look to set up an opportunity to end the point. Moving into this zone is a natural result of backcourt pressure.

Frontcourt Zone: The frontcourt zone extends forward from the service line to the net. This is the finishing zone where you look to finish points with your volley or overhead.

Tactical Key: You must adjust your racket swing to your position on the court. The closer you move to the net, the shorter your backswing.

Term # 9: The 9-foot, Depth Line
Key Thought: *Keeping your opponent deep gives you more time to read, react, and recover.*

Depth is the second component of baseline pressure. At the beginning of every point, the player who hits the deepest shot will gain the initial control of the rally. Keeping the ball deep makes it difficult for your opponent to step into the midcourt and attack. If you can play from just inside the baseline, this advantage is even more significant.

Depth Line: To help you visualize depth, imagine there is a line drawn halfway between your opponent's service line and the baseline *(see diagram 3-9).*

Your goal is to hit your rally shots so that they land beyond the depth line *(shaded area in diagram 3-9).* Keeping the ball deep will push your opponent back pinning them in the backcourt zone. Forcing your opponent back behind the baseline has five advantages: **1)** You have more time to read the situation. **2)** You have more time to react to your opponent's next shot. **3)** You have more time to recover to the tactical center after your shot. **4)** Your opponent has fewer angles making it difficult for them to launch an attack against you. **5)** Since your opponent must hit the ball further to keep you behind your baseline, you are more likely to get a short ball which will then allow you to attack.

Tactical Key: Avoid trying to create depth with power. Instead, lift the ball with a higher trajectory over the net.

Term # 10: The 9-foot, Approach Line
Key Thought: *Never pass up an opportunity to get to the net.*

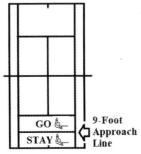

Diagram 3-10

Moving forward into the frontcourt to finish points at the net is a natural result of a forcing baseline game. The question you must answer is simply this: When should I approach?

Approach Line: The 9-foot, approach line is an imaginary line located halfway between your baseline and the service line. When you are behind the approach line, you should hit an attacking shot, but stay back and continue to rally. However, when you are inside of the approach line, you should hit an approach shot and follow it forward to the frontcourt where you can put your opponent's next shot away with a volley.

Tactical Key: Always attack the short ball with a two-shot play, i.e., an approach shot followed by a volley or overhead. Avoid the mistake of always going for an outright winner.

Term # 11: The Three Spins
Key Thought: *When in doubt, spin it in.*

You must avoid becoming your opponent's ball machine. Most opponents feed off consistent speed, spin, and placement. When you send the same kind of ball over and over, you often find the same ball coming back shot after shot. In today's power baseline game, this ball will come back faster and faster and faster. You can challenge your opponent's rhythm and timing by changing the type and amount of spin you apply to the ball.

When you master the three types of spin, you can manipulate three essential variables for every shot: **1) Control** – the ability to keep balls in play. **2) Change of Pace** – the ability to hit with either power or touch. **3) Vary the Strike Zone** – the ability to force your opponent to play from outside of their comfort zone.

Drive Shots: The drive is a shot hit with heavy pace and only a slight amount of topspin. The drive shot is hit low over the net and travels quickly through the court. The speed of the drive shot will challenge your opponent's timing and footwork.

Topspin Shots: The topspin shot can still be hit with pace but uses topspin to pull the ball down into the court. Topspin allows the ball to be hit higher over the net, which reduces your net errors. The ball will also bounce higher. A deep topspin shot forces your opponent to either move back, which pushes them behind the baseline or to hold their position hitting the ball in their higher strike zone.

Slice Shots: The slice is a shot hit with backspin. You can employ the slice in three ways. First, as a change-of-pace shot that floats deep with little pace. I call this a nothing ball. Second, the slice shot can be hit lower over the net with more speed and spin. I call this the chip. The chip will skid and stay low on the bounce forcing your opponent to hit from their low strike zone. Finally, you can use the slice to hit a drop shot that lands short in the court forcing your opponent to rush forward just to get their racket on the ball.

Tactical Key: Remember, your opponent is not a wall. They can miss any shot, at any time, and sometimes for no reason at all. So, make it your goal to always get one more ball back into play.

Term # 12: The Three Arcs
Key Thought: *The net is a more significant obstacle than you may think.*

Although the net is only three feet high at the center of the court and three feet, six inches tall on the singles sideline, it is a formidable obstacle. Just as you avoid aiming for the boundary lines, you must also keep a safe margin for error over the top of the net. Trying to skim the ball low over the net is counterproductive. First, too many of your shots will fail to clear the top of the net, and second, when your shots clear the net, they will tend to land short in the court opening the door for your opponent to move in and attack. Just like the three spins, I teach my players that there are three arcs they must master. I call them the laser, the loop, and the lob.

The Laser: You use the laser when you drive the ball about one to three feet over the top of the net. Laser balls emphasize pace over spin. The laser shot is an attacking shot that can sometimes result in a winner. However, the low trajectory of the laser makes it a low-percentage shot that can also result in an error. Knowing when to employ the laser is an important key to error management.

Tactical Key: The laser is an attacking shot that should only be used when the opportunity to end the point with a winner outweighs the risk of making an error. **1)** When you need to hit a passing shot against an opponent, who is at the net, or **2)** When you are inside the baseline and can contact the ball while it is still above the height of the net.

The Loop: You use the loop when you hit the ball three to eight feet over the top of the net. You can choose to hit the loop shot with either topspin or slice. However, the key is to keep the ball deep. The topspin loop will travel more quickly through the court than the sliced loop which floats slowly toward the opponent's baseline. When hit deep, the loop shot will give you time to recover back to the tactical center.

Tactical Key: The loop is your point-building shot that you should use when you are in a neutral or pressuring position. You can add variety by changing the pace or spin.

The Lob: You use the lob in two situations: **1)** Your opponent is in an aggressive position at the net, and you need to force them back by hitting the ball over their head, or **2)** Your opponent is in the backcourt but has forced you deep behind the baseline, wide of the sideline, or combination of the two. When hitting a lob, you should lift the ball eight or more feet over the top of the net. The amount of arc you put on the ball depends on the situation. If you are only moderately out of position sending your shot on a lower trajectory of 8 to 10 feet will give you time to recover. However, if you are forced well out of position, you will need to lift the ball even higher Aggressive lobs are hit with topspin so that when the ball lands it will kick back toward the fence making it nearly impossible to run down. Defensive lobs are often hit with slice and lifted higher into the air. Just remember, a successful lob must land deep in the opponent's court. Your aim should be to land the ball beyond the 9-foot, depth line *(see term # 9)*.

Tactical Key: When you are in trouble during a point, throw up a defensive shot by aiming high, deep, and crosscourt giving yourself time to recover for your opponent's next shot.

Chapter 3 Summary
Key Thought: *"Words are but pictures of our thoughts."* – John Dryden, English Poet

Every time you hit a shot, you are answering three tactical questions: First, where to send the ball. Second, what kind of shot you should send, and third, where to position after your shot. In chapter 3, I have touched on each of the three tactical questions. Not with the complete answer, but with the tactical vocabulary I use for answering those questions. I call this the TPC terminology.

Throughout the rest of this book, when I use these terms, I hope the picture of what they represent will appear instantly in your mind. You will use the targeting system to decide where to send the ball. The three playing zones, three spins, and three arcs to determine what kind of shot you should hit, and the tactical center to decide where you should position. As you proceed through the following chapters, the importance of this terminology cannot be understated. For us to communicate effectively, we must be using a common vocabulary.

Your first job in building a tactical game plan will be to familiarize yourself with the information found in the first three chapters of this book. If you understand this terminology, you will more readily assimilate the tactics discussed in the following chapters. At this time, you should go back and review these chapters and make sure you have an understanding of these essential concepts. Only then will you be ready to move on to chapter 4 where I will teach you how to build points using the four point-building phases. However, if as you proceed some term seems unclear, you do not have to worry. The first three chapters will still be there for you to go back and review.

See you on the court.

Chapter 4
The Tactical Battle

The Four Point-building Phases
Key Thought: *Meticulous planning will enable everything a man does to appear spontaneous.*
– Mark Caine, American author

Research
The first task in developing the **Tactical Point Control System** was to identify the components that comprise a tennis point. My research led me to five key areas that I believe serve as the framework of a perfect tennis point: **1)** The basic game situations; **2)** The normal progression of a point through each game situation; **3)** Relationship of player court position to game situation; **4)** How points end; and **5)** Average number of shots per point. The following four sections detail the core information I uncovered while conducting my research.

The Basic Game Situations
Research into game situations centered around the eight basic shots that are used when playing a tennis point: **1)** The serve; **2)** The return; **3)** The groundstroke; **4)** The approach; **5)** The volley; **6)** The overhead; **7)** The passing shot; and **8)** The lob.

Next, I divided the eight basic shots into the game situations in which each shot most frequently occurred: **1)** Serving *(starting the point)*, **2)** Returning *(starting the point)*, **3)** Baseline rally *(groundstroke patterns)*, **4)** Transition *(approach/attacking shots)*, **5)** Net play *(volleys and overheads)*, **6)** Counterattacking play *(passing shots and lobs)*.

Point Progression Through the Six Basic Game Situations
After matching the eight basic shots with the six basic game situations, the next step was to map out the natural progression of a point as it advances through each of the six situations.

Using this process, I established the following order of progression: **1)** Serve, **2)** Return, **3)** Baseline Rally, **4)** Transition, **5)** Net Play, and **6)** Counterattack. I also noted a few exceptions to this progression; for example, a serve and volley play that skips over the baseline rally, or a long groundstroke point that concludes with an error or a winner during the baseline rally. However, when you eliminate errors or early winners, a basic tennis point will progress through each of the six game situations as listed above. In the following chapters, I will often refer to such a point as the perfect tennis point.

Relationship of Court Position to Game Situation

In chapter three, I divided each end of the tennis court into three playing zones: **1) Backcourt** – which extends from the baseline back to the back fence, **2) Midcourt** – which extends from the baseline forward to the service line, and **3) Frontcourt** – which extends from the service line forward to the net. *(Turn back to chapter 3 diagram 3-8 to review the three playing zones)*

Next, I placed each of the six basic game situations into the court zones where they would most often occur. Thus, I placed the serve, return, baseline rally, and counterattacking situations in the backcourt zone, the transition situations in the midcourt zone, and the net-play situations in the frontcourt zone. With this information, I determined that the natural progression of a perfect tennis point would be for it to start with a serve and then advance to a finishing shot in the frontcourt.

How Points End

Using standard tennis statistical measurements, I determined that a tennis point can only end in one of three ways:

- **A Forced Error**: which is defined as a point-ending error caused by the quality of the incoming shot.
- **An Unforced Error**: which is defined as a point-ending error made on a shot that the player would typically make.
- **A Winner:** which is defined as a point-ending shot hit completely out of a player's reach.

My research came from two sources. The first source was my high school and collegiate team match charts that recorded not only the score but also whether the point was won or lost by an unforced error, forced error, or a winner. The second source was from the analytics of the ATP and WTA professional tours.

What I discovered was not entirely unexpected. About twenty percent of all tennis points end with a player hitting a winner, twenty percent end with a player committing an unforced error, and approximately sixty-percent of all tennis points end with a player committing a forced error. Thus, at every level of tennis, nearly eighty-percent of all tennis points end not with a winner, but with an error *(forced or unforced errors combined)*.

Average Number of Shots Per Point

My research on the average number of shots per point indicated that on the professional tours the average point length in each of the Grand Slam tournaments is slightly less than four shots per point. Just as importantly, this research also reported that less than 20-percent of all points lasted a total of 9 shots or more. What I found surprising was that my match charting for over thirty years as a high school and collegiate coach was nearly identical.

Number of Shots Per Point *(College and High School Tennis)*

- **First Four Shots:** Sixty percent of all points
- **Shots Five to Eight:** Twenty-five percent of all points
- **Shots Nine or more:** Fifteen percent of all points

The research on the number of total shots hit during a point indicated that even at the highest levels of tennis, the ATP and WTA professional tours, errors or winners occur well before the point can advance through all seven game situations. In fact, these statistics reveal that over sixty percent of all points will end in the first four shots, i.e., the serve *(0-1 shots),* the return *(2 shots),* the server's second shot *(3 shots)* or the return's second shot *(4th shot).* The research also indicated that points of five or more total shots occurred less than forty percent of the time. Although my match charting at the high school and collegiate levels is less complete, the results are very similar. Thus, I firmly believe that those basic percentages will hold true for all level of tennis.

Tactical Key: You must play each point with controlled aggressiveness. Which, I define as choosing the most effective shot for the game situation. The **Tactical Point Control System** simplifies decision-making by giving you a well-researched game plan for every situation.

The Four Point-Building Phases
Key Thought: *Avoid the hit and hope mentality.*

Building upon my research into the components of point-building, I devised a system that divides the tennis point-building process into four distinct phases. **Phase One: The First-Exchange** the first four shots of the tennis point. In this phase, both players are close to the baseline, often playing from the backcourt. However, each player's job is slightly different as the player serving can often be more aggressive than the player who is returning. **Phase Two: The Baseline-Rally** on the fifth shot, the point advances into phase two and the emphasis switches to the ***baseline rally***. Unlike the first-exchange, in the baseline-rally phase, both players are in relatively the same situation, i.e., building the point by trading groundstrokes from the baseline. **Phase Three: The Approach-and-Volley** which occurs when a player receives a short ball that allows them to move forward into the frontcourt, and **Phase Four: The Pass-or-Lob** which occurs when a player sends the ball short allowing their opponent to advance into the frontcourt.

It is during phase three and four where the point takes a dramatic turn. Here the point progression diverges into two distinct pathways. One player will enter phase three on the offensive with an approach and volley attack, while the second player enters phase four on the defensive as they counterattack or defend against their opponent's attack with either a passing shot or lob.

The Point-Building Blueprint
Key Thought: *Be decisive and play with a plan.*

In the **Tactical Point Control System**, I use the **Four Point-building Phases** as the blueprint for building a perfect tennis point. I call it a perfect point because it is the kind of point I want my players to play. I understand that most points will be far from perfect; however, all points, even the less than perfect ones, have many similarities.

My goal in developing the Four Point-building Phases was to identify those similarities and then to mold them into a blueprint which would successfully guide my players through the process of building a tennis point. For example, every point will begin in the first exchange, and many points will also advance into the baseline-rally.

Tactical Key: Most points are imperfect points. In fact, sixty percent of points will end within the first four shots, and approximately eighty percent of those points will conclude with an error.

When you make it your goal to play perfect points, you not only give yourself more opportunities to hit winners, but also provide your opponent with many more opportunities to make errors. One of the first keys to playing successful tennis is to learn how to force errors from your opponent while at the same time managing your own errors. Thus, I give my players what I call the TPC error management guidelines. The guidelines outline seven important keys to error management.

TPC Error Management Guidelines

- Eliminate double faults.
- Get your return in play.
- Never hit a rally shot into the net.
- Balance control *(getting your shot in play)* with the objective of pressuring your opponent *(forcing errors)*.
- Get your approach shot into play, giving yourself the opportunity to hit a volley.
- Get your first passing shot into play, making your opponent prove they can hit a volley.
- Get your first volley into play increasing, the pressure on your opponent.

Of course, no one can play error-free tennis for an entire match. However, if you make a concerted effort to play perfect points, you will reduce your errors in the first-exchange and baseline-rally phases. Consequently, when your errors occur in the approach-and-volley or the passing shot-and/or-defend phases, you will start winning more points than you lose.

Tactical Key: You will win more points from opponent errors than you can ever hope to win by hitting winners. Therefore, give your opponent more opportunities to commit errors by extending more points into the baseline rally.

Watching a professional tennis match, it may appear as though their tactics are unplanned or spontaneous. However, nothing could be further from the truth. What you are witnessing is an outgrowth of years and years of planning and practicing. Shots that appear spontaneous are simply their preplanned responses to the situation unfolding before them.

When playing their best tennis, professional tennis players are performing in the autonomous stage. In this stage, shot selections are really nothing more than an instantaneous reaction to a situation they have programmed into their subconscious mind. Sometimes it is called playing by instinct or the ability to see the court. However, very few players are born with this preprogrammed instinct for the game of tennis. Instead, this instinctual game plan is built slowly over time as a player becomes aware of how to employ their strengths in ways that either exploit their opponent's weaknesses or tactical mistakes. The goal of the Tactical Point Control System is simply to speed up the learning process.

Tactical Key: The primary goal of the Tactical Point Control System is to make point playing automatic. Instead of making strategic decisions on the fly, you make instantaneous shot decisions based on your game plan as determined by the characteristics of the incoming ball. When you have automated your game plan to the point where your reactions are more instinctual than impulsive, you will be able to play your best tennis.

Phase One: The First-exchange
Key Thought: *A good start leads to a strong finish.*

The first-exchange is composed of the first four shots of the tennis point. Why four shots? Because to succeed in tennis you must always be thinking one shot ahead. Nowhere is this more important than in the first exchange. If you start thinking of the serve and return as stand-alone shots, the temptation to go for a point-ending ace or return winner becomes hard to resist. Going for the one-shot kill is a mindset that ultimately results in too many errors.

Since every point begins with a serve and every successful serve must be returned, the serve and return are without a doubt the most important shots you will hit during a tennis match. If you fail to get either shot into play, you lose the point without even giving your opponent an opportunity to commit an error. Since you will win more points by forcing your opponent to make errors than by hitting winners, you cannot afford to give away free points and still expect to win.

Following close behind your serve or return, your second shot is the next most important shot in every point. As stated earlier, even at the professional levels of tennis, a point rarely progresses beyond four shots. This means if you get your first and your second shot into play, you have significantly increased your odds of winning the point.

Tactical Key: Consistently advancing the point into the baseline rally is a key to successful point building. I call this getting the point off to a good start.

First-Exchange Shot Sequence
Key Thought: *Hit every shot with a purpose.*

- **Shot # 1: The Serve.** Develop an efficient serve technique. Aces come from increased power, improved accuracy, and tactical surprise. However, you must maintain a favorable ratio of aces to double faults. If power is not your weapon, you must become an expert at hitting your serving targets. A great option is the outside serve into both the deuce and ad courts. The outside serve will open the court for your second shot.

Second serves must be hit deep with good spin. Aim your second serves into the returner's body or force them to return with their backhand. As much as possible, you must have a plan for using your serve to enhance your serve +1 shot *(the 3ʳᵈ shot of the rally)*.

- **Shot # 2: The Return.** When returning first serves, you must think defensively. My research indicates that most points are won on the first shot *(the serve);* therefore, your primary goal must be to get your return into play. The best place to aim your return is right through the middle of the court giving the server no angles for their second shot.

When returning second serves, you should think offensively. Against many players, the second serve may be the weakest shot you will see. You must take advantage of this weakness by preparing yourself to attack. Attacking the deep middle is a prime target. Think of hitting the ball directly at the server's feet.

Server's will target most of their second serves into your backhand, so you must turn your backhand into a solid return. However, statistics also indicate that forehand returns account for most return winners. Therefore, when returning a second serve, you should position yourself to use your forehand return as often as possible. You can attack with your forehand in three different ways: **1)** Inside-out to your opponent's backhand corner, **2)** inside-in to your opponent's forehand corner, or **3)** Straight down-the-line.

- **Shot # 3: The Serve + 1.** Get in the habit of looking to hit a forehand with your second shot. Try to contact the ball early and on the rise from on or inside the baseline. Practice running around your backhand so you can take advantage of the strength of your forehand groundstroke. Against a right-handed opponent, the best primary target for your forehand groundstrokes will be into target-3 using target-4 as your change-up target where you can catch your opponent by surprise. Against a left-handed opponent, just reverse the order of your targets using target-4 as your primary and target-3 as your change-up target.
- **Shot # 4: The Return + 1.** After a first-serve return, your second shot may need to be defensive. Keep this second shot deep and with enough trajectory that you can recover to the tactical center of your opponent's next possible shots. After a second-serve return, you can often position yourself to attack. Try to hit your return +1 shot from as close to the baseline as possible. On this shot, both time and court position are critical. You can crowd the server by taking the ball early and sending your return + 1 shot deep into your opponent's court. By taking both time and position from your opponent, you keep them on the defensive. If you back up or stay deep after your solid return, you give your opponent time to get back in the point.

Make it your goal to hit as many return +1 shots with your forehand as possible. If your opponent is right-handed, use target-3 as your primary target and target-4 as your surprise secondary pattern. Reverse these targets if your opponent is left-handed. Never forget that a deep middle return followed by a run-around forehand is a powerful combination.

Tactical Key: Don't wait for your opponent to make an error, force them into mistakes. Use your weapons early never letting your opponent have time to feel comfortable.

Serving Options

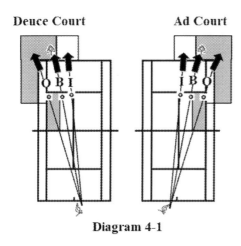

Deuce Court   **Ad Court**

Diagram 4-1

O – Outside Serve: This serve is hit into the outside of the service box and will force the returner out wide of the singles sideline. It opens the opposite side of the court for your second shot.

B – Body Serve: This serve is hit through the center of the service box and is aimed at the returner's inside hip. It jams the opponent often resulting in a weak or short return.

I – Inside Serve: This serve is hit into the inside half of the service box. Since the distance from server to baseline is shortest through the center of the court, the inside serve will challenge your opponent's footwork and reaction time. With little time to react, the returner is often forced to block or chip their return. The result is a shot that lands short in the court.

The Server's Second-Shot Option

Deep Middle Shot: This is the most conservative shot option and can be used effectively in combination with any of the three serves. The deep middle shot is aimed deep through the center of the baseline. Its purpose is to force your opponent to step back and hit their second shot from behind the baseline. It is an excellent **neutralizing shot** against a dominant returner who likes to hover on the baseline and attack the second shot with their forehand.

Crosscourt Shot: This is the second most conservative option for your second shot. Like the deep middle shot, it can also be used effectively in combination with any of the three serves. The purpose of this shot is to establish a crosscourt rally angle. It is a great set-up shot for entry into the **Base-X rally pattern** *(see chapter 7)*. You simply reply to your opponent's return with a crosscourt shot. From the center of the court, this could be either an inside-out forehand or forehand pull-shot.

Open-Court Shot: This is an aggressive second-shot option and is most often used with an outside serve. The purpose of this shot is to attack the open court away from your opponent. You simply hit down-the-line returns crosscourt and crosscourt returns down the line. Serves hit into the middle can be directed into the open court using either an inside-out or forehand pull-shot. *(see chapter 7)*

Opponent's Weakness: This is another aggressive second-shot option that can be used in combination with any of the three serve placement options. The purpose of this shot is to attack your opponent's weakest groundstroke, in most cases their backhand. You will simply direct your second shot into the opponent's weakest groundstroke. To accomplish this may require either a down-the-line, crosscourt, or inside-out shot.

Return of Serve Options

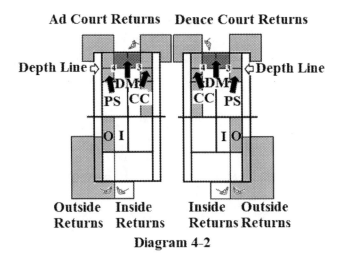

Ad Court Returns   Deuce Court Returns

Depth Line

Outside Inside   Inside Outside
Returns Returns Returns Returns

Diagram 4-2

DM – Deep Middle Return: This return does not require you to change the direction of the serve making it a safe return option. Deep returns force the server to step back and hit a more neutral shot from behind the baseline. This makes the deep middle return an excellent choice to neutralize the powerful server.

CC – Crosscourt Return: This return is hit off an outside serve forcing your opponent into the crosscourt corner. It is a safe return in that it requires no change of direction. The crosscourt return is a great entry shot into the Base-X Rally pattern *(see chapter 7)*.

PS – Pull-Shot Return: This return is hit off an inside serve and forces your opponent into the down-the-line corner. Since the pull-shot employs the natural shoulder and hip rotation of your body, it is a safe return. This is also a great entry shot into the Base-X Rally pattern *(see chapter 7)*.

Inside-Out Return: The inside-out return is sometimes used on an inside, or a body serve. The flight path of the inside-out return is the same as the crosscourt return with the exception that it employs an inside-out hitting motion. *(not shown in diagram 4-2, see chapter 5)*

Down-the-Line Return: The down-the-line return is an aggressive return off an outside serve. This shot should be hit straight up the court using a 90-degree change of direction. It is the lowest-percentage return and should only be used in two instances: **1)** Your opponent sends you a weak return that bounces up into your ideal contact zone, or **2)** You are anticipating an outside serve and have decided to attack it aggressively. Every down-the-line return opens the opposite corner of your court for a second shot attack from your opponent. Therefore, this return must be used sparingly and only when you know you can force your opponent into a defensive position. *(not shown in diagram 4-2, see chapter 5)*

No Hit Zone: You must avoid hitting the soft floating return into the short center area of the court sometimes referred to as the service-T. This is where the big server wants the ball. From here they can attack into either corner of your court with their big forehand. Returns that land short must be hit with pace, otherwise they just set up your opponent's attack.

The Returner's Second-Shot Options

Deep Middle Shot: This is the most conservative shot option and is often used effectively in combination with the deep middle return. This shot is aimed deep through the center of the baseline. The purpose is to force your opponent to step back to hit their next shot from behind the baseline.

Hitting your first two shots into the deep middle is an excellent **neutralizing play** against a powerful server who likes to hover on the baseline and attack with their forehand weapon.

Crosscourt Shot: This is also a conservative second-shot option that can be used effectively with any of the return options. The purpose of this shot is to establish a crosscourt rally angle. It is a great set-up shot for entry into the Base-X rally pattern *(see chapter 7)*. You simply reply to your opponent's second-shot with a crosscourt shot. From the center of the court, this could be an inside-out forehand or forehand pull-shot.

Open-Court Shot: This is an aggressive second-shot option and is most often used as the follow-up shot to a crosscourt angle, inside-out angle, or an attacking pull-shot that has forced your opponent well behind the baseline. The purpose of this shot is to attack the open court away from your opponent. You simply hit your opponent's down-the-line shot back crosscourt and your opponent's crosscourt shot back down-the-line. When your opponent sends their shot into the middle, you can aim your shot into the open court using your forehand. Depending on the opening you can attack the middle ball using either an inside-out or forehand pull-shot swing pattern.

Opponent's Weakness: This is an aggressive second-shot option that can be used with any of the return options. The purpose of this shot is to attack your opponent's weakest groundstroke, in most cases their backhand. You will direct your second shot into the corner of your opponent's weakest groundstroke. To accomplish this may require either a down-the-line, crosscourt, or inside-out shot. Combining this second shot with a return into the opponent's weakness is a powerful one-two punch that will often force an error or an opportunity ball for you to attack.

Tactical Key: In the first-exchange, you must be able to start points by getting your first shot in play; however, you must get your second shot into play to win them.

First-Exchange Checkpoints

Checkpoint # 1: Are you winning points in the first-exchange? Stay with your tactics; they are allowing you to dominate play.

Checkpoint # 2: Are you advancing points into the baseline-rally? Stay with your tactics; they are allowing you to build points with consistent play.

Checkpoint # 3: Are you consistently losing points in the first-exchange? You are not executing your game-plan. Reevaluate the situation using the following criteria:

- Are you playing your style of point? **Focus on your execution**, the problem is often not in your tactics but your execution of those tactics.
- Are your tactics appropriate for this opponent? If not, **make subtle changes** within the context of your playing style. Do not abandon your primary strategy.
- Are you deep in the second set and your tactics including your subtle changes are not working? **Now is the time to try something drastic**. At this point, you have nothing to lose.

Phase Two: The Baseline-Rally
Key Thought: *Work hard to make things easy.*

In the perfect point, the baseline rally phase begins with the fifth shot of the tennis point. This would be the server's third shot, and in most point-building scenarios, the third shot will be a groundstroke struck from the backcourt. Much like the first-exchange, the server will have the opening shot in the baseline rally. However, unlike the first-exchange, the server is not in complete control of this situation. In fact, the point will often enter the baseline rally in a neutral position, with neither player having gained an advantage over the other.

Although there are variations that I will discuss in chapter 7, there are basically two fundamental baseline shots: **1)** The crosscourt, and **2)** The down-the-line.

The Crosscourt Shot is the basic point-building shot.

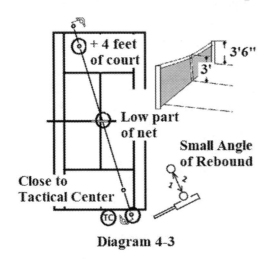

Diagram 4-3

The crosscourt shot is the highest-percentage shot in tennis.

+1: Compared to the down-the-line shot it has four feet more court in which to land.

+1: It is hit over the lowest part of the net, i.e., the net is 3'6" high on the sideline, but 3' high at the net strap.

+1: When you send the ball crosscourt, you are close to the tactical center of your opponent's next shot options.

+1: When you hit crosscourt the angle of rebound is very small.

+4: The **high-percentage score** for the crosscourt shot

The Down-the-Line Shot is the most used attacking shot.

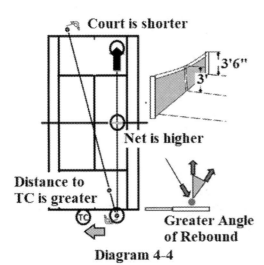

Diagram 4-4

The down-the-line shot is the lowest-percentage shot in tennis.

-1: Compared to the crosscourt shot it has four feet less court in which to land.

-1: It is hit over a higher part of the net, i.e., the net is 3'6" high on the sideline, but 3' high at the net strap.

-1: When you send the ball down-the-line, you are further from the tactical center of your opponent's next shot options.

-1: When you hit down-the-line, the angle of rebound will cause the ball to drift toward the singles sideline *(tendency to make your shot go wide)*

-4: The *high-percentage score* for the down-the-line

During the baseline-rally phase, the quality of your shot is based on the effectiveness of your shot selection. Chapter 7 will detail the shot selection guidelines I want my players to utilize when playing from the baseline. However, there are **eight key components** that I teach my players to employ during the baseline rally.

- **Shot Tolerance:** Consistency is the biggest weapon in tennis. Make every point a mental and physical battle, and you are on your way to breaking your opponent's will to win.
- **Shot Accountability:** You are responsible for where your shot lands in your opponent's court. Managing your shots is a huge key to your success in tennis
- **Depth:** When you hit the first ball of the rally deep, you gain the initial advantage in the point.
- **Trajectory:** On every shot, your first obstacle is not your opponent, it is the net. Using a safe trajectory over the net eliminates net errors from your game.
- **Spin:** There are two kinds of spin, topspin and slice. Applying the correct spin to the ball will be your major source for control.
- **Power:** Hitting with pace makes the ball feel heavy on your opponent's strings preventing the touch and feel they need to control their shot. Hitting the ball soft gives your opponent nothing to work with which upsets their timing and keeps them from hitting the shot that they want.
- **Court Position:** You must always be aware of both your vertical and horizontal position on the court. When you always recover to the tactical center of your opponent's next possible shot options, you give them less open court for their next shot
- **Time:** Every player needs time to reach the ball, organize their feet, and to make a proper swing. When you take away an opponent's time, it makes it difficult for them to run their favorite plays and often forces them into a defensive shot pattern.

Baseline-Rally Checkpoints

Checkpoint # 1: Are both you and your opponent playing from behind the baseline? If winning, you can out-rally your opponent. If losing, you need to become more aggressive.

Checkpoint # 2: Are you rallying from on or inside the baseline? If winning, you are playing aggressively and dictating play. If you are losing, you might be playing too aggressively. Move back slightly and focus on your execution and just try to get more balls in play.

Checkpoint # 3: Are you behind the baseline and defending against an opponent who is inside the baseline? Focus on hitting your shots deeper into your opponent's court as this will force your opponent back. Once the rally is neutral, you should step forward and start taking some balls on the rise. You need to force your way into a more aggressive position.

Phase Three: Approach-and-Volley
Key Thought: *Have an aggressive mindset but choose the most effective shot for the situation.*

The approach-and-volley phase begins when you decide to advance forward into your frontcourt. At this juncture, the pressure of the point is intensified. You are moving forward in anticipation of ending the point with your next shot, while your opponent is under pressure to somehow ward off your attack. In this situation, you must guard against two substantial mentality traps which can sabotage your ultimate success in the approach-and-volley phase.

Mentality Trap # 1: You must avoid being overly aggressive. To accomplish this, you must refuse to let the excitement of the moment tempt you into going for a huge kill-shot.

Mentality Trap # 2: You must avoid the overly timid approach caused by the overestimation of your opponent's ability to counter your attack with their passing shots and lobs.

Understanding the Situation
The approach-and-volley phase is based on the boxing principle of the one-two knockout punch. The first punch is the approach shot and is used to set-up the second punch which is the knockout volley. When hitting your approach shot, you must always pay close attention to the delicate balance between your priority to keep your shot in play and your objective to set-up or finish the point. The key is to choose an approach shot that meets the requirements of the situation.

There are three types of approach-and-volley attacks. **1) The planned approach** which is a predesigned approach-and-volley play like the serve-and-volley. **2) The short ball approach** which occurs when your opponent sends you a short ball, and **3) The sneak approach** which occurs when your shot places your opponent in a vulnerable or defensive position.

The Approach Shot
Key Thought: *Short balls must be attacked, and short high-bouncing balls must be punished.*

When you receive a short ball, you will have four different options: **1)** You can remain patient and continue to build the point from the baseline, **2)** You can increase the pressure to force an error from your opponent, **3)** You can go for an outright winner, or **4)** You can launch an approach-and-volley attack. The choice you make will depend on three important variables. The type of short ball you receive, where you are positioned in the midcourt, and your personal playing style. *(see chapter 11 for details)*

The Volley
Key Thought: *Hit crisp, clean, angle volleys.*

The volley should be the most rewarding shot in a tennis point. Why? Because when it occurs, you are positioned to end the point with a winner. You should never pass up the opportunity to end a point. However, the key is control. When hitting a volley, placement is always more important than power. There are no style points for how pretty or how powerfully you end the point. Just be decisive and hit your volleys with confidence. You cannot be indecisive in this situation. You must play to win.

Tactical Key: Your opponent will often attempt to counter your approach with a lob. Do not fear this option. Instead, develop your overhead into a powerful weapon that never misses. Once you perfect your technique, confidence is the key. The overhead is the one shot in tennis that you must learn to attack with fearless power. If your opponent thinks they can neutralize your attack by simply throwing up any old lob, they will not feel pressure when you approach.

Tactical Key: Punish the lob with your overhead! Make your opponent feel fear whenever you move forward to the net.

Approach-and-Volley Checkpoints

Checkpoint # 1: Are you passing up easy chances to approach? Be more aggressive. Remind yourself between every point to attack short balls and come to the net.

Checkpoint # 2: Are you making errors on your approach? Focus on your execution. The only bad approach shot is the one that isn't in.

Checkpoint # 3: Are you making errors on your volley or overhead? Be decisive and play with confidence. Hit crisp, clean, angled volleys and pound your overhead right up the middle of the court.

Tactical Key: Strike fast! Strike hard! No Fear!

Phase Four: Passing Shot-and/or-Lob
Key Thought: *Get the ball in play!*

If you send your opponent a short ball, expect them to attack. In this situation, you must avoid the temptation to surrender the point. Instead, immediately ready yourself to launch a counterattack. The quicker you recognize the situation, the better your chances to neutralize the attack. Remember, every time your opponent comes to the frontcourt they open areas of weakness for you to attack.

You can learn to effectively turn your opponent's attack into an opportunity for you to win the point. In fact, if you are a great counterpuncher with solid passing shots and a dependable lob, you may decide to invite your opponent to the net, especially if they are the kind of player who wants to avoid playing from the frontcourt.

Tactical Key: Avoid the temptation to panic when your opponent moves forward into the frontcourt. Simply get your first passing shot in play. Make your opponent hit volley winners. You will be surprised how often that first volley is missed or just sets up an easy pass for your second shot.

Sometimes the quality of your opponent's approach shot will force you to defend. In this case, you must find a way to extend the point by just getting one more ball in play! When pressured, run every ball down and always make an attempt, no matter how desperate, to at least get your racket on the ball. Never pass up the opportunity to make your opponent hit one more shot. Why, because your opponent is always capable of missing their next shot, no matter how easy it might be. Nothing is more destructive to your opponent's confidence than to miss an opportunity to end the point with a winner. Losing one point that they should have won can deflate your opponent's momentum and can become the turning point of the game, maybe even the match.

Tactical Key: Many players fail to realize the importance of playing out every point. A match can turn on one lost opportunity. So, make your opponent work for every point.

Checkpoints for the Passing Shot-and/or-Lob Phase

Checkpoint # 1: Are you sending your opponent too many short balls? Use more trajectory on your shots to keep them deeper. **Focus on your execution and aim for the 9-foot, depth line**.

Checkpoint # 2: Are you missing your first passing shot? Focus on your execution. Pick a side and just get your passing shot in play. Avoid giving away free points when your opponent is at the net. **Force them to hit a volley.**

Checkpoint # 3: After your passing shot, are you getting caught behind the baseline? Resist the temptation to retreat. Instead, step inside the baseline and hold your ground. Usually, a volley will be sent on an angle or dropped short. **From inside the baseline, you are in a position to run down the ball and hit another shot.**

Checkpoint # 4: Are your lobs getting pounded with overheads? Lob for the baseline. When you try to hit the lob over your opponent's head, your shot will often fall short. **Learn to lob the court, not your opponent.**

Chapter 4 Summary

Although this chapter has emphasized the building of a perfect tennis point, the perfect point will always be the exception and not the rule. Most points will end with an error, and usually, that error will come in the first few shots of the point. Since sixty percent of all points will end in the first-exchange, you must work hard to manage your errors by staying consistent and keeping balls in play. Remember, you will always win more points on opponent errors than you can win by hitting winners, so make sure to play solid errorless tennis in the first-exchange, manage your errors in the baseline rally and then go for your shots in the approach-and-volley and passing shot-and/or-lob phases. Make consistency the bedrock foundation of your tennis strategy.

In the following chapters, I will show you some essential tactics for playing in each of the four point-building phases. There will also be some chapters filled with drills for helping you perfect those tactics. Study the tactics, then get out on the court and use the drills to practice those tactics. If you do, you will be surprised how quickly your game will improve.

See you on the court.

Chapter 5
The Tactical Battle

Phase One: The First-Exchange

Key Thought: *Think ahead but play each point one shot at a time.*

The first-exchange is composed of the first four shots of the tennis point: the serve, the service return, and then the server's second shot followed by the returner's second shot. Thus, whether you serve or return, the first-exchange encompasses your first two shots in every tennis point. When starting a tennis point, I believe it is vitally important that you always think at least one shot ahead. Therefore, the Tactical Point Control System will teach you to think of your serve and your service return as two-shot plays. I call these two-shot plays your serve+1 or return+1 combination.

Tactical Objective

Key Thought: *It is a good thing to win points in the first-exchange; however, you must avoid losing them.*

Points won in the first-exchange are called free points. They save energy and put tremendous pressure on your opponent. However, points lost in the first-exchange are equivalent to points donated to your opponent: First, because you are not giving your opponent an opportunity to make an error, and second because you are not testing your opponent's fitness or mental toughness.

This is especially true if consistency is the strength of your game. Unless a consistent player can advance the point into the baseline rally, they can never take advantage of their greatest strength, i.e., keeping the ball in play. Conversely, aggressive players who want to avoid playing long groundstroke rallies should look to attack immediately. The aggressive player needs to win as many points in the first-exchange as possible. Their goal is to finish the point within their first three to four shots. Thus, they favor short rallies of seven to eight shots. Although the goal is slightly different, both types of players must know how to play successfully in the first exchange.

Tactical Key: To win you must give your opponent multiple opportunities to make errors. Losing points in the first-exchange limits those opportunities, which in turn dramatically reduces the odds of your winning the match.

The Two Lanes of Momentum

Key Thought: *Get your first two shots into play.*

In a tennis match, there are two pathways where match momentum can be established. I refer to the two pathways as the serving lane and the returning lane. To win a tennis match, you must establish and maintain momentum in at least one of these pathways. In high-level tennis, the momentum lane is most often the serving lane. To maintain momentum in this lane, you must be able to hold your serve game after game after game. When you hold each of your service games, you are establishing the momentum of your service game over the momentum of your opponent's return game. When both players established momentum in their serving lane, the player who breaks their opponent's serving momentum by winning a return game will have positioned themselves for the win. However, to solidify a service break, a player must also win their next service game. Players often have the tendency to let down after a break which results in a loss of their next service game. When this happens, the momentum shift was only temporary as the set is again even. The recipe for successful tennis is to break your opponent's serving momentum while at the same time maintaining the momentum of your own serve.

In high-level tennis, a single break of serve often determines which player will win the set. However, when neither player can break their opponent's serving momentum, the set advances into a tiebreaker. During a tiebreaker, the server still has the advantage, but now the pressure on the server has increased. Instead of winning a return game, in a tiebreaker a player needs only to win one return point to break the server's momentum.

Of course, the reverse of this situation can also occur. If both players have established momentum in the returning lane, the key to the set will come down to which player can break their opponent's return momentum by holding serve. In this case, should neither player manage to hold their serve, a tiebreaker will again decide the set. However, this time, the returner has the advantage.

Part One: The Serving Lane

Key Thought: *If your serve isn't in, you have no chance to win.*

The serve is the first shot of every tennis point, and it is the only shot over which you have complete control. You must use this first-shot advantage to put pressure on your opponent. Although the primary goal is to get your serve into play, just getting your serve in the service box will not put enough pressure on your opponent. The Tactical Point Control System will teach you the importance of serving into smaller and more specific targets within the service box *(see diagram 3-2 in chapter 3 ad well as diagram 4-1 in chapter 4)*. Aiming for smaller targets serves two fundamental purposes: **1)** A more specific target will help you get more serves into the service box, and **2)** Each specific target possesses a set of tactical advantages that can be used to either set-up your second shot or to neutralize the effectiveness of your opponent's return.

Tactical Key: You cannot control your opponent's next shot; however, you can influence it. Knowing how to influence your opponent's shot options is critical when developing your tennis tactics.

The Serving Progression
Key Thought: *Practice your serve, it is your number one weapon.*

Learning to use your serve effectively is a four-step progression. The **first step** is to recognize the three serving targets and to understand how to employ them in ways that can force a weak or advantageous return. **Step two** is to develop each of the four types of serves, i.e., flat, slice, topspin, and power. The **third step** is to create a two-shot plan, i.e., know what shot combinations you are going to use in a match. **Step four** is where the hard work really begins. In this final step, you must get out on the court and practice your serve and second-shot combinations until you have mastered at least one strong first serve and one consistent second serve combination.

Of course, the more serve combinations you can master, the more effective your service games will become. As you apply this four-step progression to your service game, resist the temptation to rush the process. One of the most significant serving errors is to over-use a serve that you have not mastered. For example, a beginning player often thinks that the only effective first serve is the power serve, which often leads to double faults and service failures.

Instead, make it your goal to build your serving tactics by using the four-step progression as described in the proceeding paragraphs. Remember, on first serves; it is better to over-use the one serve combination you can control, then to try to fool your opponent with multiple serve combinations that are inconsistent or out of control. Your primary serve combinations must be built around your most reliable and most consistent serve. Use the other options sparingly and only as change-ups to keep your opponent from getting too comfortable with their returns.

Tactical Key: Never throw away points by merely blasting away. Every shot should be measured and hit with a purpose. Throwing away points can break your momentum by giving your opponent a spark of life in what should have been a hopeless situation.

In today's tennis, the first-exchange is composed of four rapid-fire shots. I believe the reason for so many points ending in the first-exchange is simply this: most players have only a vague idea of how to play through this phase of the tennis point. The players who understand this phase have a well-practiced plan that allows them to react quickly and decisively. They use their serve to set up their second shot. Thus, they make fewer mistakes, force more errors from their opponent, and ultimately hit more winners. Conversely, the players who rely on pure instinct react slowly and tentatively which leads to errors, weak shots, and lost points.

The Big Four
Key Thought: *Choose the correct serve for the situation.*

Power Serve: The power serve is a first serve option that relies on speed over accuracy. Since pace is your weapon, you must aim for big targets. The power serve is best used when hitting into the inside target. To use the power serve effectively, you need to maintain a service accuracy of at least sixty percent. If you can raise your accuracy to sixty-five percent or above, the power serve should become your primary first serve option.

Flat Serve: The flat serve should be your primary first serve option. It is hit with eighty percent power and emphasizes control. You can aim your flat serve into any of the three serving targets; however, the inside or body targets are the best choices.

Slice Serve: You will hit your slice serve with a combination of pace and spin. If you are right-handed, the slice serve will break wide in the deuce court. For left-handers, it breaks wide in the ad court. The slice also skids and stays low on the bounce making it a difficult serve for your opponent to attack. You can use the slice serve as either a first or second serve option. As a first serve, it typically emphasizes pace over spin and is aimed so that it will break away from the returner. For a right-handed server, this would require an outside serve in the deuce court, and an inside serve in the ad court *(reverse this if you are left-handed)*. However, when used as the second serve, you should emphasize spin over pace aiming it into either the returner's body or into their backhand return.

Topspin Serve: The topspin serve is a primary second serve option. It usually emphasizes spin over pace. However, when pace is applied, it can become an effective first serve that is directed into the returner's body or wide in the ad court *(deuce court for left-handed servers)*. The topspin serve will bounce high and works well as a second serve into the returner's backhand side.

Seven Keys to Serving Success

- **Get your first serve in play.** It is hard to win when forced to rely on your second serve.
- **Have a pre-planned and well-practiced ritual for each time you step up to serve.**
  - o   Make this ritual a part of your designated between point routine.
- **Start every service point with a two-shot plan.** serving target and second shot
- **Make the returner move to hit the return.** two-step rule
- **Vary the pace, spin, and placement of your serve.** Avoid becoming a ball machine.
- **Make the returner use their weakest return.** Usually their backhand
- **You will only be as good as your second serve.** Take control of your double-faults

The Outside Serve

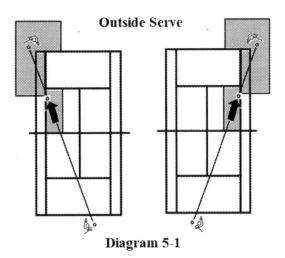

Diagram 5-1

Description: The outside serve is hit on an angle so that the ball will cross the singles sideline before crossing the baseline. The extreme angle as shown in *diagram 5-1* will pass through the singles sideline before crossing the back service-line. Effective outside serves are aimed into the outer half of the service box. Although you can hit this serve with pace, it is often more effective when combined with spin. If you are right-handed, you will use a slice serve in the deuce court, and topspin serve in the ad court *(diagram 5-1)*. If left-handed, you will use your slice serve in the ad court, and your topspin serve in the deuce court *(diagram 5-1)*.

Tactical Key: The outside serve will force the returner out wide of the singles sideline *(shaded area in diagram 5-1)*. Thus, creating an open court in the opposite corner for your second shot.

The outside serve emphasizes control over pace. The serve's placement will force the returner out wide of the singles sideline increasing the distance the returner must travel to the tactical center. This added distance complicates the returner's ability to recover and opens the opposite side of the court for your second shot.

Since the primary goal of the baseline rally is to create open court, the outside serve is a very potent weapon in the arsenal of the baseline player. Even if the serve does not set up an outright winner, it will force the returner to hit their second shot on the move, which often results in a weak reply. When your opponent sends you a short or weak reply you will have established positive momentum as the point advances into phase two, the baseline-rally.

Tactical Key: If you are a consistent baseliner, you should make the outside serve your primary option. You may not have a dominant serve that can threaten your opponent with pace; however, if you can use your first serve to open the court, you can still pressure your opponent by forcing them out of position.

The Body Serve

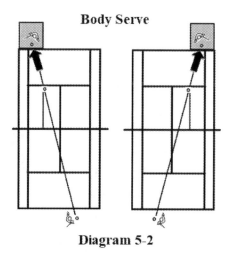

Body Serve

Diagram 5-2

Description: The body serve is hit through the center of the service box and aimed directly into the returner's body. You can hit the body serve using either pace or spin. Using pace makes it difficult for the returner to move their body away from the path of the incoming ball. Whereas, spin can create problems if the returner moves in the wrong direction. For example: If you are right-handed and serving in the deuce court, by aiming a slice serve into the returner's inside hip the returner must move inside *(toward the center of the court)* to get away from the ball. When they move to the outside, the ball will continue to break into their body making it extremely difficult to hit the return *(diagram 5-2)*. Left-handed servers can do the same thing with a slice serve into the ad court. Right-handed servers can get similar results using topspin in the ad court; whereas, a left-hander would use topspin in the deuce court.

Tactical Key: The body serve is used to jam the returner. This forces the returner to shorten their swing and prevents them from stepping forward into their shot. Jamming the returner makes it difficult for the returner to attack the serve and often results in a weak return that lands in the center of the court. This short ball sets up a second-shot opportunity for you to move forward and attack with your forehand.

The body serve with its large margin for error can be hit with more pace than the outside serve. As a first serve, you can jam your opponent forcing a weak return. As a second serve, it is effective at keeping your opponent from stepping in and attacking with their return. A weaker return allows you to be more aggressive with your second shot. The body serve is a great way to neutralize an aggressive returner.

Tactical Key: You will not hit many aces with a body serve; however, you will neutralize your opponent's return giving yourself the opportunity to attack with your second shot.

The Inside Serve

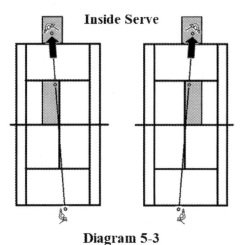

Diagram 5-3

Description: The inside serve is aimed over the lowest part of the net and into the inside half of the service box. The advantage of the inside serve is the shortened distance the ball must travel to get past the returner. When hit with pace, a well-placed inside serve can get to the returner so quickly that they have little time to react. This time-pressure often forces the returner to stretch or even lunge for the ball. Lunging for the ball forces a blocked or chipped return that often falls short and in the middle of the court.

    If you are right-handed and serving to the deuce court and your opponent contacts the ball late, their return will fade to your forehand side *(diagram 5-3)*. If left-handed, the return will drift to your forehand in the ad court *(diagram 5-3)*. When you can anticipate where the ball will land, you can be ready to attack this weak return with your forehand weapon.

Tactical Key: A well-placed inside serve will force the returner to block or slice the return. This takes away your opponent's ability to attack and gives you the opportunity to hit your next shot with your forehand.

Although the inside serve is hit over the lowest part of the net, it is also hit into the shortest part of the service box *(net to service line)*. This short target area makes the inside serve a lower-percentage serve for many players. However, if you are tall, you can use your height and higher contact point to compensate for the shorter distance.

Tactical Key: Shorter players should use the inside serve as their change-up serve. First, they get the player leaning to the outside with their outside serve, and then they surprise them by hitting an inside serve. *(see control combo below)*

The Control Combo
Key Thought: *First establish a pattern; then break the pattern.*

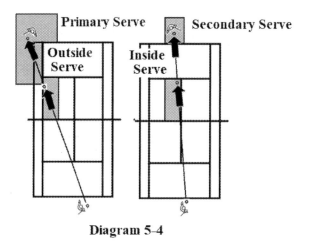

Primary Serve   Secondary Serve

Outside Serve   Inside Serve

Diagram 5-4

Primary Serve: When using the Control Combo, you will aim eighty percent of your serves into the outside target. Your goal is to angle your serve through the singles sideline forcing your opponent out wide. Forcing the returner outside the singles sideline opens the opposite side of the court for your next shot. When you can consistently push your opponent out wide, they will adjust in one of two ways: **1)** they can remain at the same depth but shift out a little wider, or **2)** they can move in closer to or even inside the baseline to cut down the distance to your angle serve. Either of these adjustments weakens your opponent's ability to react to your secondary option, the inside serve.

Tactical Key: The outside serve does more than just opening the court. It also pressures your opponent's backhand. If the returner is right-handed, in the deuce court you can pressure your opponent's second shot by forcing them to cover the open court with a running backhand; whereas, in the ad court, you immediately pressure the returner by forcing your opponent to hit a backhand return.

Secondary Serve Option: Once your opponent shifts their position to cover the outside serve, you can pressure their return by aiming your change-up serve into the inside target. Since you have forced your opponent to shift their position either forward or wide, you do not have to blast your inside serve with a lot of power. A well-placed flat or spin serve will do the job. When using a spin serve your objective is to make the ball break away from the returner and toward the center of the court. If you are right-handed, you will use a topspin serve in the deuce court, and a slice serve in the ad court. Reverse these spins if you are left-handed.

Tactical Key: When you hit the inside serve from the deuce court side, you will be aiming your serve into a right-handed opponent's backhand. Therefore, this makes the control combo exceptionally effective vs. a right-handed opponent on the deuce court side.

The Power Combo
Key Thought: *If you have a big serve, pound it through the inside target!*

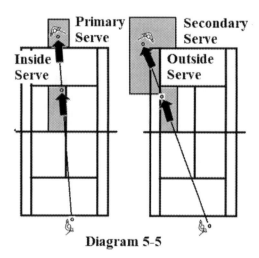

Diagram 5-5

Primary Serve Option: When using the power combo, you will hit eighty percent of your first serves into the inside target. The distance between the server and the opponent's baseline is shorter through the inside target than it is through either of the other two targets. This shorter distance translates into less time for the returner to react. If you create pressure using your power serve into the inside target, your opponent will do one of two things: **1)** They will start leaning toward the center of the court in anticipation of your big serve, or **2)** They will move back further behind the baseline hoping to give themselves more time to react to your power. When your opponent shifts position to handle your inside serve, they are setting up your secondary service option to the outside.

Tactical Key: Pressuring the reaction time of the returner, often results in returns that land short and in the middle of the court setting up an attack with your forehand weapon.

Secondary Serve Option: The outside serve is your change-up serve, so your objective is to surprise your opponent. Now that you have your opponent reacting to your power serve by moving back or toward the center, it is time to change-up your play by hitting a spin serve wide into the outside target. A good outside serve will often force a short ball that you can hit into the open court.

Tactical Key: The Power Combo is aggressive with massive first-strike potential. If you possess a consistent power serve and can accurately place it into the inside target, you will force errors, hit aces, and create opportunity balls that you can attack with your powerful forehand. However, if you lack the booming power serve, your best choice of attack will probably be the Control Combo.

Second Serves
Key Thought: *You are only as good as your second serve.*

To consistently hold your serve, you must get a high percentage of first serves into play. However, you must also have a second serve that is reliable, and that can neutralize your opponent's ability to attack with their return. Think about your own game. How many times each week do you go out and practice your second serve? Do you practice playing points starting with your second serve? Do you take the time to warm-up your second serve before every match? The answer to each of these questions is essential. If you want to succeed in tennis, you must establish a daily habit of working on your second serve.

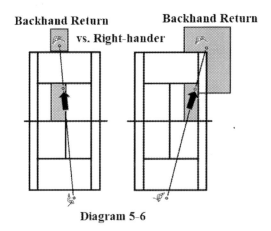

Diagram 5-6

On second serves you still possess the first shot of the point; however, the overall temperature of the situation has changed. You are now in a must get the ball in the service box situation. This added pressure forces you to serve more conservatively. Meanwhile, your opponent, who understands that you must back off on your serve, steps forward to hit an attacking return with an aggressive mindset.

Although your serving targets have not changed, you are forced by the situation to simplify your tactics while at the same time reducing the aggressiveness of your second serve. Tactically, you must do two things. First, you must apply more spin to your serve, and second, you must aim your serves into more conservative targets. This usually calls for a serve into either your opponent's body or backhand. See the shaded areas in *diagram 5-6*.

Tactical Key: When you double fault, immediately check your emotional temperature. If you are still feeling confident, go ahead and use your first serve on the next point. However, if you are nervous or feeling anxious, start the next point using your second serve as your first serve. Starting with your second serve gives you two opportunities to adjust and restore confidence in your second serve. Once you regain confidence in your second serve, start leading out with your first serve once again.

Serve + 1: *The Server's Second Shot*
Key Thought: *Most points are lost within the first four shots. This means if you get your first two shots in play, you have significantly increased your chances of winning the point.*

You should always step up to serve with a two-shot plan: **1)** The target into which you will direct your first serve, and **2)** The target into which you will aim your second shot.

Tactical Key: Until you miss your first serve, I do not want you thinking about your second serve. That would be negative thinking, and it will affect your first serve percentages. You must always expect to get your first serve in play.

On those occasions when you do miss your first serve, you must switch your mindset immediately from attacking to neutralizing. Since you only have a second or two to decide on a course of action, you must already have a default plan ready to go. In other words, I tell my players to have two second-serve options. One that is semi-aggressive and one that is conservative. That way you have a simple decision to make: Do you use plan A or plan B?

The Second Shot: Serve +1 Options
Key Thought: *Always think of the first-exchange as a two-shot play. Let your serve set up your second shot so that it either pressures or neutralizes your opponent's next shot.*

Like all shots in tennis, some serve +1 options are more aggressive and carry a high-risk/high-reward factor while others are more conservative and are higher-percentage in nature. If you are an attacking player with a big serve, the high-risk/high-reward options might fit with your mentality and playing style. However, if you are a consistent player, the more conservative higher-percentage options will be your primary choices. In most cases, you will use your first serve to pressure and your second serve to neutralize. Just remember, whichever option you choose, you must be able to get points started in the first exchange.

The Five Reads

Key Thought: *"I have good anticipation, and good reaction to the ball because I've played so many matches in my life."* – Martina Hingis, a professional tennis player, ranked #1 in the world for 209 weeks and winner of 5 Grand Slam Titles

To pressure your opponent, you must have a predetermined plan for your serve and your second shot. Since you have complete control over your serve, it is the easy part of the plan. It is your second shot that tends to be the problem. How many times have you hit a perfect serve, and then missed the opportunity to follow up your first-shot advantage because you were unprepared for your second shot? Worse yet, how many times has this lack of preparation lead to your committing an unforced error.

It is the second shot that makes the game plan work. As you practice, you must develop serve+ 1 options for each of your serve targets. As you build your tactical plan, you must keep in mind that your second-shot must be both flexible and decisive.

When you know where you will aim your serve, a solid serve + 1 option must account for each of the following. **1)** Your opponent's position when hitting their return. **2)** The location where your opponent is most likely to send their return. **3)** The primary target for your second shot. **4)** The type of shot you should hit *(drive, loop, slice)*. **5)** Where you should position after your shot, and **6)** A check-down or secondary target for those occasions when your opponent has managed to neutralize your first-shot advantage.

Your second shot does not have to be a winner; however, it must be a well-practiced shot that you can consistently hit into the target area. A successful second shot should increase the pressure on your opponent making them more likely to commit an error or send you an opportunity ball. Only go for an outright winner when you are ahead in the game by two or more points, i.e., when the score is 30-love, 40-love, or 40-15.

Matching Your Second Shot to Your Baseline Tactic

Key Thought: *"Five guys on the court working together can achieve more than five talented players who come and go as individuals."* – Kareem Abdul-Jabbar

You should think of each of your shots as part of a team working together to accomplish your objective. Some shots build points, some set-up opportunities to attack. Some shots can finish points. Other shots can force your opponent into making an error. The key is to combine your shots into patterns that build toward an opportunity for you to win the point. The tactical point control system gives you repetitive patterns that will help you build a successful point.

Serve + 1: *The Five Second-Shot Options*

Key Thought: *When you step up to serve, you should have already decided where you will send your second shot.*

Your second shot must be a tactically-sound shot that increases the pressure on your opponent. Making your opponent increasingly uncomfortable forces errors and creates opportunity balls. Remember, you will only go for the outright winner if you are ahead in the game by two or more points. *Diagram 5-7* illustrates the five primary second-shot options. The five shots will be described in the following paragraphs. As you read about each shot, refer to *diagram 5-7* for their illustrations.

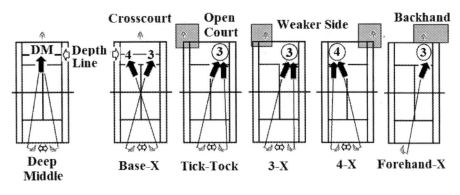

Diagram 5-7

Tactical Key: If you are missing your second-shot forehands, check your grip. Often a server will fail to shift all the way from their continental service grip to their semi-western forehand groundstroke grip. Hitting with an in-between grip *(eastern forehand)* will alter your contact point and often cause an unforced error.

Option # 1: Middle Deep *(diagram 5-7)*
Key Thought: *Use the middle-deep option to neutralize a powerful opponent.*

Definition: Ideally, you will aim your middle-deep shot through the center of the court; however, the primary goal is to keep the ball deeper than the 9-foot, depth line. One of the best ways to accomplish this goal is to aim your second shot right at the feet of your recovering opponent.

You can employ the middle-deep shot after serving into any of the three service targets. When hit aggressively it is a potent offensive weapon that can be used to transition into any baseline rally pattern. However, it is most often used as a check down option for those instances when your opponent has neutralized the advantage of your serve, i.e., they have forced you behind your baseline by sending their return into the deep middle or deep into one of the corners of your court. Once you have neutralized your opponent's advantage with a middle-deep shot, you to transition into any of the five baseline rally patterns.

When facing an aggressive opponent, you can use the deep middle option early in the point. I teach my players a three-deep pattern, in which you hit three consecutive shots beyond the 9-foot, depth line. These shots do not need to be hit through the center of the court, but the ball should cross through the baseline before crossing the singles sideline. The goal is to push your opponent back making it difficult for them to launch an attack. Then, when you get a shorter ball, you can either transition into your preferred baseline pattern or launch into an attack of your own.

Purpose: On second serves, the middle-deep option is a strong second-shot option. The middle-deep option is simple to employ and is a great way to set up your third shot. If possible, attack this ball with your forehand taking time from your opponent by hitting it early and on the rise from on or inside the baseline. If hit aggressively, the deep-middle shot will push your opponent back behind the baseline putting them on the defensive. When pushed back, your opponent will be forced to lift the ball by hitting off their back foot resulting in a neutral or even a defensive type shot.

Pushing your opponent back behind the baseline accomplishes three goals: **1)** It makes it difficult for your opponent to angle their next shot away from you. **2)** It makes it difficult for your opponent to launch an effective attack. **3)** It can often force your opponent into sending you a short opportunity ball which you can then attack with your next shot *(serve + 2 or fifth shot of the point)*.

Tactical Key: Unless you go for too much pace, the deep-middle shot is an effective shot for neutralizing your opponent's aggressive return while providing opportunities to establish momentum in the rally.

Option # 2: Base-X *(diagram 5-7)*
Key Thought: *Use the percentages to get your second shot in play.*

Description: The base-X option is a crosscourt option. Like the middle-deep option, you can combine it with any serve or service target. The key to this option is its simplicity. If your opponent sends the return to your right, aim your second shot crosscourt on a 4-to-4 angle. If your opponent sends the return to your left, aim your second shot crosscourt on a 3-to-3 angle.

Although the base-X option is a conservative tactic, it also provides you with two excellent offensive opportunities. **1)** When your opponent sends their return down the line, your crosscourt shot will attack the open court away from your opponent. **2)** If your opponent returns crosscourt, you can place your crosscourt shot behind them. When you catch your opponent on the run, hitting behind them will often force an error, and sometimes it will even result in an outright winner.

Purpose: The base-X is a conservative second-shot option that you can employ with either a first or second serve. You will simply respond to your opponent's return by aiming your crosscourt shot deep and through the baseline. Resist the temptation to go for a short-angled shot until you are pushed out near one of your singles sidelines. From this wide position, you have the space to send the ball on a short-angle, i.e., a shot where the ball crosses the singles sideline before it crosses the baseline. I instruct my players to beat an angle with a better angle.

Even though your goal is to establish the baseline rally, you cannot afford to play overly cautious. Do not wait for your opponent to miss. Instead, step forward taking the ball early and on the rise. Use your groundstroke weapons as early in the point as possible and play to win.

However, resist the temptation to aim for the lines. Instead, aim for the center of the diagonal deep target box. When you hit aggressive shots into the center of the deep target boxes, you will keep your opponent pinned behind the baseline. I always remind my players to hit aggressive shots into conservative spots.

Tactical Key: The base-X option makes for a smooth transition into the base-X rally pattern. The base-X is my fundamental pattern. It is an excellent counterpunching option as it tempts your opponent to risk the down-the-line shot. When they do, you have an opportunity to counterpunch with a crosscourt shot into your opponent's open court.

Option # 3: Tick-Tock *(diagram 5-7)*
Key Thought: *Attack your opponent's open court.*

Description: The tick-tock option is used to attack your opponent's open court. Most often the tick-tock option is combined with an outside serve. The concept is simple, use your outside serve to force your opponent wide of their singles sideline, and then hit your second shot into the open court away from your opponent. For example: If your opponent sends their return down the line, you will respond with a crosscourt shot. However, if your opponent sends their return crosscourt, you will send your shot down the line.

The key to this combination is execution. You must stay relaxed and let your racket do the work. Players often tighten up when they see an open court. They know this is an excellent opportunity to end the point and they try to force the ball through the opening. However, when they are tight, they cannot control the ball, and they end up giving the point away with a wild shot into the net, or past the baseline or sideline.

You must resist the temptation to go for an outright winner and just hit a quality shot. Be content to make your opponent hit their next shot on the move. Most of your opponents are not as efficient on the move, and their next shot will give you an even better opportunity to finish the point.

Purpose: Attacking the open court is an aggressive one-two punch option that can reap quick rewards. For most players, it is their best and possibly their only real first-strike option. However, since you are aiming for the open court, you will sometimes be forced to use a low-percentage down-the-line shot. It is crucial that you not force the down-the-line shot. If your opponent's crosscourt return is deep or pushes you out wide of the singles sideline, switch to your check down option and send your second shot either crosscourt or into the deep middle.

Beat an Angle with a Better Angle
Always remember the axiom to beat an angle with a better angle. Thus, whenever your opponent has sent an effective crosscourt return, instead of forcing a down-the-line shot into the open court, check down and send your second shot back crosscourt. In this case, you will be hitting behind your opponent. If you catch them on the run trying to cover the open court, you will often force an error and sometimes even hit a clean winner.

Tactical Key: The tick-tock option is the classic one-two punch that can lead to an easy winner. When your opponent is frustrated or tight, this is a great play to use. Forcing your opponent to hit on the run will lead to errors or short opportunity balls that will let you advance to the net.

Option # 4: 3-X *(diagram 5-7)*
Key Thought: *Attack your right-handed opponent's backhand corner.*

Definition: In the 3-X option, you direct your second shot into your opponent's 3-target box. If both you and your opponent are right-handed, you will be directing your shot into their backhand corner making the 3-X option a great way to attack your opponent's weaker shot. You can further this backhand attack by using the 3-X option to set up a crosscourt inside-out forehand attack on the 3-to-3 rally angle. If your opponent's backhand is weak, you can often overpower it with your inside-out forehand attack

Lefty Advantage: If you are left-handed and your opponent is right-handed, you can use the 3-X pattern to set up a 3-to-3 rally, but now you are hitting your outside forehand into your opponent's outside backhand corner. Once again, you are trying to overpower your opponent's backhand but this time with the strength of your forehand *groundstroke*.

Purpose: You can use the 3-X option in combination with any serve or service target. The 3-X option is used to attack a right-handed opponent's weaker backhand. If your opponent has trouble with low balls, you could use a slice shot keeping the bounce low and forcing them to hit from their lower strike zone. If your opponent has trouble with high bouncing balls, you could use a looping topspin shot forcing them to hit from their upper strike zone. If your opponent has trouble handling pace, you could use your inside-out forehand to drive the ball into your opponent's backhand corner as you look to overpower them with the speed of your shot.

Attack a Weakness: No matter which tactic you choose, once you have discovered your opponent's weakness, you should exploit it whenever possible. Again, depending on your opponent's return, you may have to direct this shot down-the-line, in which case it is a higher-risk option.

Tactical Key: Remember, you do not have to overwhelm your opponent with your second shot. If pressured, loop the ball back deep with heavy topspin so that you push your opponent back behind the baseline and into their backhand corner. The next shot your opponent sends will often be weak or short allowing you to become more aggressive.

Option # 5: 4-X *(diagram 5-7)*
Key Thought: *Attack your left-handed opponent's backhand corner.*

Definition: You can combine the 4-X option with any serve or target combination; however, like the 3-X option, it works best when combined with an inside or body serve. In the 4-X option, you direct your second shot into the 4-target in your opponent's end of the court. You can use this option to attack a right-handed opponent's forehand or a left-handed opponent's backhand groundstroke. As you play, pay attention to your opponent's weakness. Use slice if your opponent has trouble hitting from their low strike zone. Use a topspin loop if your opponent's weakness is the high-bouncing ball. If it is the pace that gives your opponent trouble, drive the ball using the added speed to overpower them.

Purpose: If you are right-handed and your opponent is right-handed, you will use this option when you believe you have an advantage using your outside forehand in the 4-to-4 rally angle. This option is especially useful when you face an opponent who likes to run-around their forehand to hit inside-out backhands. Hitting inside-out backhands places your opponent in a difficult recovery position often leaving them open for a 4-to-3 down-the-line attack.

Attacking a Left-hander: If you are right-handed and your opponent is left-handed, the 4-X option will set up a 4-to-4 rally. However, now you can drive your forehand into your opponent's left-handed backhand. If you are left-handed facing a left-handed opponent, use your inside-out forehand to drive the ball into your opponent's backhand corner.

Tactical Key: Although the 4-X option is the least used option, you should not underestimate its importance. If you are right-handed, you need it to attack a left-handed opponent's backhand with your right-handed forehand.

Option # 6: Forehand-X *(diagram 5-7)*
Key Thought: *You can never hit too many forehands.*

Description: In the forehand-X option, a right-handed player will run around their backhand to hit an inside-out forehand shot into target 3. *(Left-hander into target 4)* Usually this will occur on balls hit into the center of the court; however, if your forehand is your weapon, you should be prepared to use it at every opportunity. *(See the forehand-X groundstroke pattern in chapter 6.)* You can combine the forehand-X option with any serve and serve target. Players who own an attacking serve and powerful forehand often combine it with an inside serve.

Ad Court Attack: If you are right-handed and serving from the ad court, you can set up the forehand-X option with an outside serve. After hitting your outside serve, you will simply take two steps toward your backhand corner and prepare to attack the return with your forehand weapon.

Purpose: If you are right-handed, you will set up the Forehand-X attack by directing your second shot into target-3. This is the ultimate strength into weakness attack as you are using your powerful forehand groundstroke to overpower your opponent's weaker backhand side.

Left-hander vs. Left-hander: If both you and your opponent are left-handed, you will send your second shot into target-4 to set up your forehand-X attack.

Tactical Key: You do not need to overpower your opponent with your second shot. Instead, force your opponent into their backhand corner by aiming deep into the center of the target box.

Serving Checkpoints

Checkpoint # 1: Are you getting sixty-five percent *(2 out of 3)* of your first serves in play? If not, you need to be less aggressive with your first serve.

Checkpoint # 2: Are you winning seventy-five percent *(3 out of 4)* or more of your first serve points? If not, you might need to be a bit more aggressive with your first serve.

Checkpoint # 3: Are you getting eighty percent or more of your second serves into play? If not, you need to be less aggressive with your second serve.

Checkpoint #4: Are you winning fifty percent or more of your second serve points? If not, you might need to be more aggressive with your second serve.

Part Two: The Return Lane

Key Thought: *Without a clear plan of action, breaking serve at the advanced levels of tennis will be difficult.*

Unlike the serve, where you have complete control over the first shot of the point, your return strategy is more reactionary in nature. Every time your opponent serves, they possess the first-shot advantage. Therefore, your opponent's serve will determine the type and location of your serve return. On your opponent's first serve, this first-shot advantage almost always places you immediately on the defensive. Thus, your first task as a returner is to neutralize your opponent's first-strike advantage. Against a strong server, this is a difficult task. However, with the right mindset coupled with a tactically sound return plan, you will find success.

The Returning Mindset

Key Thought: *"Put first things first."* Steven Covey, Habit 3, from The Seven Habits of Highly Effective People

Adopting a proper mindset for returning serve means prioritizing your tactics. Why? Because, when returning serve, the odds of winning the point are stacked against you. According to statistics collected from the 2015 Australian Open, almost thirty percent of all points consisted of a one-shot rally, i.e., the serve. In most cases, these points were lost because of a missed return. In fact, the average rally length for both the men and the women was just 3.8 shots per point. This means that most shots ended on the returner's second shot. With these statistics in mind, I give my players three mental keys for a successful return

Key # 1: You must have a tactical return plan.
Key # 2: You must use a return ritual before every serve.
Key # 3: You must read the serve quickly and then react according to your return plan.

When returning first serves, you must prepare for a bang-bang exchange. There is little time for tactical decisions. Overthinking slows your reaction time making it even more difficult to get your return into play. To succeed, you must simplify your return tactics. Too many players try to match the server's first-shot advantage with an aggressive point winning return of their own. Like going for a serving ace, trying for a winning return often results in an error. This is a deadly mistake. For unlike the server, a returner has only one chance to get their return into play.

More importantly, when you fail to get your return into play, you allow the point to end without even giving your opponent the opportunity to make an error. Thus, I equate a missed return with a server's double fault. Unless you get a high percentage of returns into play, winning tennis matches will be tough.

Seven Keys to Successful Returns

- **Get your return in play.** Do not give away free points.
- **Keep the return deep beyond the 9-foot depth line**. The player who hits the first deep ball will have first chance to control the point.
- **Against pressuring serves, send your return to the deep middle.** Avoid changing the direction of a fast serve.
- **Against weaker serves, push your opponent into a corner.** Make your opponent move to hit their second shot.
- **Vary your return position.** Avoid giving your opponent the same look on every serve.
- **Keep the ball out of the short middle.** Avoid hitting to the area of the service T.
- **Use a modified swing.** Shorten your backswing and use your feet to attack the ball.

Basic Return Targets
Key Thought: *Know how to neutralize your opponent's serve.*

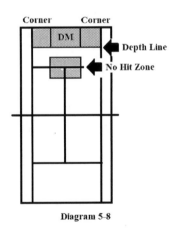

Diagram 5-8

To break serve consistently requires four key ingredients: **1)** Get your return in play; **2)** Keep the ball deep *(beyond 9-foot depth line)*; **3)** Push your opponent into a corner; and **4)** Avoid hitting into the short middle, i.e., the area around the service T. *(Diagram 5-8)*

The Art of Returning Serve
Key Thought: *"For every action, there is an equal and opposite reaction."* – Newton's Third Law of Motion

Since the server is in complete control at the start of every point, your game plan for returning must be defensive in nature. This also means your second-shot plan must be more conservative than when you are serving. By no means does this imply that you will never be able to attack; however, it does infer that in the return game, your first order of business will always be to advance the point into phase two, the baseline rally. When you employ an overly aggressive return and second-shot combination, you will make too many errors. Remember, it is impossible to break your opponent's serve without first keeping the ball in play.

Get Your Return in Play: Although you need a reliable two-shot plan when returning serve, your primary focus must first be on getting your return into play. To make returning more consistent, I teach my players three basic concepts for their service return.

- **Position**: where to position, depth, tactical center, and specialized positioning,
- **Read**: ball location, inside, outside, or into the body.
- **React:** where to send your return, shot direction.

Tactical Key: Think ahead but play each point one shot at a time.

Return Position

Key Thought: *Tennis is a game of positioning. If you are in the right position, you win!*

In general, if your opponent is a power server, position further behind the baseline. On the other hand, if the pace of your opponent's serve does not pressure you, start closer to or even inside the baseline. A good indicator for adjusting your depth is to recognize where you are contacting the ball. If you are regularly returning from the low strike zone, move forward until you are striking the ball at waist level or slightly higher. However, when you are regularly returning from the high strike zone, you should move back taking the ball on the way down, again from the waist level or slightly higher. For the basic positions, see *diagram 5-9*.

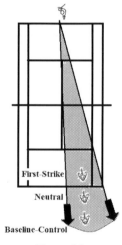

Diagram 5-9

Position 1: First-Strike Position: Attacking players want to play as close to or inside the baseline as possible. From position 1, you must shorten your swing and rely on quick reflexes.

Position 2: Neutral Position: Located right behind the baseline, this is the neutral return position. It places you at the tactical center of your opponent's widest possible serves. From position 2, you must use an adjusted swing and good footwork patterns.

Position 3: Baseline-Control Position: Located five feet or more behind the baseline, this is a defensive position. It is often the choice of players who like to return using a full groundstroke swing. It is also a solid choice against power servers who try to blast their serve past you.

Tactical Center: Lateral positioning is simply a matter of lining up at or near the center of your opponent's widest possible serve options. This positioning is also dependent upon the quality of your opponent's serve. If your opponent can serve effectively into only one of the two targets, you can shade toward the side of the service box they favor.

Tactical Key: Shifting slightly toward your opponent's stronger serve will tempt them to serve into the slight opening you have created. This slight shift in position is a great tactic as it encourages your opponent to use their weaker or less consistent serve. Forcing your opponent to use a weaker serve often results in missed serves. However, if your opponent starts to hurt you by hitting into this opening, it is time to readjust back to the tactical center.

Do not become locked into a return position. Throughout the match, you should be searching for that ideal spot from which you can neutralize your opponent's first serve and counterattack their second.

Sometimes you will find this position early. Sometimes you will find it late. Just believe in yourself and keep searching. Do not give up. You are never out of the match until it is over.

Position 1: First-Strike Position

If you prefer the first-strike point style, you will move in close to or even inside the baseline. Playing closer to the baseline gives you two distinct advantages: **1)** You can angle your return more effectively, and **2)** Your return will get back to your opponent quicker, giving them less time to recover.

However, moving closer to the baseline also means that the serve will get to you faster giving you less time to react to the ball. Therefore, when you choose to return from the first-strike position, you must also modify the fundamentals of your return by using a shortened backswing and simplified footwork patterns. These adjustments will allow you to react quickly to the speed of the incoming serve.

If you choose to return from the first-strike position, which most players should on second serves or when facing an opponent with a weak first serve, you must modify or simplify your return fundamentals. There are two ways to make this modification: **1)** You can go to a continental grip and block or slice your returns into play, or **2)** You can use your normal grips but completely modify your groundstroke using a shorter backswing and follow-through. Both methods are used successfully by many of the top professional players. Study the following two tactical notes to see which option best suits your ability and purposes.

Tactical Key # 1: The block and slice technique will employ a preparation and swing pattern that closely approximates your volley technique, but with a slightly extended follow-through. Your goal is to transfer the server's pace into your return without risking a big swing. Footwork is important. As often as possible, you want to strike the ball as you step onto your front foot. This is the same footwork pattern you would use when hitting your volley. To remind my players to contact the ball on their front foot, I use the phrase: *"step on the ball."*

Tactical Key # 2: The modified groundstroke technique has more in common with your normal groundstroke. The difference is found in its shorter backswing and reduced racket speed. The key is to relax and let your racket do the work. Your focus should be on contacting the ball in the center of your string bed. From start to finish, the swing should be smooth and controlled. I tell my players to point the tip of the racket at the side fence on the backswing and that their follow-through should finish with the tip of the racket pointed toward the sky. Additionally, you should time your footwork so that on contact with the ball your weight transfers from the back to the front foot. Although, I like my players to step into the ball, the modified swing can be used effectively from the open stance, which is often necessary against more powerful serves.

Position 2: Neutral Position

The neutral position is the most used position for returning serve. It is located just behind the baseline putting you into position to cover both the inside and outside serve. The neutral position gives you a bit more time to react to your opponent's serve. However, when returning a first serve, you will still need to use the modified groundstroke technique. On weaker second serves, you can often use your full groundstroke technique.

Position 3: Baseline Control Position

When your groundstroke fundamentals are the strength of your game, you may want to use those same fundamentals when returning serve. However, at the higher levels of tennis, you will have to move back well behind the baseline to give yourself enough time to take a full swing at the ball.

By starting several steps behind the baseline, you can often contact the kick or topspin serve as the ball is descending rather than as it is rising. Taking the ball on the descent is more natural and allows you to use your full groundstroke swing. Moving back also gives you more time to run around your backhand allowing you to hit more forehand returns. This is not the typical return position strategy; however, it is being used more and more by the big hitters at the top levels of the game.

Tactical Key: Although the baseline control position is located well behind the baseline, the actual start position is still determined by the guidelines of general positioning. Remember, the exact position from which you return should never be fixed. It must be adjusted to your opponent's serving potential and the intent of your return.

Baseline control positioning is a conservative approach to returning serve. From behind the baseline, you cannot return the ball on sharp angles through the sideline, so you must be content with keeping your return deep and hitting through the baseline. This positioning is excellent for getting the point started which is the first key to return success; however, it has disadvantages if your objective is to play a first-strike point.

Tactical Key: The further you position yourself from the net, the more the net becomes an obstacle to your return. Therefore, you must add more arc to your return. This extra arc will ensure your return clears the net and lands deep in your opponent's court. If you move back to get more serves in play but keep sending the ball short into your opponent's court, you had better be very good at playing defense because your opponent will always be on the attack.

Always remember, your return position is not fixed. If you want to play a more aggressive point, you should position more aggressively. Better yet, you can sometimes disguise your intent by using one of the special positioning techniques outlined later in this chapter.

Concept # 2: Read the Serve
Key Thought: *See the ball early!*

Your opponent will aim their serve into one of the three targets explained in the first part of this chapter. Thus, when returning, you can expect an inside, outside, or body serve from your opponent *(see diagram 5-1, 5-2, and 5-3)*. Good returners read the direction of their opponent's serve before the ball crosses over the net. The sooner you determine the path of the ball, the better your chance of hitting a solid return.

Focus on the Ball: When you return, avoid watching your opponent's serving motion; instead, focus immediately on the ball. As your opponent readies to serve, you must keep your feet alive. This keeps you ready to react and avoids the heavy foot syndrome caused by blood pooling in your feet. Remember, the ball is your target.

- **See the Ball Early:** Begin watching the ball as soon your opponent bounces it in their service preparation.
- **See the Toss:** Follow the ball up with the server's toss, taking a small step forward.
- **See the Contact Point:** When the server's racket contacts the ball spring forward into your split step.
- **See the Flight Path:** Don't sink on your heels but be ready to spring forward in the direction of the incoming ball.
- **See the Bounce:** There are two reasons this is critical: **1)** You must immediately determine if the served is in or out and make an immediate call, and **2)** The flight path of the ball will change, so to make solid contact you have got to sight in on the ball, i.e., your target.

Tactical Key: We teach our players to remember the 5S's for a successful return: **See, Step, Split, Spring, and Swing**

Ball Location: *Inside, Outside, or Body Return*

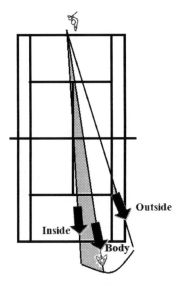

Diagram 5-10

Inside Return: When located at the tactical center, any serve that does not cross the front of your body requires an inside return *(shaded area in diagram 5-10)*. There are three types of inside returns: **1)** The inside-out return will send the ball back crosscourt. **2)** The inside pull-shot sometimes called the inside-in return which sends the ball back down-the-line. **3)** The inside middle shot which sends the ball back deep to the middle of your opponent's court.

Outside Return: Any serve that crosses the front of your body and is headed toward the outside of the court requires an outside return *(unshaded area in diagram 5-10)*. There are four types of outside returns: **1)** The deep middle return will send the ball directly back to the server. **2)** The deep crosscourt return will send the ball back crosscourt with the ball crossing the baseline before crossing the singles sideline. **3)** The crosscourt angle return will also send the ball crosscourt; however, the ball will cross the singles sideline before crossing the baseline. **4)** The down-the-line return will send the ball straight up the near sideline.

Body Return: On serves aimed directly into your body, you will either slide laterally toward the inside of the court or laterally toward the outside of the court. When you slide to the inside, you will hit an outside return, and when you slide to the outside, you will hit an inside return.

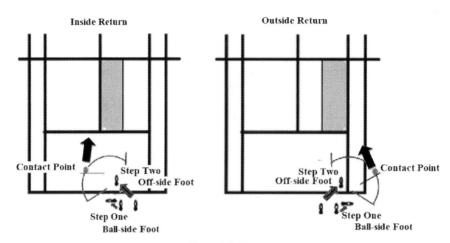

Diagram 5-11

Footwork: As the ball crosses the net, you should recognize immediately if the ball is directed toward your inside or your outside return. Make a unit turn toward the ball with your upper body and step in the direction of the ball with your ball-side foot. As you step with your ball-side foot, your eyes must continually track the ball. You must make a conscious effort to see the ball as it bounces in your service box. Next, you will step toward the ball with your off-side foot *(the foot on the opposite side of the ball)*. In the deuce-court *(as shown in diagram 5-11)*, this would be your right foot on an inside return and your left foot on an outside return. This step will turn your front shoulder toward the ball. Your goal should always be to step into your return with your off-side foot. Remember our key phrase: ***"Step on the ball."***

Tactical Key: If the ball is further away from your position, you must add small adjustment steps as you scramble to get your ball-side foot set behind the ball. Sometimes you can reach the ball with just a few adjustment steps before going into the three-step footwork pattern described above. Other times you will be forced to hit off the ball-side foot using an open stance *(without stepping into the ball with your inside foot)*.

Concept # 3: Where You Send Your Return

Key Thought: *When you set up to return, know what you will do if the serve is sent to your inside, to your outside, or into your body.*

Since eighty percent of all tennis points will end with an error, you must give your opponent plenty of opportunities to make mistakes. Taking this fact into consideration, I provide my players with two primary goals when returning.

- **Goal # 1:** Get the point started. If you make an error on your return, you are losing the point without even giving your opponent the opportunity to make a mistake.

- **Goal # 2:** Extend the point beyond the fourth shot. When returning serve, you will win more points by advancing the point through the first-exchange and into the baseline rally than you can win with your return or second shot *(return +1)*.

Tactical Key: Over-aggressive return and second-shot combinations will result in far too many errors. These errors will bolster your opponent's confidence and cause you to doubt your own ability to compete. You must make your opponent work to hold serve, i.e., force the server to hit more than two shots to win the point.

Basic Return Options
Key Thought: *Neutralize any advantage; counterattack any opening.*

If all you do is react to your opponent's serve, consistency in your return game will become a problem. Moreover, without a consistent return, you will have a difficult time breaking your opponent's serve. What you need is a game plan, and that game plan begins with an understanding of the basic return options.

When you set up in the ready position, you do not know where your opponent will send their serve. Therefore, you should have already determined where you will hit an inside return, outside return, and body return. In fact, you must make these decisions on the practice court if you hope to successfully implement them in a match.

You will have several return options for each type of return. I will illustrate them as in the diagrams and explanations that follow. However, the key to breaking your opponent's serve is to always rely on your best returns. If you are forced to depend on a return you cannot consistently hit inside the court, your return game will suffer. The secret to winning tennis is to always find a way to play from your strength.

The Outside Return
Your opponent will often attack with an outside serve. This serve is aimed into the outer half of the service box and is hit, so the ball crosses the front of your body as it heads toward the outside of the court. The objective of the outside serve is not to end the point but to push you into the corner or even outside of the doubles sideline, *the shaded area in diagram 5-1 at the beginning of this chapter.*

The Server's Intent: Your opponent's goal is to force you wide of the singles sideline opening the opposite corner of the court for their second shot. Thus, when you understand what your opponent is trying to do, you can neutralize the advantage they are attempting to create.

Outside Return Options: When receiving an outside serve, you have four directional choices for your return: **1)** deep middle, **2)** deep crosscourt, **3)** short-angle crosscourt, or **4)** down the line. The deep middle and deep crosscourt returns are relatively high-percentage shots and are excellent options for keeping your return in play. When returning your opponent's first serve, they are your best options for neutralizing your opponent's attack.

On-the-other-hand, the short-angle and down-the-line returns are higher-risk options and should be used sparingly *(see high-risk characteristics in chapter 3)*. The short-angle and down-the-line returns are your counterattack options. They are most effective when attacking your opponent's weak second serves.

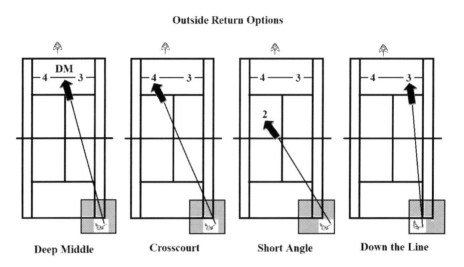

Outside Return Options

Deep Middle   Crosscourt   Short Angle   Down the Line

Diagram 5-12

Option # 1: Deep Middle Return

Key Thought: *This is your primary return for neutralizing your opponent's first serve.*

The deep middle return is often employed when facing a powerful first serve. The beauty of this return lies in its simplicity. As you can see in *diagram 5-12*, you are returning the ball directly back in the direction from which it came. If you are a bit early at contact, your shot will go crosscourt. If you are right on time, your return will go to the middle, and if you are a bit late, your shot will go down the line. In each instance, there is a good chance that your shot will land inside the court. Since you are less focused on direction, you can concentrate on keeping the ball deep which will force your opponent to back off the baseline. When your opponent moves back, you will have taken the sting out of their next shot.

Tactical Key: The deep middle return can be used as the entry shot into any of the baseline patterns. I teach my players to use the three-deep pattern against aggressive opponents. In the three-deep pattern, you send your first three shots deep *(return, return+1, and return+2)*. This pattern pushes your opponent back behind the baseline making it difficult for them to launch an attack. It also increases your chances of receiving a short ball giving you an opportunity to launch an attack. However, the best reason is simply this: It gives your opponent three opportunities to make an error.

Option # 2: Deep Crosscourt Return

Key Thought: *This is a high-percentage shot used to neutralize the advantage created by an outside serve.*

The crosscourt return is the highest-percentage return, and when the ball lands beyond your opponent's 9-foot depth line, it will neutralize the server's second-shot options *(see diagram 5-12)*.

This option is an excellent entry into the Base-X groundstroke pattern and can often force the server to abandon their attack. If your opponent chooses to continue the open court attack by hitting a low-percentage down-the-line shot, they risk making an error or opening their court for your crosscourt counterattacking shot.

Tactical Key: Effective tennis strategy uses the diagonal rally which keeps the ball out of the middle third of the court. Not many points are won with outside shots; however, a deep outside shot will tempt your opponent to hit down the line. This gives you two advantages: **1)** The down the line shot is a low-percentage shot which increases your opponent's chances of committing an error, and **2)** The down-the-line shot opens the court for your next crosscourt shot, i.e., you can hit crosscourt while at the same time angling the ball away from your opponent.

Option # 3: Short-Angle Crosscourt Return

Key Thought: *The short-angle is an aggressive return used to open the court for your next shot.*

The short angle crosscourt return is an aggressive return used to force your opponent out wide of their singles sideline *(see diagram 5-12)*. It then opens the opposite corner of the court for your second shot. This makes it a great one-two punch when attacking a weak second serve. I have a saying, "beat an angle with a better angle." When your opponent forces you short and wide, go after them by hitting an even sharper angle back across the court. For accuracy, aim the short-angle crosscourt into the center of the diagonal short-target box *(short target 2 in diagram 5-12)*.

Tactical Key: There will be times when you are early on your deep crosscourt return turning it into the short-angle return. So, always be ready to take advantage of any return that forces your opponent out wide of their singles sideline.

Option # 4: Down-the-Line Return

Tactical Key: *Use the down-the-line return to attack open court or to send a ball to your opponent's weaker groundstroke.*

The outside down-the-line return is the most aggressive return *(diagram 5-12)*. However, it is also a low-percentage shot, and unless it pressures your opponent, it will simply open your court to their attack. You should use this return on only two occasions: **1)** Your only chance is to hit an outright winner, or **2)** You are inside both the baseline and singles sideline. From the midcourt zone, you are positioned to hit a clean winner down the line. The attacking down-the-line shot is both high-risk and high-reward. If you are in the midcourt and your confidence is high go for it. If not, hit the ball back deep crosscourt and continue to build.

Tactical Key: When your opponent serves wide, they want you to send your shot to their inside as this gives them a crosscourt angle into your open court. Unless you can hurt your opponent with your down-the-line return, you must avoid hitting into their trap.

Inside Return

Another service attack is to aim the serve through the inside half of the service box. The goal of the inside serve is to challenge your reaction time forcing a weak return that opens the court for your opponent's forehand attack. The inside serve does not cross the front or midline of your body and lands in the inside half of the service box, the *shaded area in diagram 5-13.*

Inside Return Options: You have three choices for your inside return: **1)** Hit it straight up the middle, **2)** Pull it down-the-line into target 4 in the ad court and into target 3 in the deuce court, or **3)** Hit it inside-out into target 3 in the ad court and into target 4 in the deuce court. However, it is best to have decided which option you will use before your opponent hits their serve.

Tactical Key: You must know where you will hit your return before you take-up the ready position. This decision can be somewhat flexible. For example, you could have a different plan for an inside, outside, or body serve. Now you have simplified the return process. Instead of making an instantaneous decision as you see the serve, you can simply react to the serve with your pre-programmed return response.

Inside Return Options

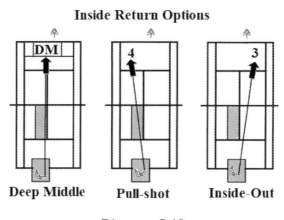

Deep Middle   Pull-shot   Inside-Out

Diagram 5-13

Option # 1: Deep Middle Return
Key Thought: *To keep your return deep, aim for the server's feet.*

Power servers follow a typical two-shot plan: Blast their serve through the inside target to attack your timing, and then hug the baseline looking to attack your short return with an aggressive groundstroke into the open court. By returning up the middle, you are less focused on direction and can concentrate on keeping the ball deep which forces your opponent to back off the baseline *(diagram 5-13)*. You do not have to hit this shot with pace, even a blocked or sliced ball that lands deep near the server's feet will force them to step back. By forcing your opponent to move back and hit off their back foot, you will take some of the sting out of their next shot.

Tactical Key: Once your deep middle return has pushed your opponent back, you can use your second shot to work your way into the point

Option # 2: Pull-Shot Return
Key Thought: *This should be your go-to return, especially when attacking a second serve.*

The pull-shot is a versatile return. It can be used defensively to neutralize your opponent's attack or offensively to hit into an opponent's weakness or away from the server into the open corner. Technically, the pull-shot has much in common with a baseball player pulling an inside pitch down-the-line. The hips and shoulders rotate naturally and powerfully through the pull-shot motion which allows a baseball player to drive the ball with tremendous power. For example, most towering home runs are hit off inside pitches. Likewise, in tennis, the inside ball is a high-percentage opportunity to go on the offensive and take control of the point. You can use the pull-shot from both the ad and deuce courts and with either your forehand or your backhand. When you are balanced and in control, the pull-shot can be an effective first-serve return; however, it is most effective when attacking a weaker second serve. Against the second serve, you should step into your pull-shot by taking the ball early and on the rise and driving it deep and through the baseline.

Tactical Key: The inside pull-shot is a high-percentage opportunity for you to go on the offensive.

Option # 3: Inside-out Return
Key Thought: *This is a great way to attack with your forehand.*

The inside-out return is hit crosscourt using the same high-percentage advantages as the outside crosscourt shot: **1)** Crosses the lowest part of the net; **2)** Has more court to land in, and **3)** Sets up a diagonal rally pattern which in turn leads into the Base-X rally pattern. Unless, you are a right-handed player on the ad side or a left-handed player on the deuce side, where the inside-out return is an excellent entry into the more aggressive inside-out forehand barrage pattern *(see chapter 7 for details).* For most players, the inside-out forehand is more offensive in nature, while the inside-out backhand is more of a neutralizing shot.

From the ad-court, a right-handed returner can use the inside-out forehand to attack a right-handed opponent's backhand. On second serves, the goal is to overpower your opponent's backhand with the pace of your forehand forcing an error or an opportunity ball. However, against your opponent's first serve, the key is to get your return in and deep so that you can attack with your next inside-out forehand.

Tactical Key: From the ad court, a right-handed returner can use the inside-out forehand to attack a right-handed opponent's backhand corner.

Body Return

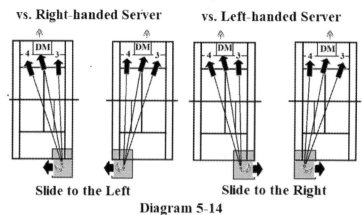

Body Return Options

vs. Right-handed Server   **vs. Left-handed Server**

Slide to the Left   **Slide to the Right**

Diagram 5-14

When your opponent sends you a body serve, i.e., a serve aimed through the center of the service box and into your body, your first objective is to move away from the path of the incoming ball. Depending on the direction you choose to slide, a body serve can become either an inside or an outside return. When facing a right-handed server, you should slide to your left. If you are also right-handed, this will allow you to use a forehand return. However, when facing a left-handed server, you should slide to your right. Although this means hitting a backhand return, it will keep you from being jammed by the natural curve of the ball *(see diagram 5-14)*.

Your options for returning the body serve would depend on the direction of your slide. If you slide toward your backhand side, you will use the forehand options, and if you slide toward your forehand side, you will use the backhand options described for inside or outside returns.

Tactical Key: I teach my players to slide left against a right-handed server and to slide right against a left-handed server.

Base-X Return Plan
Key Thought: *In most circumstances, your best return is your most consistent return.*

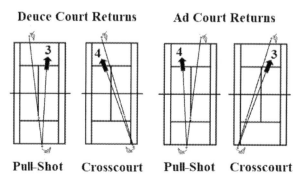

Deuce Court Returns   **Ad Court Returns**

Pull-Shot   **Crosscourt**   **Pull-Shot**   **Crosscourt**

Diagram 5-15

Our base-X return plan uses two high percentage returns. Outside serves are hit crosscourt and inside serves down the line using an inside pull-shot *(see diagram 5-15)*. If you learn to rely on these two high-percentage returns, you will have a firm foundation to fall back on whenever you face opponents who employ serves that are difficult to return.

Forehand Return Plan

Key Thought: *If your forehand is a weapon, use it as often as possible.*

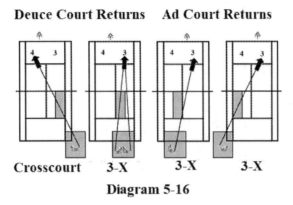

Deuce Court Returns   Ad Court Returns

Crosscourt   3-X   3-X   3-X

Diagram 5-16

This pattern emphasizes the 3-X or backhand attack into the backhand corner of a right-handed opponent *(see diagram 5-15)*. It is an excellent entry into the Forehand-X pattern. Against a left-handed opponent, you would use a 4-X attack *(not shown in diagram 5-15)*.

The Returner's Second Shot

Key Thought: *Get your second shot in if you want to win!*

When you hit your second shot, you will have already forced the server to get their second shot in play. Thus, you are just one shot away from successfully advancing the point into the baseline rally. If your opponent is an attacking player, who likes to play short points, every time you force them to hit the ball, you give them another opportunity to make an error. Conversely, if you are an aggressive player, you are increasing the odds that they will send you an opportunity ball that you can attack. In either case, the formula for a winning return game is a simple one-two concept: **1)** Get your return in play; and **2)** Get your second shot in play.

To become a dangerous returner, you must understand that the purpose of your second shot is not to end the point, or even to set-up a winner. Instead, think of your second shot as a response to the game situation. The dangerous returner is the player who can see the court and understands what shot to play based on the quality of their opponent's last shot.

Tactical Key: Whenever possible, use your return to set-up your second shot. Middle returns force short replies; angled returns open the court, and down-the-line returns force your opponent to hit on the move.

Second-Shot Options: Return + 1

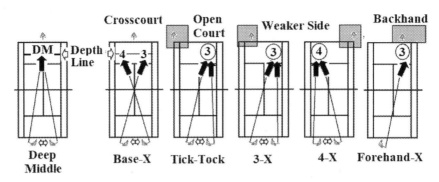

Diagram 5-17

Option # 1: Deep Middle
Key Thought: *Neutralize and Advance to Stage Two, the Baseline Rally.*

When you hit the ball deep *(beyond the 9-foot, depth line)*, your opponent must decide to either move back or to hold their ground and take the ball on the rise. When they move back, they are on the defensive and are likely to send you a short ball that you can attack. When they decide to take the ball on the rise, they are hitting a difficult shot, which makes them more likely to make an error. *See diagram 5-17.*

Tactical Note: Although you plan to send your second shot into the deep middle, depth is more important than direction. Just hit your shot deep beyond the 9-foot, depth line and then scramble to maintain your court position in the tactical center of your opponent's next shot. You have two primary goals: **1)** push your opponent back, and **2)** regain your position at the tactical center.

Option # 2: Base-X
Key Thought: *Build and advance the point into Stage Two, the Baseline Rally.*

The crosscourt groundstroke is the highest-percentage shot in tennis and is the fundamental shot in the Base-X rally pattern. The crosscourt shot crosses over the lowest part of the net and is aimed in a diagonal direction, i.e., the longest angle on the court. The crosscourt shot is usually hit using either your outside forehand or backhand groundstroke *(shown in the diagram)*. However, from the middle of the court, it could be hit with an inside-out or inside pull-shot *(not shown in the diagram)*.

If your opponent hits the ball to your left, you will direct your crosscourt shot toward target-3, and if your opponent hits the ball to your right, you will hit your crosscourt toward target-4. *(See diagram 5-17.)*

Tactical Key: The crosscourt shot has the least offensive potential of any groundstroke; therefore, you must think of it as a building shot. When hitting crosscourt, your emphasis is on consistency, placement, depth, spin, and then lastly on pace. Building shot errors are unforced errors, so resist the temptation to go for winners. Instead, your goal is never to miss a crosscourt shot wide or into the net. You will not win consistently if you give your opponent free points with unforced errors.

Option # 3: Tick/Tock
Key Thought: *You have open court, so attack.*

The tick/tock option occurs in two situations: **1)** Your return forced your opponent wide of the singles sideline, or **2)** Your opponent hits their second shot down the line. In either case, you can hit your second shot into the open court away from your opponent. Your first thought should be to hurt your opponent, by putting them on the defensive and forcing an error. Only go for an outright winner when the ball is positioned exactly where you like it, you are in good court position, and you can hit from a balanced position. If not, you should go for a good shot that will make your opponent hit on the move. *See diagram 5-17.*

Tactical Key: When you aim for the center of the deep target box and hit your shot through the baseline, it allows you to hit aggressively with the confidence that your shot will land in the court.

Option # 4: 3-X
Key Thought: *Make your opponent uncomfortable.*

A primary way to force errors is to force your opponent into uncomfortable situations. You can do this by forcing them to hit on the move, from outside of the singles sideline, from deep in the court, or with their weaker groundstrokes. Often this means directing the ball into your opponent's backhand corner *(see diagram 5-17)*. When facing a right-handed opponent, the 3-X option sends the ball into their backhand corner. This is an excellent way for a right-handed player to set up an inside-out forehand attack *(see forehand barrage in chapter 7)*. However, if you are left-handed, the 3-X option sets up a rally on the 3-to-3 angle allowing you to hit your outside forehand into your right-handed opponent's backhand corner.

Forcing your opponent to hit from uncomfortable strike zones will accomplish this same goal. Slicing the ball will force your opponent to hit from their lower strike zone while looping deep topspin shots will force them to hit from their upper strike zone. If a player has difficulty with either of these shots, you should give them plenty of opportunities to make errors.

Tactical Key: Attack your opponent's weakness as often as possible. If you are left-handed, you must make the 3-X shot a staple of your second-shot tactics.

Option # 5: 4-X
Key Thought: *Find your opponent's weakness.*

In the 4-X option, you direct your second shot into the 4-target in your opponent's end of the court. You can use this option to attack a right-handed opponent's forehand or a left-handed opponent's backhand groundstroke. As you play, pay attention to your opponent's weakness. If your opponent has trouble hitting low balls, you can use a slice shot to keep the bounce low. If their weakness is the high bouncing ball, use a topspin loop to force them back or to hit from their upper strike zone. If it is pace that gives your opponent trouble, drive the ball using the added speed to overpower them. If you are right-handed and your opponent is left-handed, the 4-X option will set up a 4-to-4 rally where you can drive your forehand into your opponent's left-handed backhand.

Tactical Key: If you are left-handed, you must make the 4X option using an inside-out forehand a significant part of your game plan against left-handed opponents. If you are right-handed, you need to be able to use it against a left-handed opponent.

Option # 6: Forehand-Barrage, The inside-out forehand attack
Key Thought: *Use your strength against your opponent's weakness.*

If your forehand is your strength and you can drive the ball inside-out, the forehand attack into your opponent's backhand corner can force errors or create opportunity balls. The inside-out forehand barrage is an excellent option when returning from the ad court side. From the ad court you can send the ball back crosscourt on your return, then run around your opponent's next shot to drive your second shot back into the backhand corner with your inside-out forehand. The goal is to overpower your opponent's weaker backhand with your forehand attack. *See diagram 5-17.*

Tactical Key: Whenever possible, you should attack using your strength against your opponent's weakness.

Specialized Positioning
Key Thought: *"Variety may be the spice of life, but consistency pays the bills."* – Doug Cooper, Outside In

One of the real keys to a successful serve is a feeling of comfort with the situation at hand. When the server glances across the net at the returner, he likes to see the same picture every time. The court itself never changes; however, you as the returner can alter the picture by where you position. When you move in, you make the service box seem smaller, which can cause the server to hit their serve into the net, and when you move back, you make the service box appear longer, which in turn can cause the server to hit their serve long.

The server also feels comfortable when they know you are going to remain in the same position throughout their service motion. You can make the server uncomfortable by showing one look, but then changing position as the service toss goes up.

An important, yet often overlooked, element in breaking serve is to make the server uncomfortable with the picture you are showing them. Every time your opponent steps up to serve, you want to make them think about three things: **1)** Where are you located this time? **2)** Why are you located there? And finally, **3)** Where will you be when they hit their serve. When you can distract the server into thinking about something other than their game plan, you reduce their serving efficiency.

Backhand Shade Position

The backhand shade is primarily a second serve strategy in which you position yourself so that you are covering up to two-thirds of the service box with your forehand. By shifting or shading toward your backhand side, you are leaving more of the forehand portion of your service box open. This tempts the server to hit into the open court to your forehand side, which is where you want them to serve.

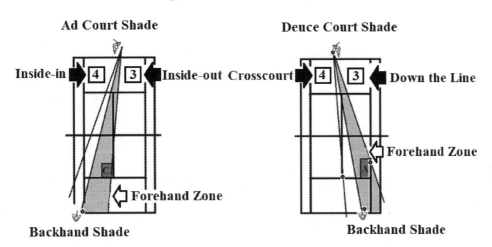

Right-handed Returner

Ad Court Shade   **Deuce Court Shade**

Inside-in ▶ 4 / 3 ◀ Inside-out   Crosscourt ▶ 4   3 ◀ Down the Line

◁ Forehand Zone

◁ Forehand Zone

Backhand Shade   **Backhand Shade**

Diagram 5-18

Diagram 5-18 shows the ad and deuce court shade position for a right-handed returner. In the ad court, the returner has shifted out wide tempting the server to hit an inside serve; whereas, in the deuce court the returner has shifted toward the middle tempting the server to hit an outside serve. From each of these positions, the right-handed returner is covering about two-thirds of the service box with their forehand. If you are left-handed, you will merely reverse this positioning by shading toward the inside in the ad court and the outside in the deuce court.

From the backhand shade position in the ad-court, a right-handed returner has two aggressive shot options: **1)** Drive the ball inside-out to the center of the Target-3 box; or **2)** Drive the ball with an inside pull-shot to the center of the Target-4 box. From the deuce-court side, the right-handed returner can: **1)** Drive the ball down-the-line using a 90-degree change of direction toward the center of the Target-3 box, or **2)** Drive the ball crosscourt to the center of the Target-4 box. If you are left-handed, you will reverse these options.

Tactical Key: How much of the forehand court you leave open will be determined by your opponent's ability to target the forehand area. If they can accurately place balls into your forehand side, you must choose to leave less of the court open.

Cat-and-Mouse Positioning

In this option, you will start out positioned in your normal return position. Then as the server makes the toss to hit their serve, you will reposition into a new return position. You can use the Cat and Mouse in two ways:

- **Depth Switch:** to switch from your normal return position into a more aggressive or less aggressive position.
- **Lateral Switch:** to switch from your usual position into the more aggressive backhand shade position.

The cat-and-mouse switch is used when your opponent has fallen into a specific serve pattern which allows you to anticipate the location of their next serve.

Bait-and-Switch Positioning

When using the bait-and-switch, you show a return position that is unexpected, something different than your normal return position. Then when the server makes their toss, you move into a different position. The goal is to bait your opponent into serving into a specific location or into using a particular type of serve and then switching into a position to cover that serve. For example, you might start out in the first-strike position tempting your opponent to hit a hard serve; and then, on the server's toss slide back to the baseline control position. Another example might be for you to start out using an extreme backhand shade position tempting your opponent to serve to your forehand side and then, on the server's toss slide back toward your normal return position.

Tactical Key: You can use the bait-and-switch position to take away your opponent's best serve by tempting them to go with a weaker option. This tactic can often result in a missed first serve which gives you an opportunity to attack their weaker second serve.

Chapter 5 Summary

The Serve

The first part of chapter 5 is devoted to helping you develop a two-shot game plan for your service games. You can reduce the main point of this discussion down to this: When you step up to serve you must know where you intend to hit your first-serve and where you will hit your second shot. Having a plan for your first two shots will help you get more points started. More importantly, since most tennis points last less than four shots, just getting your serve and second-shot into play, will help you win many more points. The Tactical Point Control System is predicated on playing each point with a plan, and that plan always begins in the First-Exchange.

The first key to holding serve is to get a high percentage of your first serves in play. If your first serve is a reliable weapon, you can survive with a percentage of around sixty percent. If you get it up to sixty-five percent, you will be darn near unbeatable. However, if your first serve is not a significant weapon, then your first-serve percentage needs to climb upwards towards eighty percent. Why is the first serve so important? First, because there usually is a substantial drop in quality between a first and second serve. This means that your opponent can be more aggressive against your second serve than they can against your first.

Second, even if the drop off between your first and second serve is negligible, there is an important psychological reason for getting your first serve in play. That reason is your opponent's mindset. Most opponents will shift from defending against your first serve to attacking your second. This shift in mindset signals a significant change in your opponent's mental focus and tactical decisions. Kind of like shifting from 'I hope I can get this serve back,' to 'I'm going to win this point.' This is a significant shift in both mental focus and confidence.

Third, your opponent is probably going to move forward taking up a more aggressive return position on or just inside the baseline. From this position, the returner is both thinking about and positioning themselves to attack. Thus, winning a point with your second serve becomes much more difficult.

Tactical Key: The most prominent mentality trap when serving is the assumption that you must hit your first serve hard. Blasting away with your serve, even if you manage to hit a few aces, is not worth the price you will pay for a low first-serve percentage. Giving your opponent a steady diet of second serves will lead to lost service games, and lost service games will lead to lost matches.

How important is your second serve? Well, if you don't have a good one, you'll probably lose the match. In tennis, you can often hide your weakest shot. But, if your second serve is soft, it is difficult to hide. You know that whenever you miss your first serve, your opponent is going to attack. Knowing your opponent is about to pounce, puts even more pressure on your first serve, which makes it even harder to get it in play. The question is, what are you going to do about it. My suggestions in order of importance:

- Get more first serves in play
- Improve your second serve
- Have a tactical plan for how you will employ your second serve

The Return

The second part of chapter 5 is devoted to your return, which after the serve, is the second most important shot in tennis. However, despite its importance, the service return is probably the least practiced of all the tennis shots. In the Tactical Point Control System, I place a tremendous amount of emphasis on the First-exchange. I believe that if you improve this phase of your game, you will be on your way toward becoming a successful tennis player.

As stated in chapter three, most points last fewer than four shots, which means if you can get your return and your second shot in play, you have significantly increased your chances of winning the point. You have now forced the server to get their third shot into play. If your opponent is a big server who likes to play short first-strike points, the more shots you force them to hit, the better the chance they will grow impatient and make an error.

Conversely, if you are the attacking player, the more times you force your opponent to return one of your aggressive shots, the better the chance they will send you an opportunity ball which will allow you to finish the point with a winner. In either case, the primary formula for a winning tennis game is a simple one-two plan:

- Get your return in play
- Get your second-shot in play as well

See you on the court.

Chapter 6
First-Exchange Drills

Purpose: The first-exchange drills develop the first four shots of the tennis point, i.e., the serve, the service return and then the server's second shot followed by the returner's second shot.

Drill Principles: Before going into the first-exchange drills, I need to cover the four fundamental principles that govern all my drills: **1)** Drill Theory; **2)** Pressure Training; **3)** Shot Accountability; and **4)** Shot Tolerance.

Drill Theory: The point-phase drills are games in which players compete against either another teammate *(keeping score)* or against a set standard *(required number of consecutive shots into a target)*. Each drill simulates a part or segment of a tennis point. You will be taught to play within a tactical framework where you must strategize, or problem solve for each shot. You will learn to hit each shot with a purpose. In some drills restrictions and stipulations are used to mold the drills so that they simulate specific game situations. By playing within the defined parameters of each drill, you will learn discipline, increase your willpower, and be forced to problem-solve in match-like situations. Each drill is timed, has a specific number of repetitions, or ends when you achieve the desired score. Every drill uses recordable results allowing you to see how well you are performing in each practice and to measure and track your improvement.

Pressure Training: The real test of your tennis ability will be demonstrated by how well you compete under the pressure of an actual tennis match. Practice should be challenging requiring you to train at the top of your playing range. During a tennis match, you will face four kinds of pressure: tactical pressure, mental/emotional pressure, momentum pressure, and physical pressure. In practice, you must prepare yourself to succeed under the same kinds of pressures you will face in an actual match. To prepare for pressure, you must be pushed to reach your potential, in other words, you must learn to practice using pressure situations. Most of the drills will require you to keep score. Keeping score requires mental energy, the same kind of mental strength you will need in an actual match. Keeping score also increases pressure, because when you keep score, it means there will be a winner and a loser. Besides keeping score, the drills will also test your willpower. In match play, most players will react to stressful situations with shots and tactics that are comfortable; however, a quality opponent will often take away your favorite shots and strategies. Pressure drills will force you into uncomfortable situations forcing you to stretch your limits. Frequently you will be asked to execute shots and to use tactics that might feel uncomfortable; however, learning to adopt a positive attitude in response to these challenging situations is merely a matter of willpower.

Shot Accountability: You are responsible for where your shot lands on the opponent's side of the court. Shot accountability is the most significant key to success in tennis. To win a match against an equally skilled opponent, you must be able to hit the ball into a specific target area. Accuracy is critical to building a point using your strength *(offense)* as well as neutralizing the advantage of your opponent *(defense)*. Practice is where shot accountability is learned; however, to master shot accountability, you must hold yourself accountable for where you send the ball. Not just sometimes, but all the time.

Shot Tolerance: How many consecutive shots can you keep in play? More importantly, how many can you send back to a specific target without becoming so uncomfortable that you either error by going for too big of a shot or miss by becoming tentative and trying to play too safe. To successfully implement the **Tactical Point Control System**, you must work hard to develop your shot tolerance.

The Three Learning Stages

- **Cognitive *(Mental)* Stage:** In this stage, your focus is on gaining an understanding of how to perform a particular skill. In the cognitive stage, your coach will guide you through the performance with verbal cues and visual demonstrations. You can also learn by watching other athletes in practice or on video as they perform the required movements. Another excellent visual cue is to watch yourself performing the skill either in a mirror or on video. Just remember, your goal in the cognitive stage is to develop a motor program or internal representation of the specific skills that will allow you to advance into the associative stage.
- **Associative *(Practice)* Stage:** In this stage, your focus moves from merely learning the skill to performing the skill with both accuracy and consistency. During the associative stage, the control of your performance advances from visual and verbal to proprioceptive control which is your ability to feel the performance as it is taking place.
- **Autonomous *(Automatic)* Stage:** This stage begins when you can perform the skill at a high level of proficiency. In the autonomous stage, the performance of the skill takes less thought as the perfected motor program attains a high level of proprioceptive control allowing your mind to focus less on performance and more on the other aspects of the sport such as tactics and strategy.

Developmental Drills
Key Thought: *All players must have dependable serves and returns; however, advanced players must be able to both serve and return with consistency, accuracy, and power.*

I teach the first-exchange with three developmental drills. Each of the three drills develops one of the critical components of the serve and the return. A fourth component, competitive success, is an integral part of each of the three developmental drills.

- **Consistency**: I expect my players to get a minimum of 80-percent of their second serves into play *(shot tolerance)*.
- **Accuracy:** I expect my players to direct a minimum of 60-percent of their second serves into the correct service target *(shot accountability)*.
- **Power**: I expect my players to maintain at least 50-percent of their first serves in the power range *(ball hits the back fence before second bounce)*.
- **Competitive Success**; I expect my players to maintain less than a 20-percent error ratio on their service returns *(shot tolerance and accountability)*.

Base Serving Drills

Set-Up: All serving drills will use the set-up shown in *Diagram 6-1*. The black circles along the baseline represent the positioning of target cones.

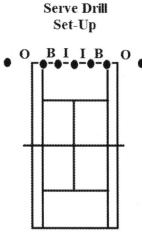

Serve Drill Set-Up

Diagram 6-1

O – Outside Target: The first cone used for the outside target is placed ten feet outside the doubles sideline. The second cone is placed on the intersection of the baseline and the singles sideline. All serves that land in the service box and then pass between these cones are outside serves. This includes serves that pass outside of the first cone.

B – Body Target: The first cone used for the body target is located on the intersection of the baseline and singles sideline. The second cone is positioned midway between the singles sideline and the center hash mark. All serves that land in the service box and then pass between these cones are body serves.

I – Inside Target: The first cone used for the inside target is located midway between the singles sideline and the center hash mark. The second cone is placed on the center hash mark. All serves that land in the service box and then pass between these cones are inside serves.

Drill # 1: Second Serve Consistency

Purpose: To teach the server to be consistent with the second serve.

Set-up: Two players serve on the same end of a full singles court.

Sequence: One Shot: Each player uses their second serve.

Directions: Drill consists of two rounds. **Round # 1:** Player # 1 serves ten serves to the deuce court while player # 2 serves ten serves to the ad court. **Round # 2:** Players switch sides with Player # 1 now serving ten serves to the ad court while player # 2 serves ten serves to the ad court.

Scoring: Server keeps track of the number of successful serves for each round. The score is reported to a coach who will keep a record of made serves on the practice score sheet.

Standard: The server should be successful on 80 percent of their second serves *(8 out of 10)*.

Tactical Key: Each player should work to develop a serve ritual that they will follow religiously throughout each repetition of the drill.

Drill # 2: Second Serve Accuracy

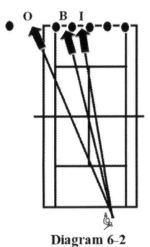

Diagram 6-2

Purpose: To teach the server to be both consistent and accurate with the second serve.

Set-up: Two players serve on the same end of a full singles court.

Sequence: One Shot: Each player uses their second serve.

Directions: Drill consists of two rounds. **Round # 1:** Player # 1 serves six serves to the deuce court, two serves into each of the serving targets as shown in diagram 6-2, while player # 2 serves six serves to the ad court, 2 into each of the serving targets *(not shown)*. **Round # 2:** Players switch sides with Player # 1 now serving 6 serves to the ad court, two into each of the serving targets, while player # 2 serves six serves to the ad court, two into each of the serving targets.

Scoring: A successful serve is counted each time the ball lands in the service box and then passes between the cones that correspond to the serving target *(see diagram 6-1 and 6-2)*. The server keeps track of the number of successful serves for each round. The score is reported to the coach who will keep a record of made serves on the practice score sheet.

Standard: The server should be successful on sixty-six percent of their second serves *(5 out of 6)*. A successful serve is hit into the appropriate target, i.e., inside, body, or outside serves.

Tactical Keys: 1) Each player should work to develop a serve ritual that they will follow religiously throughout each repetition of the drill, **2)** Each player should make a mental note of the serving targets where they are the most consistent. Then they should build a game plan that takes advantage of their serving strengths.

Drill # 3: Serving Power

Purpose: To develop power, depth, and penetration with your first serve.

Set-up: Two players serve on the same end of a full singles court.

Sequence: One Shot: Each player uses their first serve.

Directions: Drill consists of two rounds. **Round # 1:** Player # 1 serves ten first serves into the deuce court while Player # 2 serves ten first serves into the ad court. Round # 2: Players switch sides. Player # 1 now serves ten first serves into the ad court while Player # 2 serves ten first serves into the deuce court. Players should aim their power serve through the inside target. *(see diagram 6-1)*

Scoring: Server gets one power point for every serve that lands in the service box and then hits the back fence before the second bounce. Although the server is aiming for the inside target, any serve that lands within the service box is considered successful.

Standard: The server should have five power points. *(5 of 10 or fifty percent)* A .power point is awarded for each successful serve that hits the back fence before the second bounce.

Tactical Keys: 1) Each player should work to develop a serve ritual that they will follow religiously throughout each repetition of the drill, **2)** All players must have a dependable serve. Advanced players must also be able to hit their first serve with both accuracy and power.

Keys for First Serve Success

- Use a serving ritual before each serve. There are no exceptions to this rule.
- Location on first serves is as important as power.
- Aim your power serve through the inside target.
- Adopt an aggressive mindset for first serves: Strike first, strike hard, no fear!

Two-Shot First-Exchange Drills
Key Thought: *Get your first two shots in play.*

The two most important shots in the first-exchange are the serve and the return. These two shots will account for more than fifty percent of the total shots you will make in a match. They are the get the point started shots. If you double-fault or miss your returns, you are giving away free points. Why, because when you fail to get one of these shots into play, you are losing the point without giving your opponent an opportunity to make an error.

Scoring Note: To simplify scoring, the server keeps track of successful serves and the returner keeps track of made returns.

Drill # 1: Two-Shot Second Serve and Return Drill

Purpose: 1) To teach the server to be consistent with the second serve; and **2)** to prepare the returner to consistently get the return into play using the deep middle return.

Set-up: Two players work cooperatively on opposite ends of a full singles court.

Sequence: Two shots: **1)** Second Serve; and **2)** Return using deep middle option. The server must move to the return and catch the ball. This gets the server used to moving quickly after their serve. Do not waste time in this drill by hitting additional shots.

Directions: Drill consists of two rounds. **Round # 1:** Player # 1 will use a second serve, to hit ten serves, five to the deuce court and five to the ad court. Player # 2 will return using the deep middle option. Player # 1 will keep track of the number of made serves, and player # 2 will keep track of the number of successful returns. **Round # 2:** Then the two players will switch roles with player # 2 serving and player # 1 returning.

Scoring: The server keeps track of the number of made serves, and the returner keeps track of the number of made returns. A service ace counts as a missed return. At the end of each round, the results are reported to the coach who then records them on the practice score sheet.

Standard: 1) The server should make eighty percent of their second serves *(8 of 10 serves),* and **2)** the returner should return eighty percent of the good serves. The return percentage is calculated based on the number of successful serves received.

Tactical Keys: 1) Server should aim their serve into either the returner's body or backhand side. **2)** The returner should aim their return at the server's feet. This will help to keep the return deep and in the middle of the court.

Drill # 2: Two-Shot Inside/Outside Serves and Returns

Purpose: 1) To teach the server to control the direction of their serve; and **2)** To teach returners to use the base return plan.

Set-up: Two players work cooperatively on a full singles court.

Directions: Drill consists of two rounds.

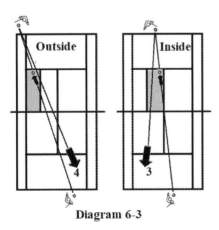

Diagram 6-3

Round # 1: Player # 1 will use a second serve to hit twenty serves. Ten serves into the deuce court, five serves into the outside target, and five serves into the inside target. Then, ten serves in the ad court, five serves into the outside target, and five serves into the inside target. Player # 2 will return outside serves crosscourt and inside serves with a pull-shot down the line. **Round # 2:** After player # 1 has hit all twenty serves, player # 1 and player # 2 will switch roles with player # 2 serving and player # 1 returning. The server will keep track of the number of good serves into each target box. Returner will keep track of the number of the number of successful returns.

Scoring: 1) The server keeps track of the number of made serves. **Note:** I want the server to aim for the correct target; however, scoring is based on the number of successful serves. **2)** The returner keeps track of made returns. A service ace counts as a missed return. **Note:** I want the returner to work on using my base return plan by hitting inside serves down the line using an inside pull-shot and outside serves crosscourt using an outside shot. However, scoring is based on returns kept in play.

Standards: 1) Servers are expected to get eighty percent of their serves into play. *(16 of 20).* **2)** Returners are expected to get eighty percent of their returns into play. Returner's percentage is based on the number of successful serves they receive.

Tactical Key: To employ serving and returning tactics, you must be able to direct your shots into specific targets. If you cannot place your serve or return, your first-exchange tactics will be weak.

Four-Shot First-Exchange Drills
Key Thought: *Get your first four shots into play.*

The first-exchange consists of the first four shots in a tennis point: **1)** The serve, **2)** the service return, **3)** The server's second shot *(serve +1),* and **4)** The returner's second shot *(return +1).* Since statistics indicate that most points will end during the first four shots of the point, you must be able to play successfully through the first exchange. This is a pivotal element to becoming a successful tennis player. Use the following drills to master this phase of the game. If you consistently lose points with errors in the first-exchange, you will have a difficult time winning matches against top-level players.

Scoring Note: In each drill, the server and returner start with a specific number of points. They lose one of these points each time they make an error, or their opponent hits a winning shot. At the end of each round, they will report the number of remaining points to the coach at the end of the drill. Thus, at the end of each drill, percentages can be calculated for winning percentage when serving and returning.

Drill # 3: Four-Shot Second Serve and Return Drill

Purpose: This is a four-shot drill used to develop the skills needed to complete the first exchange. In this drill, you are not required to aim your serve into any specific target; however, you should practice aiming into the returner's body or backhand. When returning, practice using the base return pattern. You should hit outside serves crosscourt and inside serves with a pull-shot down the line.

Set-up: Two players are working cooperatively on a full singles court.

Sequence: Four shots: **1)** Second Serve; **2)** Service Return; **3)** Server hits a groundstroke; and **4)** returner hits a groundstroke. The sequence ends after the fourth shot. Do not waste time hitting additional shots. Remember the focus of this drill is on the first exchange.

Directions: The drill consists of two rounds. **Round # 1:** Player # 1 uses a second serve to start five service points to the deuce court followed by five service points to the ad court *(player gets only one serve to start each point, a second serve)*. Player # 2 will return each serve using the base return plan. After the serve and the return, both players will hit one additional shot. **Round # 2:** After player # 1 serves ten serves, the players will switch roles with player # 2 serving and player # 1 returning.

Scoring: In each round, both players start with ten points. Each player will subtract one point from their total every time they make an error, or their opponent hits a winning shot. At the end of each round, the players record their score *(points left after errors)*.

Standard: At the end of practice, the coach will compute each player's winning percentage for both serving and returning. Servers are expected to maintain a percentage of 70 to 80 percent. Returners are expected to maintain a percentage of 40 to 60 percent.

Tactical Key: To succeed in the return game, you must understand the one fundamental difference between serving and returning: When you are serving most of your points will be won in the first-exchange; however, when you are returning you will win most of your points in the baseline rally

Keys for the First-exchange

- Location is the key for your second serve, i.e., deep and into body or backhand.
- Return using base plan, i.e., outside returns crosscourt, inside returns down the line.
- The four-shot serve and return drill is excellent for working on second serves and returns while reinforcing the need to react quickly when your opponent sends you an aggressive, penetrating shot or return.

Drill # 4: Four-Shot Body Serve and Return Drill

Purpose: 1) To teach the server how to neutralize attacking players with big returns by jamming them with the deep body serve. **2)** To prepare the returner to slide away from the body serve and aim their return deep at the server's feet.

Set-up: Two players competing on a full singles court.

Sequence: Four shots: **1)** Body Serve, **2)** Deep Middle Return, **3)** Server hits a groundstroke, and **4)** Returner hits a groundstroke. Do not waste time by hitting additional shots.

Directions: This drill consists of two rounds. **Round # 1:** Using their second serve from the deuce court, Player # 1 will hit five serves into the returner's body and then from the ad court will hit five serves into the returner's body. The serves should be either slice or topspin serves with good depth in the service box. Player # 2 will slide away from the body serve and hit a deep middle return. After the serve and return each player will hit an additional groundstroke, and when possible, the server will use an attacking forehand for their second shot. **Round # 2:** After player # 1 has hit ten serves, the two players will switch roles with player # 2 serving and player # 1 returning. Repeat the same shot sequence.

Scoring: In each round, both players start with ten points. Each player will subtract one point from their total every time they make an error, or their opponent hits a winning shot. At the end of each round, the players record their score *(points left after errors)*.

Standard: At the end of practice, the coach will compute each player's winning percentage for both serving and returning. Servers are expected to maintain a percentage of 70 to 80 percent. Returners are expected to maintain a percentage of 40 to 60 percent.

Tactical Key: The Body serve is an excellent second serve option. However, it will not work unless you aim deep in the service box. If you hit your second serve short, you are inviting your opponent to step inside the baseline and attack. When you keep the ball deep and aimed into the returner's inside or backhand hip, it will keep the returner from stepping into their return. The result a weak and often short return that you can attack with your forehand.

Tactical Keys for Body Serve

- A right-hander's slice serve will break into the returner's inside hip in the deuce court and outside hip in the ad court. The kick serve will break into the returner's outside hip in the deuce court and inside hip in the ad court.
- A left-handed player's slice serve will break into the returner's inside hip in the ad court and outside hip in the deuce court. The kick serve will break into the returner's outside hip in the ad court and inside hip in the deuce court.
- The key is to keep your spin serve deep in the service box. This freezes the returner behind the baseline and does not allow your opponent to step into their return, thus forcing a weak return.

Drill # 5: Four-Shot Tick/Tock Drill

Purpose: 1) To teach the server to use an outside serve followed by a second shot into the open court. **2)** To prepare the returner to attack with a down-the-line return.

Set-up: Two players are playing competitively on a full singles court.

Sequence: Four Shots: **1)** Outside Serve; **2)** Down-the-Line Return; **3)** Server's groundstroke into open court, and **4)** Returner's groundstroke crosscourt. Do not waste time by hitting additional shots. In this drill, you will be practicing a specific point segment, i.e., the first four shots of a tennis point.

Directions: This drill consists of two rounds. **Round # 1:** Player # 1 serves five outside service points into the deuce court followed by five outside service points into the ad court (player # 1 gets one serve to start each point). Player # 2 will return each serve with a down-the-line return purposely setting up the server's tick-tock attack. Player # 1 will then attack by hitting their second shot crosscourt into the open court. If player # 2 hits a crosscourt return, player # 1 will attack with a 90-degree down-the-line shot. Player # 2 will run down the ball and hit a second groundstroke, aiming crosscourt with enough arc to counter the attack. **Round # 2:** After player # 1 has served ten outside service points, the two players will switch roles with player # 2 serving and player # 1 returning. Repeat this same shot sequence.

Scoring: In each round, both players start with ten points. Each player will subtract one point from their total every time they make an error, or their opponent hits a winning shot. At the end of each round, the players record their score *(points left after errors)*.

Standard: At the end of practice, the coach will compute each player's winning percentage for both serving and returning. Servers are expected to maintain a percentage of 70 to 80 percent. Returners are expected to maintain a percentage of 40 to 60 percent.

Tactical Key: One of the most important tactics is to open the court by pushing your opponent outside the singles sideline. The easiest way to open the court is with an outside serve, making this one-two punch play an essential part of your tennis tactics. You must be able to both employ it when serving and defend against it when returning.

Drill # 6: Four-Shot Inside Attack Drill

Purpose: 1) To teach the server to attack the inside target with a powerful first serve. **2)** To prepare the returner to cover the inside serve.

Set-up: Two players competing on a full singles court.

Sequence: Four shots: **1)** Inside First Serve, **2)** Deep Middle Return, **3)** Server hits a groundstroke, and **4)** Returner hits a groundstroke. Do not waste time by hitting additional shots.

Directions: This drill consists of two rounds. **Round # 1:** From the deuce court, player # 1 will use a first serve to hit five service points into the inside target and then five service points from the ad court *(server gets one serve to start point)*. The first serve can be either a flat or power serve. Player # 2 will hit a deep middle return. After the serve and return each player will hit an additional groundstroke. When possible, the server uses an attacking forehand to hit their second shot. **Round # 2:** After player # 1 has hit ten serves, the two players will switch roles with player # 2 serving and player # 1 returning. Repeat the same shot sequence.

Scoring: In each round, both players start with ten points. Each player will subtract one point from their total every time they make an error, or their opponent hits a winning shot. At the end of each round, the players record their score *(points left after errors)*.

Standard: At the end of practice, the coach will compute each player's winning percentage for both serving and returning. Servers are expected to maintain a percentage of 70 to 80 percent. Returners are expected to maintain a percentage of 40 to 60 percent.

Tactical Key: Because the distance on the inside serve from the server to the baseline is the shortest of all serves, the inside serve will get to the returner much quicker. This gives the returner less time to react and forces them to stretch or reach to make the return.

Tactical Keys for the Inside Serve

- Servers attack with the first serve; returners neutralize attack with a deep middle return.
- This drill teaches the server to take immediate control of the point with their first serve.
- This drill teaches returners to neutralize an inside attack.
- Reduce second shot angles by returning difficult first serves to the deep middle.

Drill # 7: Four-Shot Second Serve and Aggressive Returns

Purpose: 1) To teach returners to attack second serves with their forehand. **2)** To teach returners to use the forehand-shade or cat-and-mouse positioning tactics.

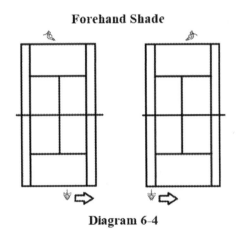

Forehand Shade

Diagram 6-4

Set-up: Two players competing on a full singles court.

Sequence: Four Shots: **1)** Second Serve; **2)** Forehand Return; **3)** Server's Second-Shot Groundstroke; and **4)** Returner's Second-Shot Groundstroke *(forehand when possible)*. Point ends on fourth shot. Do not waste time by continuing to hit.

Directions: This drill consists of two rounds. **Round # 1:** From the deuce court, player # 1 will start five second-serve points *(only one serve to start point)*. Player # 2 will use either the forehand shade or cat and mouse positioning to set up a forehand return. *(When using the cat-and-mouse make your shift on the ball toss.)* After the serve and return each player will hit an additional groundstroke. When possible, the returner will strike their second shot with their forehand groundstroke. Then using a second serve, Player # 1 will start five points from the ad side with Player # 2 using the forehand shade or cat-and-mouse return position. **Round # 2:** After player # 1 has hit ten serves, the two players will switch roles with player # 2 serving and player # 1 returning. Repeat the same shot sequence.

Scoring: In each round, both players start with ten points. Each player will subtract one point from their total every time they make an error, or their opponent hits a winning shot. At the end of each round, the players record their score *(points left after errors)*.

Standard: At the end of practice, the coach will compute each player's winning percentage for both serving and returning. Servers are expected to maintain a percentage of 70 to 80 percent. Returners are expected to maintain a percentage of 40 to 60 percent.

Tactical Key: To break serve you must be able to pressure your opponent's second serve. When you can pressure the second serve, you put more pressure on the opponent's first serve.

Tactical Keys for Using the Forehand Shade Positioning

- The forehand shade puts pressure on the server's second serve.
- When in the forehand shade, you will be surprised how easy it is to cover the serve.
- Use the inside-out forehand from the ad court *(right-handers)*.

Drill # 8: Six-Shot Serve and Volley

Purpose: To teach the serve and volley attack.

Set-up: On a full singles court, two players working cooperatively for the first two shots and then competitively on the last three shots.

Sequence: Five Shots: First two shots are cooperative with neither player trying to end the point. Shots three to five are competitive with players looking to end the point. **1)** Second Serve and follow the serve toward the net, **2)** Return directly back to the server, **3)** Server hits a volley, **4)** Returner looks to hit a passing shot, **5)** Server seeks to end the point with a second volley and, **6)** Returner tries to reach volley and hit lob over net player. Net player tries to position under lob as if to hit an overhead, but instead catches ball with non-hitting hand. This teaches the server to position correctly under a lob. Point ends on sixth shot. Do not waste time by continuing to hit.

Directions: This drill is composed of two rounds. **Round # 1:** Using their second serve, Player # 1 will serve five points to the deuce court followed by five points to the ad court. On each point Player # 1 will follow the serve toward the net. Player # 2 will hit the return directly back toward the server who is moving forward. This ensures that the server will get to practice the first volley. Player # 1 hits volley. Player # 2 attempts passing shot and player # 1 tries to end the point with a volley. **Round # 2:** After Player # 1 serves ten total points, the two players switch roles with player # 2 serve and volleying and player # 1 returning.

Scoring: In each round, both players start with ten points. Each player will subtract one point from their total every time they make an error, or their opponent hits a winning shot. At the end of each round, the players record their score *(points left after errors)*. **Note:** Returner must get lob into play or they lose the point *(sixth shot)*.

Standard: At the end of practice, the coach will compute each player's winning percentage for both serving and returning. Servers are expected to maintain a percentage of 70 to 80 percent. Returners are expected to maintain a percentage of 40 to 60 percent.

Tactical Key: The serve-and-volley attack is an aggressive, first-strike attack. The server completely bypasses the baseline rally and advances the point directly from the first-exchange to the attack and finish. This is a high risk/high-reward attack that you must know how to execute and how to defend when used against you.

Tactical Keys for the Serve and Volley

- The server must follow the direction of their serve.
- The server must advance as close to the service line as possible before the opponent contacts the ball.
- The server must split-step as the returner contacts the ball.
- It is important to remember that the split step is not a stop, but a momentary pause as the server prepares to spring forward immediately in the direction of the return.

Drill # 9: Seven-Shot Second Serve with Chip and Charge Return

Purpose: To teach the chip and charge attack.

Set-up: On a full singles court, two players play the first three shots cooperatively and the last three shots competitively.

Sequence: Seven Shots: **1)** Second Serve, **2)** Service Return and follow to the net, **3)** Server hits groundstroke at returner, **4)** Returner hits a volley, **5)** Server hits a passing shot, **6)** Returner hits a put-away volley and **7)** Server runs down volley and throws up a lob. Returner will position under lob as if to hit overhead but will catch ball with non-hitting hand. This teaches the returner to position correctly to hit an overhead. Point ends after seventh shot. Do not extend the point by hitting more shots.

Directions: This drill is composed of two rounds. **Round # 1:** Using their second serve, Player # 1 will serve five points to the deuce court followed by five points to the ad court. Player # 1 will start each point with a second serve. Player # 2 will hit return and follow shot to the net, *i.e., follow the angle of the shot.* Player # 1 hits groundstroke directly at returner; this ensures that player # 2 will get a chance to hit a volley. Player # 2 will then hit a volley. Then Player # 1 attempts passing shot and player # 2 tries to end the point with a volley. Player # 1 then throws up a lob and player # 2 positions under it for an overhead, but instead catches ball with non-hitting hand. **Round # 2:** After Player # 1 serves ten total points, the two players switch roles with player # 2 serving and player # 1 using a return and volley attack.

Scoring: In each round, both players start with ten points. Each player will subtract one point from their total every time they make an error, or their opponent hits a winning shot. At the end of each round, the players record their score *(points left after errors)*. **Note:** Server must get their lob into play or they lose the point *(seventh shot)*.

Standard: At the end of practice, the coach will compute each player's winning percentage for both serving and returning. Servers are expected to maintain a percentage of 70 to 80 percent. Returners are expected to maintain a percentage of 40 to 60 percent.

Tactical Key: Often the best approach shot is a biting slice known as a chip. On outside serves, you should approach down the line. On inside serves, you should hit your approach shot into the opponent's backhand corner.

Tactical Keys to the Chip and Charge

- Always follow the angle of your return.
- Get as close to the service line as possible before your opponent contacts ball.
- Split step as your approach shot bounces in your opponent's court. This will ensure that you can change directions to cut off the passing shot.
- Always move forward and on a diagonal to the ball.
- If the ball is below the net, you must volley deep.
- If the ball is above the net, you can go for the angle put-away.

Chapter 6 Summary
Key Thought: *Will plus drill equals skill.*

Over eighty percent of the total shots you hit during a match will occur in the first exchange. This means that to be a successful tennis player, you must prioritize the practicing of the first-exchange shots, i.e., the serve and service return followed by the second shot by each player. This second shot will usually be a groundstroke; however, depending on the type of point you decide to play, it could be a volley.

Most players practice their serve and their groundstrokes. However, the return and volleys are often neglected. This is especially true of the return. Too many players think of it as a groundstroke, but it is a specialized shot. To become a dangerous returner, you must practice your return game. The following two sections describe three plans for returning serve. You must decide which will work best for you.

Tactical Key: *Your return plan must match your style of play.*

Return Strategy: When returning first serves, you must expect a bang-bang exchange. There will be no time to make tactical decisions on the fly and still get your return into play. This means your return tactics must remain simple. As discussed in chapter two, most tennis points end within the first five shots; therefore, the first step toward success in your return game is to get your return into play. The second step is to follow your return with a successful second-shot.

On the second serve, there will be less pressure, and you can be more aggressive. However, the key to success on the second serve is no different than on the first. Get your first two-shots into play.

Baseline Control
If you are a consistent baseline player and have tremendous confidence in your groundstrokes, you may prefer to return from the deep position. From this deep position, you will give yourself more time to react to your opponent's serves, which then allows you to use a full groundstroke swing when

returning serve. Although you have competent groundstrokes, there are three critical elements which you must account for when returning from far behind the baseline.

- You have increased your distance to the outside serve; therefore, you must either have the footwork agility to cover the outside serve, or you must be confident that your opponent is unable to hit this serve effectively.
- The further you position from the net, the more the net becomes an obstacle to your return; thus, you must put more arc on your return to make sure your shot will clear the net tape.
- The deeper you play, the greater the distance to the 9-foot, depth-line on your opponent's side of the court. Therefore, you will need to hit with more arc or more pace to ensure that you are not sending your opponent a short ball and inviting them to move forward and attack.

Furthermore, baseline control positioning is a conservative approach to returning. Yes, you can neutralize your opponent's serve, but it will be difficult to go on the attack. This tactic for positioning is an excellent choice for getting points started and advancing them into Stage Two, the Baseline Rally. If the Baseline Rally is the strength of your game, then this is a great option. However, if you need to play a more aggressive point style, this positioning may not be the one for you.

Tactical Key: Although the baseline control player will return from deeper behind the baseline, their start position is never completely fixed. You must always adjust your return position according to your opponent's serving potential, the intent of your return, and the point-building style you want to employ.

First-Strike

If you prefer to play a more aggressive point style, you should choose to play closer to or even inside the baseline. Playing close to the baseline gives you two distinct advantages when it comes to attacking: **1)** Your angle returns will be more effective; and **2)** You have moved closer to your opponent which means your return will get to them quicker giving them less time to recover. However, this also means that the serve will reach you quicker as well. To return from the first-strike position often requires a modification in your returning fundamentals, i.e., a shortened backswing and simplified footwork patterns.

There are two ways to modify your swing: **1)** You can go to a continental grip and block or slice your return into play, or **2)** You can use your regular grips but modify your groundstroke using both a shorter backswing and follow-through. Both methods are used successfully by many of the top professionals. In fact, you might want to incorporate both tactics into your return strategy. Study the following two tactical keys for a brief description of how to modify your swing.

Tactical Key # 1: The block and slice technique – When playing first-strike tennis, your return swing will often approximate that of a volley with a minimal backswing, but a slightly extended follow-through. The goal of this return is to neutralize the serve by blocking or chipping *(slicing)* the ball back deep often at the returner's feet.

Tactical Key # 2: The modified groundstroke technique – When using this approach, your return swing will have more in common with your groundstroke. The basic technique is to shorten your backswing and to reduce your swing speed letting your racket do the work. The swing from backswing, through the contact point, and into the follow-through should be smooth and controlled. I tell my players to point the tip of the racket at the side fence on the backswing and that their follow-through should finish high with the tip of the racket pointed toward the sky. Additionally, you should time your footwork so that your weight transfers from the back to the front foot on contact with the ball. When used correctly, you can attack down-the-line or with sharp angles not by hitting hard, but by merely making solid contact with the ball.

See you on the court.

Practice Scoring Sheet

Base Serving Drills

Round # 1`	Made Serves	Percentage
Deuce Court Server		
Ad Court Server		
Round # 2	**Made Serves**	**Percentage**
Deuce Court Server		
Ad Court Server		

For the base serving drills record the total number of made serves for each player. Then after practice, the coach will compute the score, i.e., 6 of 10 serves for 60 percent.

Two-Shot Serving Drills

Round # 1	Made	Percentage
Server # 1		Serving --
Returner # 1		Returning --
Round # 2	**Made**	**Percentage**
Server # 2		Serving --
Returner # 2		Returning --

For the two-shot serving drills, record the total made serves and returns for each player in the made column. Remember an ace serve counts as a missed return. Then after practice, the coach will compute the score, i.e., 6 of 10 serves for a 60 percent serving percentage. However, if the returner missed one return it would be 5 of 6 serves for an 83 percent returning percentage, i.e., the returner's total and the percentage is based on the number of good serves they had an opportunity to return. In the above example, the server only made three serves; thus, the returner had only three return attempts.

Four-Shot Serve and Return Drills (also 6-shot and 7-Shot)

Round # 1	Points remaining	Percentage
Server # 1		Serving --

Returner # 1		Returning --
Round # 2	**Points remaining**	**Percentage**
Server # 2		Serving --
Returner # 2		Returning --

For the four-shot serve and return drills you are not keeping track of serve and return percentages, but the winning percentage of serve and return points. Remember that points can be lost both with errors or opponent winners. Each time you lose a point, you subtract one point from your total of ten. At the end of the round, you will report the points remaining to your coach. After practice, the coaches will compute the scores and percentages.

Chapter 7
Phase 2: The Baseline Rally

The Base-X Rally Pattern
Key Thought: *A tennis point is like a tug-a-war, you are either ahead, even, or behind. The winner will be the player who can get ahead and then maintain momentum shot by shot without making an error.*

The Fifth Shot Checkpoint *(the server's third shot)*
In the Tactical Point Control System, the fifth shot is a pivotal juncture in the point building sequence. At the beginning of the baseline rally, the fifth shot is a reliable indicator of which player has gained control of the match momentum. Since few points last deep into the baseline rally, the fifth shot is often a key predictor of the outcome of the match.

Because of its tactical importance, I instruct my players to use the fifth shot as a checkpoint for measuring match momentum. To make this easier, ask yourself this question: On the fifth shot of the tennis point, am I ahead, behind, or even? The answer to this question will help you quickly determine what is happening during the point, and ultimately in the match.

- **Ahead:** You are winning a large majority of points before the fifth shot. This means either you are dominating the first-exchange with an aggressive first-strike mentality, or your opponent is weak, error prone and inconsistent. In either case, you are putting yourself in a strong position to win. Continue attacking in the first exchange.
- **Behind:** You are losing a large majority of points before the fifth shot. This means your opponent is dominating the first exchange and you are in danger of losing the match. You must determine whether you are losing because of your opponent's aggressive play or because you are making unforced errors. In either case, you must find a way to extend more points past the fifth shot and into the baseline rally. To extend the point you must have a solid two-shot plan that takes advantage of shots that you can control and can get into play. High risk shot selections will only lead to more errors making it even more difficult for you to switch the match momentum back to your side.
- **Even:** Most points are advancing past the fifth shot and into the baseline rally. This means that you are doing a good job of getting the point started. It also means you are in for a difficult match. However, it is a match you can win. Now, you must lean on your

groundstrokes and use the baseline rally to build points to your advantage. This means managing your errors, neutralizing your opponent's game plan, and taking advantage of every opportunity to attack.

The fifth-shot checkpoint measures how effectively you are performing during the first exchange. I tell my players, it is great if you are winning points in the first exchange, and conversely, there is no problem if you are occasionally losing in the first exchange. However, if you are losing too many points in the first-exchange, it will become very difficult to win the match.

This is especially true if your groundstrokes are the strength of your game. If you allow your opponent to eliminate or neutralize your greatest strength, it will be very difficult for you to win the match. For baseline players, the first step to tennis success is to consistently advance points into the baseline rally where you can employ your groundstroke weapons.

Whether you are an aggressive or consistent baseliner, you must adopt the mindset that the first-exchange is but the start of the point. To start the point, you must get your first two shots into play on every point.

Tactical Key: When you learn to use the fifth-shot checkpoint you will know what you need to do to build, switch, or maintain the momentum of the points. When serving, your goal is to be ahead on the fifth shot. When returning, your primary goal is to be even.

Point Momentum

Key Thought: *For every winner, there's a loser. And that person didn't really need to lose. They just didn't understand the game plan.* – Buzz Aldrin, U.S. astronaut

The baseline rally is fluid in nature. Every shot has the potential to change the flow of momentum within the point. This makes every shot an important shot. Choosing the right shot builds momentum. Choosing the wrong shot destroys it. In my experience as both a player and a coach, momentum is shifted more often by the wrong shot selection than by the right one. In other words, your mistakes can cost you more than you can gain by hitting great shots.

Tactical Key: In the typical tennis match, more points are won by forcing errors than by hitting winners.

The most efficient way to increase your point-winning percentage is to reduce your errors. To minimize errors, you must understand two critical variables. **1)** The strengths of your game and **2)** The basic principles of situational tennis. You must quickly differentiate the situations which require a controlled response from those which call for a more aggressive one.

Tactical Key: When your opponent attacks you with a shot that drives you back, pushes you wide, or challenges your shot-making technique, you should respond with control by hitting a neutral shot. However, when your opponent sends you a ball that is weak, short or opens the court, you should choose an aggressive shot that attacks into one of their weaknesses. Learning how to play situational tennis is an essential step toward reaching your full tennis potential.

Point Building
Key Thought: *Don't hit and hope. Play with a plan!*

Without a clear set of objectives for the baseline rally, it is difficult to establish a consistent game plan. Thus, I give my players four fundamental playing goals for the baseline rally.

- Put your opponent on the defensive.
- Force your opponent into committing an error.
- Win the physical battle.
- Force your opponent to send you an opportunity ball.

The four playing goals will vary depending upon your opponent's specific strengths and weaknesses. Thus, in every match, you must continually evaluate how your strengths and weaknesses stack up against the strengths and weaknesses of your opponent. Then as the match progresses, you will use this information to adjust your baseline game plan, so you can make use of your best shots and preferred tactics.

The Base-X Pattern
Key Thought: *Work hard to make things easy.*

In the Tactical Point Control System, the Base-X pattern provides a point-building plan that allows you to employ consistent shot patterns, force errors from your opponent, and create openings into which you can attack. The Base-X pattern is the foundation upon which my baseline rally tactics are built. A foundation that is secure because it rests squarely on the bedrock of three high-percentage shots.

- **The Outside Crosscourt Shot:** When your opponent sends you a deep crosscourt shot, you respond with a crosscourt shot. *(You hold the rally angle.)* This is your point-building shot.
- **The Inside Pull-shot:** When your opponent sends you an inside or down-the-line shot, you respond with a crosscourt shot. *(You switch the rally angle.)*. This is your counterattacking shot.
- **The Outside Switch:** When your opponent sends you a crosscourt opportunity ball, i.e., a shot that is weak, lands short, or opens the court, you will respond with a down-the-line shot. *(You switch the rally angle.)* This is your attacking shot.

Tactical Key: The **switch shot** plays an important role in tennis tactics. In simple terms, it is a shot that changes the angle of the rally from either crosscourt to down the line or from down the line to crosscourt. Tactically, the switch shot is an offensive shot used to attack open court. However, it does not come without risk as most tennis errors occur when attempting to change the angle of the rally.

The Outside Crosscourt Shot: *The Building Shot*

Key Thought: *The player best able to win crosscourt rallies will probably win the match.* – Allen Fox, author of the book Think to Win

The crosscourt shot will not provide many immediate opportunities to win points. However, if hit with consistency, it will force your opponent to hit more balls which increases the chances of their making an error. It also tempts your opponent to hit down the line, which is the lowest-percentage shot in tennis. Hitting down the line not only leads to errors but when your opponent's shot is aimed to your inside, it opens your opponent's court allowing you to counterattack with an inside pull-shot *(see diagram 7-2)*.

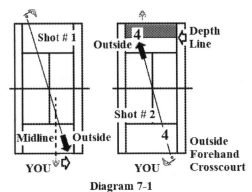

Diagram 7-1

Definition: An outside shot occurs when your opponent sends you a ball that crosses the midline of your body and is headed toward the outside of your court *(shot # 1 in diagram 7-1)*.

Guideline: When you receive an outside ball from your opponent, you should hold the rally angle by sending the ball back crosscourt with no change of direction *(Shot # 2 in diagram 7-1)*

Diagram 7-1 illustrates an outside ball sent crosscourt to a right-handed player on the 4-to-4 rally angle *(see chapter 3 for my targeting system)*.

Tactical Key: The outside crosscourt shot is the highest percentage shot in tennis. Make the crosscourt groundstroke the fundamental building block of your groundstroke game.

The Inside Pull-Shot: *The Counterattack Shot*

Key Thought: *When your opponent hits down the line, hit your next shot into the open court!*

Definition: An inside shot occurs when your opponent sends you a ball that does not cross the midline of your body and is aimed toward the inside of your court *(shot # 1 in diagram 7-2)*. An extreme inside shot is hit down the line *(shot # 3 in diagram 7-2)*

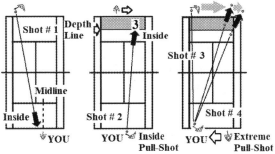

Diagram 7-2

The inside pull-shot is the highest-percentage **switch shot** in tennis. The middle pull-shot *(shot # 2 in diagram 7-2)*, and the extreme pull-shot *(shot # 4 in diagram 7-2)*, which is hit off an opponent's down-the-line shot, share many of the characteristics of the crosscourt shot. However, the pull-shot has one huge advantage. It can be angled away from your opponent forcing then to hit on the run. When you move inside the baseline and take this ball early, and on the rise, it can even be hit for a winner.

Guideline: When you receive an inside ball, you should switch the angle of the rally by hitting an inside pull-shot into the open court away from your opponent. Like a baseball player pulling an inside pitch down the baseline, the pull-shot uses a natural shoulder and hip turn making it a highly efficient way to switch the rally angle.

Tactical Key: The inside-pull shot is reactionary as it is your response to your opponent's down-the-line shot. Although it is an aggressive shot, it is a counterattacking shot, because you cannot utilize a pull-shot until your opponent sends you an inside ball.

The Outside Switch: *The Attacking Shot*

Key Thought: *Force errors from your opponent. Don't make them.*

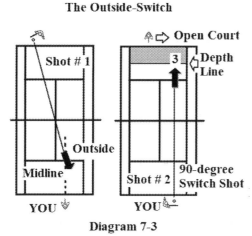

The Outside-Switch

Diagram 7-3

Definition: The outside switch occurs when you choose to send your shot down the line. *(Shot # 2 in Diagram 7-2)* The best time to use this shot is after your crosscourt shot has either pushed your opponent back behind the baseline or out wide of the singles sideline.

Guideline: When you decide to go down the line, move forward taking the ball early and as close to the baseline as possible. Avoid aiming your shot at the sideline as the ball will tend to drift wide. Instead, send your down the line shot straight up the court. I call this a 90-degree change of direction. When using the outside switch, focus on depth rather than angle. *(Shot # 2 in Diagram 7-2)* Unless you can pressure your opponent or hit a clean winner, avoid using the outside switch shot when you are outside the singles sideline. From a wide position, the best shot is usually back crosscourt. *(Beat an angle with a better angle)*

Tactical Key: The down-the-line shot is the lowest percentage shot in tennis. **1)** you are hitting over the highest part of the net. **2)** you are hitting into a shorter court. **3)** The angle of rebound is high, which tends to make the ball drift toward the sideline, and **4)** you are further from the tactical center of your opponent's next possible shots.

The Tactical Center: *The Final Piece of the Foundation*
Key Thought: *To win you must control the Tactical Center of the court.*

The tactical center is a position located halfway between the widest shot angles into which your opponent can send the next ball. Controlling the center of the court is a critical component of baseline pressure. Every time you send your opponent the ball, you must recover to the tactical center of your opponent's next possible shot options. Failure to recover, will leave open court for your opponent, which results in your having to hit more shots on the move. There are two essential requirements for maintain the tactical center:

- **You must hit shots that are good for your court position**. This means that unless you can hit a clean winner, you must choose a shot that gives you enough time to recover to the tactical center.
- **You must be willing to expend the necessary energy to make a complete recovery**. Effort is a critical component of the physical battle and it must be expended during long rallies and or on points late in the match. *Diagram 7-4* shows you the appropriate baseline recovery positions based on the location of the ball in your opponent's court.

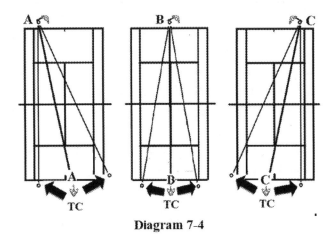

Diagram 7-4

Position A: When the ball is located at position A, the opponent's deuce court side, you will recover to position A on the baseline. This position is approximately two steps to the right of the center hash mark. From position A, any ball hit to your left is an inside shot and any ball hit to your right is an outside shot.

Position B: When the ball is located at position B, the center of the opponent's baseline, you will recover to position B on the baseline. This position is located behind the center hash mark on the baseline. When the ball is in the middle of the court, you should consider a ball hit to either side of you to be an outside shot.

Position C: When the ball is located at position C, the ad court side, you will recover to position C on the baseline. This position is approximately two steps to the left of the center hash mark. From the C position, any ball hit to your left is an outside shot and any ball hit to your right is an inside shot.

Tactical Key: When you are consistently positioned in the tactical center, the court seems smaller to your opponent. Thus, they see less open court which increases the pressure on their next shot.

Employing the Base-X Rally Pattern
Key Thought: *Establish a pattern.*

Establishing a pattern may at first seem counterproductive to what you believe about tennis strategy. Many players have the mistaken assumption that the goal of the baseline rally is to surprise their opponent or to do something unexpected. However, if your game is built entirely on the unexpected, you are actually playing with no plan at all. Instead, you have chaos and confusion. Without a clear-cut game plan, it is easy to lose track of what you do best. Instead of replicating a winning strategy or avoiding a losing one, your game is based solely on feelings and emotions, and when you base your choices on feelings and emotions, you often make poor and misguided decisions.

When you change tactics randomly thinking you are going to fool or trick your opponent, you are really in danger of outsmarting yourself. If your game loses its rhythm, your timing suffers, and when your timing suffers, you start missing your shots. For you to establish and maintain your rhythm and timing, you must have a well-practiced baseline rally plan. A plan that takes into account the various types of shots your opponent could send your way.

In this book, you will often hear me state that consistency is the biggest weapon in tennis. However, consistency cannot arise out of chaos. Consistency is defined as something that is capable of being reproduced or repeated. To reproduce something, you need a pattern. In tennis, a pattern for consistency must be part of your game plan. It will be patterns that stabilize your game and give you confidence even when everything else seems to be going wrong.

Tactical Key: To succeed in tennis, you must have a system of shot-making guidelines that can be replicated, shot, after shot, after shot.

Crosscourt Exchange: The Building Sequence
Key Thought: *Put your best foot forward.*

When using the Base-X pattern you will establish your pattern with a crosscourt shot. This means if your opponent sends you a crosscourt ball, you will send it back crosscourt with no change of direction, and if your opponent sends you a down-the-line ball, you will send it back crosscourt with a change of direction. Thus, unless an opportunity to attack was created in the first-exchange, your third shot in every point will be sent crosscourt.

This first crosscourt shot will establish a rally angle, either an ad court 3-to-3 or a deuce court 4-to-4 angle. Once the rally angle has been determined, you must remain patient within this crosscourt pattern. Aim your crosscourt shots through your opponent's baseline and land them deeper than the 9-foot depth line. This helps you play more consistently while making it more difficult for your opponent to launch an attack against you. There are four additional reasons why holding the rally angle is a sound tactic:

- It reduces your risk and helps you manage your errors.

- It gives your opponent less open court for their next shot.
- It tempts an impatient opponent to over-hit leading to unforced errors.
- It tempts your opponent to hit down-the-line which opens the court for you to counterattack.

Holding the crosscourt angle does not mean you will never shift or change the direction of the rally; however, it does mean that you must have a good reason for making the shift. Pass up the temptation to rush into this switch because you are afraid of a long rally. Instead, teach yourself to play fearlessly. Nevertheless, no rally angle will last forever. Thus, I give my players four solid reasons for switching the angle:

- Your opponent hits down-the-line;
- You are stronger than your opponent in one of the rally angles;
- Your opponent does not move well or cannot hit on the run.
- Your opponent sends you an opportunity ball.

Tactical Key: Why crosscourt? Because when you hit crosscourt, you are using the highest-percentage shot in tennis. This is important because one of the primary goals of the baseline rally is to give your opponent multiple opportunities to make errors, and this will not happen unless you can keep the ball in play.

Inside Switch: The Counterattack or Defend Sequence
Key Thought: *Send inside shots back crosscourt with a change of direction.*

Your opponent will often send you a down-the-line or inside shot. Depending on the quality of your opponent's shot, you may find yourself in either a counterattacking or defending position. Although, your programmed response is the inside-pull-shot, *(diagram 7-2)*, the type of pull-shot will depend on the situation. When using the Base-X pattern, you have predetermined the direction of your shot; however, you must read the situation to decide if you should defend or counterattack.

- **Defending:** Your opponent sends you a ball that is difficult to reach or return. When you are defending, you will loop, lob, or slice the ball back into play. Your goal is to neutralize an attack by forcing your opponent back behind the baseline; thus, giving yourself enough time to recover to the tactical center. If successful, your opponent will often send their next ball crosscourt allowing the rally to return to a crosscourt exchange. Be patient and hold this new crosscourt angle until you receive another opportunity to change.
- **Counterattacking:** Your opponent sends you a ball that is weak or lands short in your court. When you are in a position to counterattack, step into the court taking the ball early and on the rise. This is an opportunity to aggressively drive the ball into the open court and away from your opponent. Since you can angle this shot away from your opponent, they will be forced to hit their next shot on the move. You will then read and react to the quality of your counterattacking shot. If your pull-shot forces an opportunity ball from your opponent, you will attack. If it is neutralized by your opponent's good shot, you will return to the crosscourt exchange. *(see sneak volley attack in chapter 11)*

Outside Switch: The Attack
Key Thought: *Attack down the line with a 90-degree change of direction.*

You can change the crosscourt rally angle by attacking your opponent with a down-the-line shot. *(outside switch shot diagram 7-3)* Your decision to hit this shot will take place as you recover to the tactical center. If your crosscourt shot forced your opponent wide of the singles sideline or pushed them deep behind the baseline, move in two steps and ready yourself to attack. If your opponent sends you a ball that you can easily control, attack down-the-line. The goal of the outside switch is not to win the point outright, but rather to force your opponent to hit their next shot on the move, which often results in an opportunity ball.

Tactical Key: The Base-X Pattern can be utilized in two ways. The consistent baseliner who prefers to build points with consistency will emphasize the crosscourt exchange and the inside pull-shot. They will only send a ball down-the-line when the situation is significantly in their favor. Whereas, the aggressive baseliner who wants to attack and dictate the point will utilize the down-the-line shot more quickly and more frequently as they attempt to pressure their opponent into making errors or surrendering opportunity balls that they can attack.

The Opportunity Ball: The Finishing Shot
Key Thought: *The road to success is paved with opportunity; unfortunately, many people are blind to the opening and miss the turn.*

Although your primary goal in the baseline rally is to force errors, like a tiger, you are also stalking for prey. That prey is the opportunity ball which is defined as a shot that is weak, short, or opens the court. Like a tiger, you must be ready to pounce on every opportunity ball that comes your way. Depending on your playing style, court position, and comfort level, an opportunity ball will present you with four distinct possibilities:

- Be patient and continue to build.
- Hit a more aggressive shot with the intent of creating a better opportunity ball.
- Go for an outright winner, by aggressively attacking the ball.
- Attack the net using one of the approach-and-volley tactics *(see chapter 11).*

Tactical Key: Not every opportunity ball is the same. Be on the lookout for the high-percentage opportunities, those that allow you to attack using your strengths. Attacking a low-percentage opportunity ball may not be the smart play for the situation.

How you choose to respond to an opportunity ball will be based on your playing style. Consistent players will be more likely to select options one and two; whereas, aggressive players will be more prone to choose options three and four. There are no right or wrong responses; however, there are often better ones. Since your personal playing style is based on the strengths of your game, you will have greater success when you use options that coincide with your strengths. That said, you must also account for the situation.

For example: If a consistent player is forced to move forward to a position near the service line, the situation calls for them to attack the net with an aggressive approach and volley play. Playing conservative shots when provided with a frontcourt attacking situation will never put you in a winning position.

Playing the attacking point-style requires steady nerves, consistent weapons, and an attacking nature. To be a complete player, you must develop a plan for how you will finish points in both open court and net-approaching situations. Then, based on your strengths and playing style, you must be confident in the way you decide to finish off points. Once you have learned to play bravely and without regrets, you will see your game improve rapidly.

Tactical Key: In the baseline rally, baseliners work to create open-court opportunities for a groundstroke attack, and net rushers try to force short ball opportunities that allow them to move forward and attack at the net.

The Open Court Finish
Key Thought: *Read the court.*

Baseline players thrive on attacking the open court. The aggressive baseliner possesses the consistency, the control, and the power to drive the ball through the open court before their opponent can recover or react. The same can be said for a consistent baseliner; however, the difference is that the consistent baseliner requires a more substantial opening. Where the aggressive baseliner can often hit outright winners, the consistent baseliner strives to increase pressure. If you are a consistent baseliner, you must learn to be content with forcing errors by challenging your opponent's footwork and fitness.

The Finishing Shots
The groundstroke-finish consists of the same shots that make up the groundstroke attack. However, you must discipline yourself to think of every attack as a two-shot play. The purpose of the attacking shot is to create a larger opening, i.e., a shot that forces your opponent to send a shot that is either weaker, shorter, or that creates a larger opening in the court.

Thus, finishing shots will often occur after you force a second or even a third opportunity ball from your opponent. The absolute best time to finish is when you receive an opportunity ball that is weak, short, and opens the court. However, to draw this kind of ball requires the ability to build points with **patient pressure**, i.e., a perfect blend of consistency with aggressiveness.

Tactical Key: The groundstroke finish is almost always aimed into the opponent's open court. The only exception is when you hit behind your opponent hoping to catch them off-balance or making an early break toward the open court.

The Outside Switch (*see diagrams 7-3 on page 75*)**:** One of the essential patterns in the baseliner's arsenal is to establish a crosscourt rally and then to switch the angle with a down-the-line shot. The difference in the finishing shot over the attacking shot is the size of the opening.

Therefore, to finish with an outside switch, the baseliner often requires two additional variables. **1)** They must first push their opponent further out of position, i.e., deeper behind the baseline and/

or wider than the doubles sideline, and **2)** The ball sent from the opponent must land short in the court allowing the baseliner to move forward inside the midcourt zone to finish the point.

Tactical Key: Both the aggressive and consistent baseliner works to gain these same advantages; however, the aggressive baseliner can power the ball through a much smaller opening.

When hitting a finishing shot, there are two mentality traps that must be avoided. First, if you are an aggressive baseliner, you must guard against overhitting. Going for a bigger shot than is needed will often leads to unforced errors. Second, if you are a consistent baseliner, you must guard against playing too tentatively. Going for a safe shot when a more aggressive shot is necessary will often open the door for an effective counterattack from your opponent.

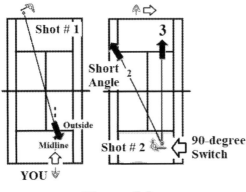

Diagram 7-5

The Short Outside Switch: *Diagram 7-5* illustrates that there are two options available when the ball is short, especially when it allows you to move inside the depth line. From the midcourt, you can choose to hit down the line into the open court or to angle the ball sharply crosscourt. The short down-the-line switch can often be hit through the open court for a winner; whereas, the sharp crosscourt shot is designed to ***wrong-foot*** your opponent, i.e., catch them moving early to cover the down the line opening.

Tactical Key: The crosscourt angle works best against quick opponents who anticipate and recover quickly to the tactical center. Against a slower footed opponent, the open court shot down the line is usually the better option.

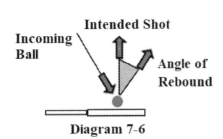

Diagram 7-6

A common error when using the outside switch is to miss your shot wide of the near sideline. The reason for this error is that when you receive a crosscourt shot, the angle of rebound off your racket strings will cause the ball to drift toward the near sideline. Therefore, when hitting an outside switch shot, it is imperative that you use a 90-degree change of direction, which means aiming your shot straight up the court and through the opponent's baseline. Using a 90-degree change of direction shot will significantly improve your chances of keeping this ball in play.

The Inside Pull-shot Attack: When your opponent hits a shot to the inside of the court, they have sent a ball that is bad for their court position. In the Base-X pattern, you will immediately respond to a down-the-line shot with an inside pull-shot. The pull-shot can be angled into the open court and away from your opponent's position. Thus, it forces your opponent to move across the baseline to the opposite corner to hit their next shot. *(see shot # 2 and Shot # 4 in diagram 7-2)*

The inside pull-shot is considered a counterattacking shot because your opponent must first send you an inside ball. If you are a consistent baseliner and can move well from side to side, a good tactic is to bait your opponent into sending the ball down the line. When they do, drive your pull-shot into the open court away from your opponent. You must make the inside pull-shot an integral part of your counterattack game plan.

Tactical Key: For a consistent baseliner, the inside ball is the preferred way to finish points.

The Inside-out Forehand Finish

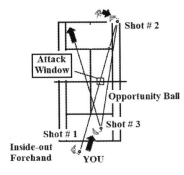

Diagram 7-7

The aggressive baseliner also employs the Base-X pattern; however, if you own a forehand weapon, the inside-out forehand attack *(shot # 1 in diagram 7-7)* should become your primary option. Whenever your inside-out forehand forces a weak backhand reply down the line *(shot # 2 in diagram 7-7)*, it opens the court for an forehand pull-shot which you can send aggressively through your opponent's open court for an outright winner. *(see shot # 3 in diagram 7-7)* If you use the inside-out forehand attack, the forehand pull-shot will soon become your favorite finishing shot.

Develop Your Playing Style

Where the aggressive baseliner possesses the weapons to end the point from the baseline with a single shot, the consistent baseliner will more often finish a point with a series of shots. In either case, each successive shot should increase the pressure on the opponent's footwork and fitness until they create an opening so large that any shot into the open court will win the point.

In contrast, the net rusher will try to get off the baseline as quickly as possible. They will charge forward at the first opportunity to advance to the net. In fact, the net rusher will often skip the baseline-rally entirely by attempting to get to the net before the end of the first exchange

BASE-X GUIDELINES
Base Shot Patterns

- **Outside Forehands** – Hit crosscourt *(no change of direction)*
- **Outside Backhands** – Hit crosscourt *(no change of direction)*
- **Inside Forehands** – Hit pull-shot into open court away from your opponent *(change of direction)*
- **Inside-Backhands** – Hit pull-shot into open court away from your opponent *(change of direction)*

Change-up Shot Patterns

- **Outside Forehand Switch** – Hit down the line *(change of direction)*
- **Outside Backhand Switch** – Hit down the line *(change of direction)*

The Mirror Play: *Closed Pattern*

Unlike the Base-X pattern which is more reactive in nature, the Mirror Play is a closed pattern, which means you have a predetermined directional objective for each of your first three to four shots. In the Mirror pattern, you will hold the angle *(no change of direction)* for the first two to three shots followed by a change of direction shot on the third or fourth shot of the rally.

I call this the mirror play because you will copy or mimic the first two to three shots sent by your opponent. For example, if your opponent hits crosscourt, you will hit crosscourt; however, if your opponent sends a ball down the line, you will hit your shot down the line. Thus, you are holding the angle of the rally. You become the mirror image of your opponent.

Then on the third or fourth shot of the rally, your pattern changes. Now if your opponent hits crosscourt, you will switch the direction of the rally by sending your shot down the line, and if your opponent hits down the line, you will change the direction of the rally by sending your shot crosscourt.

Tactical Key: *If you wait, you'll be late.* The actual number of shots you use will vary from point to point because you are not just using a pattern, you are really working to create an opportunity ball that you can attack. Thus, you are looking to switch the angle of the rally when you see weakness in your opponent's shot production or court position. You could receive an opportunity ball after your first or after your fourth shot.

If you are an aggressive player who likes to dictate play, you will love this pattern as it allows you to focus entirely on a set pattern for sending the ball. Then, when you mix this pattern with the Base-X pattern, your groundstroke patterns become less predictable allowing you to keep your opponent off balance and unsure of where you will hit your next shot.

Tactical Key: When you alternate tactics by using the Mirror pattern on some points and the Base-X pattern on others, you gain two distinct advantages. Tactically, your opponent may recognize you are playing a pattern, but they cannot be reasonably sure which pattern you are using, and Technically, your consistency and control are increased because you can focus entirely on shot-making without having to make tactical decisions about the direction of your next shot. Thus, you gain an advantage both tactically and technically in the point.

Additional Patterns

After my players have mastered the Base-X and Mirror rally patterns, I teach them five additional patterns that can be employed from the baseline. Players of every playing style can use these five patterns; however, they are most often employed by aggressive baseliners. Even net rushers, who want to avoid playing long baseline rallies, can find them useful.

The Middle-Deep Pattern

The middle-deep pattern is a more conservative form of the Base-X pattern. When using this pattern, your primary concern is keeping the ball deep. This means aiming deeper than the 9-foot depth line while hitting your shots through the baseline. Use the same Base-X guidelines but aim toward the center of the baseline. I tell my players to aim for their opponent's feet. This pattern will force an aggressive opponent to back up behind the baseline.

I call this hitting through the baseline. Your goal is for the ball to cross the baseline before it crosses the singles sideline. Hitting through the baseline reduces the odds that you will hit a ball wide. More importantly if forces your opponent to hit their shots from deeper in the court giving you four distinct advantages: **1)** You make it more difficult for your opponent to launch an attack, **2)** You give yourself more time to read your opponent's next shot, **3)** You have more time to recover to the tactical center, and **4)** You increase your chances of receiving a short ball from your opponent.

Tactical Key: You can combine the Mirror and Middle-Deep patterns. However, you must avoid hitting the ball through the singles sideline by emphasizing the concept of keeping every shot deeper than the 9-foot depth line.

The 3-X Mirror Pattern

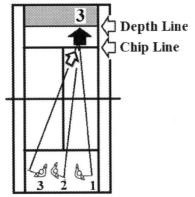

Diagram 7-8

The 3-X pattern is a variation of the mirror pattern. You will establish a 3-to-3 rally by sending your first shot to the 3-target. Then you use the rules of the Mirror pattern to continue directing your shots into the 3-target. *See diagram 7-8.* This pattern is used to attack the weaker backhand of a right-handed opponent.

Right-handed Attack: When your right-handed opponent sends a ball to your inside, you will only hit a forehand pull-shot into the 4-target box when you can put extreme pressure on your opponent. Otherwise, you will continue to hit inside balls back into the 3-target using either an outside backhand (shot # 3 in diagram 7-8), an inside-out forehand *(shot # 2 in diagram 7-8)* or down-the-line forehand *(shot # 1 in diagram 7-8)*.

You can also put pressure on your opponent by using a backhand chip *(biting-slice)* that lands somewhere between the service line and the depth line *(shot # 3 in diagram 7-8)*. The chip shot will force your opponent to hit from their lower strike zone. Most players cannot attack the low ball, which means you will draw a weak reply. This opportunity ball will then give you the opportunity to turn up the pressure on your opponent.

Tactical Key: In the 3-to-3 backhand rally, your backhand groundstroke does not have to be your strength. For this pattern to succeed, it only needs to be stronger than your opponent's backhand.

Lefty Advantage: If you are left-handed, the 3-X pattern allows you to attack your right-handed opponent's backhand with your crosscourt forehand groundstroke. Once you have established the 3-to-3 rally pattern, you will maintain the 3-to-3 angle by directing the majority of your outside shots into your opponent's 3-target box *(shot # 1 in diagram 7-8)*. This means that unless you can hurt your opponent with your backhand pull-shot into the 4-target box, you will direct your backhand either inside-out *(shot # 2 in diagram 7-8)* or down-the-line *(shot # 3 in diagram 7-8)* into your opponent's 3-target.

Tactical Key: As a left-handed player, the 3-X pattern must become one of your primary patterns for attacking a right-handed opponent.

The 3-X Forehand Barrage: *Inside-out Forehand weapon*

The 3-X Forehand Barrage is an inside-out forehand assault on a right-handed opponent's weaker backhand. In today's game, it is the ultimate strength-against-weakness attack. When using the forehand barrage, you use your inside-out forehand weapon to direct your shots into your opponent's backhand corner. The goal is to overpower your opponent's backhand with your forehand; thus, forcing either an error or an opportunity ball. The Forehand Barrage is an expanded version of the inside-out forehand finish used in the open court attack. *(see shot # 1 in diagram 7-7)*

If your opponent sends their backhand down the line, you will use your running forehand to attack crosscourt into the open court in your opponent's forehand corner. If they hit short, you have two choices: **1)** You can hit a forehand pull-shot into the open court in your opponent's forehand corner, or **2)** You can send another inside-out forehand into their backhand corner. Whichever option you choose, you should follow your shot forward to the net looking to put away your opponent's next shot with a volley or an overhead. *(see shot # 2 in diagram 7-7)*

Tactical Key: Early in the rally, hit your inside-out forehands through the baseline with plenty of net clearance.

If you are right-handed and facing a left-handed opponent, you may want to occasionally run-around your backhand to hit your inside-out forehand into a left-handed opponent's forehand corner *(3-X target)*. This will help to neutralize the power of your opponent's left-handed forehand. However, you are also opening the court for your left-handed opponent's down-the-line forehand. Therefore, I suggest that you always recover to the standard tactical center position after hitting this shot. From the standard recovery position, you will not be able to hit as many forehands, but you will also avoid opening the court for your opponent's down-the-line attack.

Tactical Key: If you are right-handed and your left-handed opponent hits their crosscourt forehand short, you should run-around your backhand and hit an aggressive forehand pull-shot into your opponent's backhand corner *(4-Target box)*.

Tactical Center: *Backhand Shade*

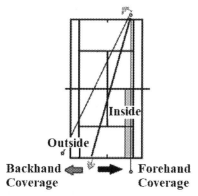

Diagram 7-9

When using the forehand barrage, you will use your inside-out forehand to hit the ball to your opponent's backhand corner. Because you want to continue to attack your opponent's backhand corner with your forehand, you will shift your recovery position *(tactical center)* toward your own backhand corner. This is similar to the backhand shade positioning you might use when returning an opponent's second serve. I tell my players to recover to a position two steps to the left of the standard recovery position. From this slightly wider position, you will be able to cover approximately two-thirds of the court with your forehand weapon *(see diagram 7-9)*.

Tactical Key: Sometimes when using the Base-X pattern, you may choose to hit an inside-out forehand into your opponent's 3-target box. However, unless you are planning to take over the 3-to-3 rally with your forehand, you should recover to the standard tactical center position after your shot *(see diagram 7-4).*

Vulnerability

Overplaying toward the backhand corner puts you in position to hit more forehands; however, it also leaves you vulnerable to a down-the-line backhand shot from your opponent. However, if you are pressuring your opponent's backhand with a combination of pace, location, and depth, you narrow the down-the-line target to a small two-foot strip. This challenges your opponent to place their backhand into a very small target area. *(shaded area in diagram 7-9)* If they miss this narrow strip, they will either send their shot wide or give you an opportunity to drive a ball into the open court opposite them *(see diagram 7-7).* Either mistake will open the door for you to win the point.

Forehand Barrage Guidelines

- Establish a rally angle that allows you to hit your forehand into your opponent's backhand corner.
- When your opponent hits short or down-the-line, use your forehand pull-shot to attack the open court away from your opponent.
- When your opponent manages to hit the ball to your outside, hit your outside backhand crosscourt and deep with no change of direction.
- When your opponent manages to hit the ball to your outside, but it lands short. Attack the open court using your down-the-line backhand.

The 4-X Mirror Pattern

The 4-X Mirror pattern is the reverse image of the 3-X Mirror pattern. Now, instead of targeting the 3-target box, you will hit the majority of your shots into the 4-target. Thus, if you are right-handed, you will be targeting a right-handed opponent's forehand; however, against a left-hander, you will be hitting your forehand into your opponent's backhand corner.

Tactical Key: The 4-X pattern is useful when facing a right-handed opponent with a weak forehand, but it is an excellent go-to plan when you are right-handed, and your opponent is left-handed.

The 4-X Forehand Barrage: *Inside-out Forehand Weapon*

If you are left-handed and facing a left-handed opponent, you must know how to employ the 4-X forehand barrage. Now the left-handed player is attacking a left-handed opponent's backhand corner with their inside-out forehand. Your goal is to overpower a left-handed opponent's backhand with your left-handed inside-out forehand weapon.

If you are left-handed and facing a right-handed opponent, you may want to occasionally run-around your backhand to hit your inside-out forehand into a right-handed opponent's forehand corner *(4-X target).* This will help to neutralize the power of your opponent's right-handed forehand.

However, you are also opening the court for your right-handed opponent's down-the-line forehand. Therefore, I suggest that you always recover to the standard tactical center position after hitting this shot. From the standard recovery position, you will not be able to hit as many forehands, but you will also avoid opening the court for your opponent's down-the-line forehand attack.

Tactical Key: If you are left-handed, be ready to run around any short crosscourt shots to hit your forehand pull-shot down the line into your opponent's 3-target box.

The Tick-Tock Pattern: *Hitting to the Open Court*

The tick-tock pattern is the most aggressive pattern. When using this play, you will switch the direction of each of your opponent's shots. Another way to think of this pattern is simply this: you will always be hitting your shot to the open court. If your opponent hits crosscourt, you hit down the line, and if your opponent hits down the line, you will hit crosscourt. This pattern is used to keep your opponent on the run.

Tactical Key: You should flow from your predetermined baseline pattern into the Tick-Tock Pattern whenever you attack your opponent's open court. Remain in the Tick-Tock pattern as long as your opponent continues to send you opportunity balls. However, if your advantage is neutralized, you should return to your best and most reliable baseline pattern as you await the next opportunity ball to attack.

The tick-tock pattern is a high-risk pattern for two distinct reasons: **1)** It often calls for you to hit the lower-percentage down-the-line switch, and **2)** Switching the direction of the ball is where most errors occur. So, by switching direction often, you are continually flirting with control.

Tactical Key: You must always keep this defensive situation in mind. Whenever you are pushed deep behind the baseline or are forced out wide of the singles sideline, send your next shot crosscourt with enough trajectory to give yourself time to recover to the tactical center of your opponent's next shot. If you follow this rule, your patterns will work. If you try to force your patterns from defensive positions, you will usually lose the point.

Checkpoints for the Baseline Rally

Checkpoint # 1: If both you and your opponent are playing from behind the baseline, you are playing **neutral points**. If you are winning, you are playing steady and can out rally your opponent. However, if you are losing, you need to move closer to the baseline and start using some of the more aggressive patterns.

Checkpoint # 2: If you are forcing your opponent behind the baseline while you are hitting from on or inside your baseline, you are playing **aggressive points**. If you are forcing errors and hitting winners, you are dictating play. However, if you are making errors and losing, you may be playing too aggressively. To avoid wild errors, move back a couple of steps and start exercising more control and patience by employing one of the less aggressive patterns.

Checkpoint # 3: If your opponent is forcing you back behind your baseline while they are hitting from on or inside their baseline, you are playing **defensive points**. You need to neutralize your opponent by hitting the ball deeper. To do this, you will need to play more aggressively in the first exchange. This will force your opponent back into the backcourt at the start of the baseline rally where it is more difficult for them to attack.

Chapter 7 Summary
Key Thought: *Focus on hitting shots. Not on hitting winners.*

In the Tactical Point Control System, the Base-X rally pattern is the foundation of my baseline tactics. Why, because it is simple to execute and highly effective in helping you maintain control of the baseline rally. When followed faithfully and implemented correctly, it allows you to control the baseline making it difficult for your opponent to launch an attack.

The Base-X pattern emphasizes the high-percentage crosscourt shot making it easier for you to manage your errors. It also keeps you close to the tactical center making it possible for you to control the center of the court. However, the primary strength of the Base-X pattern is its simplicity. Because it has a preprogrammed response to almost every situation, it makes your shot selection quick and efficient. Playing points becomes automatic as you allow the point to flow rather than trying to force the pattern of play.

The Base-X pattern makes it possible for you to establish a rhythm and pattern of crosscourt shots which allows you to maintain both consistency and control. Thus, you give your opponent ample opportunities to self-destruct with errors.

The Base-X pattern also allows for both defensive and offensive play. You play defense by hitting outside shots crosscourt forcing your opponent to risk going down the line. Conversely, you can go on the offensive whenever your opponent sends a ball short or to your inside.

When you break the Base-X pattern by hitting down the line, it can force your opponent to hit short; thus, becoming a springboard for advancing the point into phase three, the approach and volley.

When you can vary the Base-X pattern with the other patterns in this chapter, you have the tools to make your baseline game more aggressive and unpredictable. This flexibility will keep your opponent off balance making it more difficult for them to go on the attack.

See you on the practice court.

Chapter 8
Phase 2: The Baseline Rally

Forcing Errors
Key Thought: *Every shot has a purpose during practice and in match play.*

Most players falsely believe that winning more points means hitting more winners. However, studies show that even at the highest levels of tennis *(ATP and WTA),* this is just not the case. If you want to win more points, you need to stop going for winners and start emphasizing the concept of forcing your opponent to make more errors.

In chapter 7, I gave you some tactical game plans for the baseline rally. In this chapter, my goal is to teach you how to employ them. The purpose behind the X-patterns is to make point playing automatic. These patterns remove the need to think about shot selection. Instead, your shot-selection decisions are based solely on the direction of the incoming ball. This simplifies the decision-making process. However, there is another significant benefit. When you have mastered this concept, not only will your shot-making decisions become automatic, but you will also begin to anticipate the direction of your opponent's next shot. Thus, you will react quickly to your opponent's shots allowing you to cover the open court on your side of the net. This instant anticipation reduces your opponent's ability to either hit winners or force you into making errors. Not only that, but it also allows you to attack or counterattack with a suddenness that often takes your opponent by complete surprise.

Tactical Key: Once you master the X-patterns, you will no longer fear your opponent's best weapons because you now have an immediate and effective answer for any shot your opponent may attempt, no matter how hard they can hit the ball.

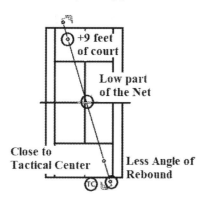

Diagram 8-1

I developed the X-patterns to take advantage of the high-percentage crosscourt shot. By emphasizing the crosscourt shot, you can avoid making careless change-of-direction errors. *(see diagram 8-1).* Not only will you reduce your errors, but the X-patterns also keep you close to the tactical center. This makes the recovery after each of your shots more manageable and efficient. When you are consistently positioned in the tactical center, you will tempt your opponent into hitting the more difficult and lower-percentage down-the-line shot. These down-the-line shots will often lead to more errors from your opponent.

The X-patterns allow you to build a strategy that is based on forcing errors from your opponent instead of attempting to blast the ball past them. Thus, both your accuracy and consistency will show radical improvement. By emphasizing the crosscourt rally patterns, your errors will be reduced, and you will find yourself winning more points, more games, and more matches.

Court Position: *The Physical Battle*

Key Thought: *Location... Location... Location... The most valuable pieces of real estate are always located in the best possible locations.*

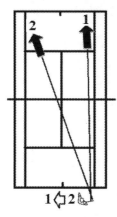

Diagram 8-2

Controlling the center of the court is the first component of baseline pressure. It is imperative you continuously recover to the tactical center of your opponent's next possible shot options. Maintaining this position has two essential requirements:

- **You must hit shots that are good for your court position.** This means that unless you can hit a clean winner, you must use a shot that gives you time to recover to the tactical center.
- **You must be willing to expend the energy necessary to recover.** *(see diagram 8-2).*

When you hit down the line *(shot # 1)*, you must recover to position 1. When you hit crosscourt *(shot # 2)* you must recover to position 2. Thus, when you hit down the line, the tactical center is further away from your position then when you send your shot crosscourt. This recovery factor is a critical component of the physical battle during long rallies and or on points late in the match.

Shot Accountability: You are responsible for where your shot lands in your opponent's court. Therefore, you must make sure the direction, pace, spin, and trajectory will always allow you enough time to recover to the tactical center.

Tactical Key: Never stand and watch your shot. Move! Plant your outside leg and push off! Recover with urgency! Your tennis success depends on it.

Consistency: *The Mental Battle*

Key Thought: *Consistency is the most powerful weapon in tennis!*

The second component of baseline pressure is consistency or your ability to keep the ball in play. In a match, you build your confidence by keeping the ball in the court. Therefore, consistency becomes a vital part of the mental battle. Consistency builds your confidence because you know you can keep the ball in play. At the same time, your consistency weakens your opponent's confidence because they begin to fear they cannot out rally you.

Shot Tolerance: The number of consecutive shots you can hit in a rally before you become uncomfortable and feel the need to end the point.

Think about this: How comfortable are you in the baseline rally? As the point progresses and the number of shots starts to build, do you begin to feel an urgency deep inside you to end the point? Are you frustrated when you face an opponent who seems never to miss a shot? Do you often feel the need to win points with your serve or your return, so you can avoid the baseline rally entirely?

The first step toward successful baseline play is to recognize your shot tolerance. If your shot tolerance is short, you need to work hard in practice to increase it. Conversely, if your shot tolerance is long, you will have just discovered one of your biggest weapons. Consistency can discourage your opponent, breaking down their will to win. Thus, giving you momentum in the mental battle.

In a match, shot tolerance is based on your confidence, and your confidence is based on your consistency, which in turn is based on your ability to keep the ball in play. Without consistency, your confidence will be difficult to maintain, and without confidence, winning is impossible.

Get one more ball back into play than your opponent, and it is impossible to lose. The tactic of consistency is so apparent to winning tennis that you grasped its importance from the first time you picked up a racket. In the beginning, consistency was the only tactical plan you needed. However, as your game has evolved, you now realize that although consistency is still the foundation of a winning game plan, ultimate success comes from learning to combine consistency with the other five essential elements that make up point building.

Tactical Key: One of the primary goals of the baseline rally is to win the mental battle. It is in this phase that you will build your confidence. You don't have to win every point to build confidence, but you do have to keep balls in play. Nothing destroys confidence faster and more thoroughly than a string of costly unforced errors.

Depth: *The Tactical Battle*
Key Thought: *Keeping your opponent deep gives you more time to read, react, and recover.*

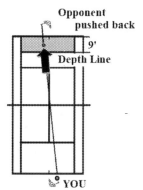

Diagram 8-3

Depth is the third component of baseline pressure. On every point, the player with the deepest shots will gain the initial control of the point. Keeping the ball deep makes it very difficult for your opponent to step into the midcourt and attack. If you can play from just inside the baseline or inside the midcourt zone, this advantage is even more significant. Almost all tennis points are won by the player who can play closer to the net than their opponent.

Depth Line: To help you visualize depth, I want you to imagine a line that is halfway between your opponent's service line and baseline *(see diagram 8-3).*

Goal: Your goal is to hit all your rally shots so that they land beyond the depth line *(shaded area in diagram 8-3).* This will push your opponent back pinning them in the backcourt.

Tactical Key: Forcing your opponent back behind the baseline has five key advantages. **1)** You have more time to read the situation. **2)** You have more time to react to your opponent's shot. **3)** You have more time to recover to the tactical center after your shot. **4)** Your opponent has fewer angles making it difficult for them to launch an attack against you, and **5)** Since your opponent must hit the ball further to keep you behind your baseline, you are more likely to get a short ball that will allow you to step into the midcourt and attack your opponent.

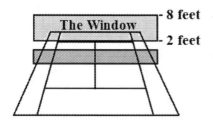

Diagram 8-4

Avoid the trap of trying to create depth with power. Instead, learn to hit the ball with a higher trajectory over the net. I call this hitting through the window.

When you are in a baseline rally, hit arcing shots that pass through the 2-foot to 8-foot window over the top of the net. Avoid trying to hit laser or flat shots under the window.

Tactical Key: Consistent depth is a powerful weapon. When you can hit three or more consecutive shots beyond your opponent's 9-foot, depth line, you will break the rhythm of their shots. This break in rhythm can often result in an error or a short ball which will then allow you to move forward and attack. The three-ball deep pattern is one of the most fundamental plays in tennis and should be a part of your game plan as well.

Spin: *The Technical Battle*
Key Thought: *When in doubt, just spin it in.*

The fourth component of pressure is spin. When you understand spin, you can manipulate three essential variables: **1) Control**: the ability to keep balls in play, **2) Pace**: the ability to change the pace by hitting with either power or touch, and **3) Strike zone**: the ability to force your opponent to hit balls outside of their comfort zone.

Control: Topspin allows you to hit the ball hard. Slice or underspin enables you to hit the ball with pinpoint accuracy and control. Both elements are critical to successful tennis tactics. I have listed spin as a part of the technical battle; however, as you will see in the following paragraphs, spin has a tremendous impact on tactics as well.

When you hit the ball hard, adding topspin increases your margin for error. The topspin groundstroke's forward spin decreases the air pressure under the ball essentially pulling it down into the court. This forward spin shortens the balls flight length allowing you to hit through the ball with tremendous pace. It also allows you to use a higher trajectory of three to six feet over the top of the net and still land the ball inside your opponent's baseline. Thus, topspin helps you to eliminate net errors from your game.

When you watch professional players from ground level, you will be surprised by the high trajectory of their rally shots. They use topspin as their control factor when hitting the ball hard. Likewise, you must do the same if you hope to hit the ball hard with consistency.

Slice, on-the-other-hand, adds backspin to the ball. It reduces your power. However, because it can be produced with such a short compact swing, it gives you tremendous control over the ball. Defensively, slice allows you to stay in points when you are pressured either by a ball that is hit short or that pushes you out extremely wide of the singles sideline.

Since the backspin causes the ball to rise over the first part of its flight, it is an excellent option for low balls or shots where there is no time for a full groundstroke swing. From the midcourt, slice gives you the ability to hit shots into small targets with both touch and control. The slice shot is the ultimate control shot when it comes to threading the ball on a sharp angle away from your opponent.

Change-of-Pace: You must avoid becoming your opponent's ball machine. Most players feed off consistent speed, spin, and placement. So, when you send the same kind of ball to them over and over, you often find the same type of ball coming back shot after shot after shot. Against better opponents, that ball will come back faster and faster and faster as they can add speed to their shots with minimal effort and without loss of control.

To challenge your opponent, you must be able to vary the pace of your shots. Changing the pace of your shots affects your opponent's timing and rhythm by forcing them to adjust their footwork and racket preparation. When you give your opponent the same shot over and over, they only need to react to the placement. However, when you change the pace of your shots, much like a baseball pitcher who mixes their fastball with their change-up, you force them to think. Thinking complicates every issue. When your opponent is forced to think, they can become distracted. They may look up to see where you are located instead of staying focused on the ball. In mid-swing, they might suddenly change their mind about the type of shot or shot-location they intend to use. Distraction destroys shot-making technique, so the more you can legally distract your opponent, the better your chances of forcing an error.

What's the best way to change-the-pace? I believe there are two simple ways. When hitting with topspin, the best way is to change the trajectory of the ball by raising or lowering the flight path or arc of your shot over the net. Whenever you change your shot trajectory, you must also adjust the pace of your shot. Thus, I want my players to think of the change of pace in terms of shot type, i.e., drive, loop, or lob, instead of merely how hard they will hit the ball. I think you will find that you automatically adjust the pace of your shot whenever you change the ball's trajectory, a fact that makes the change of pace simple to both understand and execute.

The second way to change the pace of the rally is to use slice. You will notice very quickly that there is a noticeable difference between the pace of a slice, flat, and topspin shot. The slice shot absorbs the pace of your opponent's incoming shot effectively slowing the speed of the rally. Changing the rally speed forces your opponent to manufacture their own pace rather than feeding off the speed of your incoming ball. By changing the speed of the rally, you force your opponent to dramatically alter the timing of both their footwork and swing pattern for their next shot, which often causes them to make errors.

Tactical Key: Remember, your opponent is not a wall. They can miss any shot, at any time, and sometimes for no reason at all. So never give up hope, just get one more ball back in play!

Forcing your opponent to hit from different strike zones: For most players, the ideal strike zone is somewhere between mid-thigh and the waist. If you watch them warm-up, you will see them position themselves so that the contact point is almost always the same. They should do that and so should you. However, once you understand the concept of the ideal strike zone, one of your tactical objectives should be to force your opponent to hit from the strike zones where they are the least comfortable. Spin can help you keep the ball out of your opponent's comfort zone.

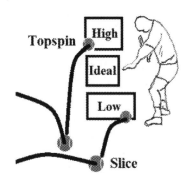

Diagram 8-5

Topspin causes the ball to kick up and back on the bounce. This gives your opponent three possible options. **1) Back up** and take the ball as it drops down into the ideal strike zone which pins them behind the baseline. **2) Move forward** and take the ball on the rise, this can be a difficult shot as the timing is entirely different from the regular groundstroke, or **3) Stay where they are** and try to hit their shot in the high strike zone, which is often a weakness, especially on the backhand side. *(see diagram 8-5)*

Slice, when hit low and with a moderate pace, causes the ball to skid and stay low on the bounce. This will force your opponent to hit from their lower strike zone, somewhere between the knee and the ankle. The low ball is a difficult ball for your opponent to attack. Thus, you will often force your opponent into hitting a neutral or even defensive shot. Neutral and defensive shots are often weak or short, which opens the door for you to launch an attack, i.e., they are opportunity balls.

Chapter 8 Summary

When you remember that your opponent is human and is fully capable of making errors, you begin to understand the importance of keeping the ball in play. You will always win more points off your opponent's errors than you can win by hitting winners. Strive to continually improve your shot tolerance, how many balls you can keep in play, while at the same time exercising shot accountability, by taking complete responsibility for the depth and placement of each of your shots. When you master these concepts, you are closing in on your tennis potential.

Forcing Errors

The key to winning the baseline rally is to find ways to increase your opponent's errors while at the same time reducing your own mistakes. This means balancing the priority of control with the need to win the point. One of the subtle ways to win more points is to know how to turn up the heat or increase the pressure on your opponent. In most cases, it is much like boiling water. Water does not boil when you first set it on the burner. However, if you keep it on the burner and keep applying the heat, eventually it boils. The same thing happens to your opponent. Keep the ball in play and keep applying the pressure. Eventually, your opponent will start to feel the heat, and when they do, the errors will begin to bubble up to the surface.

Tactical Key: Don't give up! Don't ever give up! Remember, just as many players crack under pressure when they are ahead as crack under pressure when they are behind. Just find a way to turn up the heat.

See you on the court.

Chapter 9
Phase 2: The Baseline-rally

Counterattacking from the Baseline

Key Thought: *Counterattack – an attack in reply to an attack.* – Webster's Dictionary

Now that you understand the X-patterns and the four ways to force your opponent into making errors, it is time to learn what to do when you face a tough opponent whose game style is difficult for you to overcome. This is where counterattacking comes into play, and it is an essential rung on the tennis ladder of success.

When attacked, your first reaction must be to neutralize the attack. Sometimes all it takes is to change-the-pace of the rally by sending the ball back deep with a loop, a lob, or a slice. Other times, you can counterattack into an opening or weakness created by your opponent's attack. Counterattacking is not predicated on your ability to strike the ball hard, but rather on your ability to hit the ball to specific spots in your opponent's court. On the tennis court, you will face four kinds of attacks:

- **Consistency Attack:** In this attack, your opponent challenges your ability to out-rally them from the baseline. This attack is composed of long rallies testing your mental and physical endurance as well as your technical ability to keep ball after ball in play.
- **Open Court Attack:** This attack challenges your court positioning. It occurs when your opponent sends an attacking ball into the periphery of your court coverage which then opens the opposite side of your court for your opponent's next shot. This opponent will use angle shots that push you out wide of the singles sideline or deep balls that force you back well behind the baseline.
- **Power Attack:** In this attack, your opponent tries to overpower you with their powerful weapons; usually a power serve or attacking forehand. The power attack often employs the inside-out forehand attack into your backhand corner. The goal of this attack is to force you into surrendering an opportunity ball, which allows your opponent to finish the point with a shot into the open court.
- **Net Attack:** This attack is used by players who like to move forward to the net. It can be a first-strike attack composed of a serve-and-volley or a delayed attack where your opponent waits for you to send them a short ball before moving forward to attack the net. This type of

attack is quick and determined as your opponent moves forward into the frontcourt to finish points with volleys or overheads. However, they are really hoping you panic and commit desperation errors with your passing shot attempts.

Tactical Key: Any time your opponent chooses to attack, it will create openings in their defense. Thus, counterattacking becomes as simple as finding those openings and then taking advantage of them.

Early in the match, you must test your opponent's shot-making ability. First, check your opponent's shot tolerance to determine how long they can stay patient in a rally. Second, check how your opponent reacts to different kinds of pace, trajectory, and spin. Finally, check how well your opponent performs in the backcourt, the midcourt, and the frontcourt. Then, take what you learn and apply it to your game by counterattacking with your strength into your opponent's biggest weakness.

Tactical Key: Always take away your opponent's best option and make them play with their second or third best shot. Forcing your opponent away from their game plan is the key to a successful counterattack.

The Three Stages of the Baseline Counterattack

- **Stage One:** *Recognize* your opponent's ability to attack and prepare early to either neutralize the attack or counterattack into their weakness. The earlier you prepare, the more effectively you can counter.
- **Stage Two:** *Read* the quality of your opponent's attack. **1)** If you are in immediate danger of losing the point, you must scramble and defend. **2)** If you are feeling pressure, but can still hit an effective shot, then you should counterattack.
- **Stage Three:** *React* with a preplanned response to the situation at hand. When you know what to do, you eliminate one step in the preparation process, and the time you save will often make the difference in the overall effectiveness of your response.

Tactical Key: When you follow the three-phase plan for counterattacking, even when you choose the wrong option, the quality of your shot may still win the point. Wrong choice and strong shot are always better than the right choice accompanied by a weak or missed response.

The Baseline Counterattacking Plays
Key Thought: *The right shot for the right situation.*

Based on the angle of the rally, there are two primary counterattacking shots: **1)** The Crosscourt Switch used when your opponent attacks down the line*;* and **2)** The Down-the-Line Switch used to change the angle of the rally. Although there are only two basic counterattacking shots, when you combine them with the variables of spin, pace, angle, and trajectory, there are multiple variations available to you. Just remember, you must be able to execute a shot with consistency and control for it to become one of your primary counterattacking weapons.

Tactical Key: Remember Newton's third law of motion: For every action, there is an equal and opposite reaction. This law is valid in tennis as well. Your opponent cannot attack without also making themselves vulnerable to a counterattack.

Counterattacking the Open-Court Attack
Key Thought: *Expect your opponent to attack your open court.*

The first component of the open court attack is distance, how far you must travel to reach the ball. Thus, an open court attack forces you to move laterally across the width of the court to reach the ball. The greater that distance, the more intense the pressure. According to this definition, most open-court attacks will occur on two occasions:

- **The Down-the-Line Attack:** A favorite play of all baseline players is to try to push you behind the baseline or outside of the singles sideline. When they do, they attack the open court to your inside with a down-the-line shot.
- **The Inside Pull-shot Attack:** A second open court attack occurs when you send a ball to your opponent that is not good for your court position. However, in this case, you create the open court when you purposely directed your shot down-the-line or accidentally sent a ball into the middle of the court. The inside-ball creates a dangerous situation, as it allows your opponent to attack your open court with a shot that is angled away from you.

Tactical Key: When your opponent hits their down-the-line off your crosscourt shot, they can run you no further than the singles sideline; however, when you send a down-the-line shot to your opponent, they can angle the ball crosscourt and away from you. This crosscourt shot can force you to run well beyond the doubles sideline.

The second component of the open court attack is time, how long will it take you to cover the distance between yourself and the ball. Two factors have a direct correlation to time pressure:

- **The pace of your opponent's shot.**
- **The distance the ball must travel before crossing the baseline.**

Although both time and distance are critical elements to an open court attack; since you cannot outrun even a slowly hit ball, the distance from your opponent's contact point to your baseline is always the most critical factor. Thus, the best way to eliminate or reduce the effectiveness of your opponent's open court attacks is to make sure your shots land deep in the court. When your opponent must contact the ball from behind the baseline, you will have more time to react.

Crosscourt Switch Options

Key Thought: *Recognize the situation and react accordingly!*

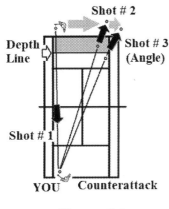

Diagram 9-1

The crosscourt counter is your response to an opponent's open-court attack *(Shot # 1 in diagram 9-1)*. When your opponent uses the down-the-line attack, you will face three possible situations:

- **Defense**: you can barely reach the ball.
- **Neutral**: you are forced to hit on the move.
- **Counterattack**: you have time to set your feet and employ an aggressive shot.

Within the three situations, you have five possible shot options. The option you choose will be predicated on the quality of your opponent's attacking shot and your shot-making ability. The first two options are defensive. They are used just to keep the ball in play. The objective is to make your opponent hit at least one more shot. The third option is a neutralizing shot. Its purpose is to check your opponent's momentum and to take away their advantage. Finally, the last two options are real counterattacks. They give you the opportunity to switch the point momentum in your favor as you turn a defending situation into an opportunity to attack.

Situation # 1: Defense

Key Thought: *At all cost, get one more ball into play!*

When your opponent has combined the pressure of time and distance in such a way that you are barely able to reach the ball, you are in a defensive situation. Your goal is to hang on and regroup with the hope of somehow getting back into the battle.

Option # 1 The Absorbing Slice: The absorbing slice is hit with underspin using a trajectory of 8 to 10 feet over the top of the net *(shot # 2 in diagram 9-1)*. It is aimed crosscourt and deep landing well beyond your opponent's 9-foot depth line, the deeper, the better. You will use the absorbing slice when you are under so much pressure to reach the ball that you are unable to organize your balance and footwork making it impossible to take a full swing at the ball. In this case, the compact swing of the absorbing slice is the best choice for getting the ball over the net and deep in your opponent's court. The purpose of the absorbing slice is not to win the point, but to just get one more ball back into play.

The underspin action of this shot will absorb nearly all the pace from your opponent's shot resulting in a return that floats high over the net and deep into your opponent's court. This slow floating action will give you the additional time necessary to recover back to the tactical center of the court. Thus, the second purpose of the absorbing slice is to buy you time to recover.

If hit deep, the absorbing slice creates a nothing-ball that can neutralize the rally by forcing your opponent to supply all the power for their next shot. This nothing ball can also lead to an unforced error should your opponent over-hit their shot in a foolish attempt to regain the advantage in the point. Hence, the third purpose of the absorbing slice is to provide absolutely no pace for your opponent to transfer into their next shot.

Option # 2 The Deep Defensive Loop or Lob: The deep defensive loop is a topspin shot hit with a trajectory of between 10 to 20 feet over the top of the net. This defensive shot is aimed crosscourt and hit with enough trajectory over the net to land beyond the 9-foot depth line on your opponent's end of the court *(Shot # 2 in diagram 9-1)*. Whenever you are under pressure and on the move, but still have time to take a full swing at the ball use the defensive loop.

Like the absorbing slice, the purpose of the defensive loop is three-fold: First, it forces your opponent to hit at least one more shot. Second, it neutralizes your opponent's attack by giving you enough time to recover back into the tactical center of the court. Finally, the defensive loop pushes your opponent back behind the baseline making it difficult for them to continue their attack.

Tactical Key: Your opponent is always capable of making an error. Getting one more ball in play and forcing that error, can sometimes change the momentum of an entire match.

The critical components of the defensive topspin loop or lob are as follows. **1)** To organize your footwork, so you are balanced and under control. This means you can get your back foot down and behind the ball. This is important because it allows you to tilt your front shoulder up and lift the ball with your legs, body, and shoulder. **2)** To shorten your backswing in preparation for the shot. **3)** To contact the back of the ball with a steep upward brushing action of the racket, and **4)** To use a buggy-whip motion on your follow through.

Tactical Key: On the buggy whip follow through, the racket will finish on the ball-side of the body with the hitting hand is positioned above the top of your head.

Situation # 2: Neutralize
Key Thought: *Rocksteady!*

Your opponent has forced you to move to reach the ball; however, you can arrive in time to get your outside foot down and to hit through the ball with balance and control. In this circumstance, your goal is to stop the opponent's momentum and to reset the baseline rally.

Option # 3 The Crosscourt Rally Ball: The crosscourt rally ball is used when you are forced to contact the ball from behind the baseline but from inside the doubles sideline. When hitting a crosscourt rally ball, your intent is to keep the ball deep and to the outside of your opponent's court position forcing them to hit their next shot from behind the baseline. You must hit this shot with topspin and a trajectory that is between 4 to 6 feet over the top of the net. Use moderate pace and aim for a spot beyond the 9-foot depth line *(Shot # 2 in diagram 9-1)*. Only use the crosscourt rally ball when you can reach your opponent's attacking shot with enough time to regain your balance and organize your footwork, i.e., you can plant your back foot. A well-placed rally ball will break the momentum of your opponent's attack and allow you to return to the Base-X pattern.

Tactical Key: Most of the time, your counterattack goal is merely to neutralize your opponent's advantage which will then allow you to go back to building points using your preferred baseline rally tactics.

Situation # 3: Counterattack

Key Thought: *A counterattack is an attack made in response to an opponent's attack.*

The true counterattack occurs when your opponent's shot is weak or short allowing you to reach the ball in time to hit an aggressive shot in return. Now, the goal is not only to stop your opponent's momentum but also to switch it into your favor by taking advantage of an opening in your opponent's defenses.

Option # 4 The Topspin Angle: The topspin angle is an aggressive counterattacking shot. It is hit when your opponent's down-the-line shot is weak or short allowing you to be fully balanced and organized for your shot. Unlike the crosscourt rally ball, this shot is angled away from your opponent so that the ball will cross the singles sideline before it crosses the baseline *(Shot # 3 in diagram 9-1)*. The purpose of this shot is to attack the movement, footwork, and shot-making ability of your opponent. If your opponent is late on their swing and sends the ball back to your inside, you are now positioned to continue your offensive by launching an inside pull-shot attack into the open court. Thus, you are flowing into the Tick-Tock pattern described in chapter 7. When this happens, you can run your opponent from corner to corner allowing you to turn-the-table from defense to offense.

Option # 5 The Short-Angle Chip: Like the topspin angle, the short-angle chip is an aggressive counterattacking shot. You will use this shot when your opponent's down-the-line or inside pull-shot is weak or lands short in the court. It is a touch shot that is angled precisely and with a biting slice that grabs the court and causes the ball to skid and stay low on the bounce. The short-angle chip is aimed low over the center of the net and into the short corner of the diagonal service box *(Shot # 3 in diagram 9-1)*. The direction and spin of the chip angle will attack your opponent's movement, footwork, and ability to hit an effective shot from their lower strike zone, i.e., between the knee and the ankle. When you see your opponent running hard and stretching to reach this low ball, you can react to their weak position with a sneak approach and volley attack.

Tactical Key: When you see your opponent out wide and stretching for the ball, especially on the backhand side, sneak to the net and be ready to pick off your opponent's weak shot with a winning volley or overhead angled into your opponent's open court. *(see chapter 11 for a detailed description of the sneak volley attack)*

Counterattacking the Power Attack

Key Thought: *Take away your opponent's strength by making them play from their weakness.*

Unlike the crosscourt counter, which is in response to your opponent's attack, the down-the-line counter is about escaping from a pressure situation before an attack begins. Thus, the down-the-line counter is employed when you anticipate an impending attack rather than after the attack has occurred. To be successful, you must be able to read the situation, understand your opponent's intent, and then be able to escape the pressure before falling prey to your opponent's attack.

Down-the-Line Counterattacking Options

Key Thought: *Balance your priority of getting your shot into play with your need to counter your opponent's attack. Give away no free points.*

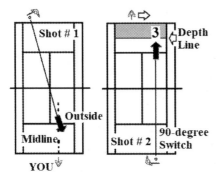

Diagram 9-2

The down-the-line switch changes the angle of the rally from crosscourt to down the line. It is an excellent counterattacking shot; however, it is not without risk. First, if you forget to use a higher trajectory, you will hit the ball into the net. Second, if you fail to adjust your pace to account for a shorter court, you will hit the ball long. Third, if you fail to account for the rebound angle of the ball off your racket strings, you will send your shot wide of the singles sideline. Finally, if you fail to account for the greater distance to the tactical center, you will be unable to cover the court adequately. So, with all these disadvantages, why would you ever choose to send the ball down the line?

Well, although the percentages might be against it, there are three tactical situations where the likelihood of your remaining in the point will depend solely on your ability to employ a down-the-line switch efficiently. The first situation occurs when you need to switch the crosscourt angle of the rally from your weakness to your strength. The second, when you need to force an aggressive opponent to hit on the move. The final situation occurs when you must escape from the dangerous backhand cage.

Situation # 1: Switch the Rally Angle by Employing the 3-X or 4-X Patterns

Key Thought: *When you hit down the line, your opponent will most likely respond with a crosscourt reply.*

As a match progresses, you will begin to recognize your opponent's strengths and favorite rally patterns. If you are employing a sound between-point routine where you analyze what is happening during each point, you will start to identify which rally situations are placing you at the greatest disadvantage. Then, as each point progresses through the four point-building phases, you can read the situation and recognize when the rally angle or shot pattern is swinging the point momentum in favor of your opponent. For example: If one of your opponent's groundstrokes is stronger than yours, you must avoid the rally angle that pits your weaker shot against your opponent's stronger one. To accomplish this, you must understand how to switch the rally angle, and you must know how to do it safely and efficiently. If in doing so, you can turn the momentum of the point in your direction as well, even better.

Tactical Key: The down-the-line counter is used to halt your opponent's point momentum by switching the rally angle or by altering the shot pattern. Remember, at all costs avoid becoming your opponent's ball machine.

The Two-Shot Plan

Breaking your opponent's momentum by successfully switching the rally angle necessitates the use of a two-shot process. The first shot is the momentum buster, and its sole purpose is to make your opponent move. This movement causes them to back off from their attack to just get the next ball in play. To force this change, you will send them a down-the-line shot *(Shot # 2 in diagram 9-2)*. This change-of-direction shot directs the ball away from your opponent breaking the current crosscourt rally angle. Your opponent must now move laterally along the baseline; thus, you have forced them to move corner to corner.

When your opponent reaches this ball, they will most likely respond by sending the ball back crosscourt. Now, the crosscourt rally diagonal has switched. When you reply to your opponent's crosscourt shot by sending your next shot back crosscourt with no change of direction, you have established a new rally angle. For example, if the original rally was on the 3-to-3 angle, it has now been changed to the 4-to-4 angle. *(see diagram 3-5 in chapter 3)*

The second shot is the momentum builder. It is used to maintain the new rally angle forcing your opponent to play from their weaker side, or at least away from their strength. Once you have established this new crosscourt angle, you will continue to build the point with your opponent until you receive an opportunity to attack, or your opponent decides to switch the angle by sending a ball down-the-line. Tactically you are running either the 3-X or 4-X rally patterns. *(see chapter 7 for details)*

Tactical Key: A smart opponent will want to play from their strength, so you must always expect them to switch the rally angle to the side of their strength. The key is to have a plan for how to neutralize or better yet, to take advantage of this switch.

When your opponent counters the new rally angle by sending a ball back down-the-line, you have three options:

- **Option # 1: Hit a Crosscourt Switch** *(Shot # 2 in diagram 9-1)* switching the rally angle back to your opponent's strength and then holding that crosscourt angle.
- **Option # 2: Hit immediately back down-the-line** *(not shown)* avoid changing the angle by sending the ball right back down the line into your opponent's weaker corner, thus preventing your opponent's attempt to return to their strength, i.e., combining the Mirror pattern with the 3-X or 4-X tactic.
- *Option # 3:* **Hit a Crosscourt Switch** *(Shot # 2 in diagram 9-1)* sending the ball into your opponent's strength, and then when your opponent sends the next ball crosscourt, follow up immediately with a second down-the-line switch *(Shot # 2 in diagram 9-2)* back into your opponent's weaker rally angle. Thus, you are reestablishing the 3-X or 4-X pattern.

Option # 1 allows your opponent to return to using their strength, never a good idea. Whereas in option #2, you completely avoid your opponent's strength by immediately sending the ball back to their weaker side. You should probably choose option #2 if your opponent's strength is overwhelming, or their weakness is the fatal flaw of their game. In either case, your best chance to win the point is to keep forcing your opponent to play from their weakness.

However, I encourage you to use option #3 whenever your opponent sends you an opportunity ball. This option allows you to challenge your opponent to hit both their strongest and their weakest shots on the move. Whenever you force your opponent to hit on the move, they are more likely to commit an error.

Tactical Key: In option #3, you are forcing your opponent to hit two consecutive shots on the run: The first shot on the move from their strength and the second on the move from their weakness. This gives you two opportunities to force your opponent into an error.

Both options # 2 and # 3 will keep your opponent from dominating the point with their more powerful groundstroke, and when possible, you always want to make your opponent play from a weakness. Some of your opponents will recognize what you are doing to them; but, some never will. In either case, you are forcing your opponent away from what they do best.

Situation # 2: Make Opponent Move to Hit
Key Thought: *Big players like to be set to hit, so keep them running.*

When you are playing aggressive baseliners, you will find some that want to stay in the middle of the court and pound the ball with their big groundstrokes. These are the players you want to keep on the move. This movement can be lateral from corner to corner, or it can be vertical between the net and the baseline. The key is to find their weakness and expose it.

Option # 1 The Lateral Counterattack: The aggressive baseliner will want to push you into a corner, and then once they push you back or push you out wide, they will attack you down the line. Therefore, the key is to make your opponent move first by hitting your down-the-line switch early in the rally *(Shot # 2 in diagram 9-2).* However, this is both a dangerous and challenging task. Difficult because the down-the-line switch is a low-percentage shot, and dangerous because it also opens the opposite corner of the court for your opponent to attack.

As you can see, the down-the-line switch calls for a delicate balance between control and aggressiveness. You must remember that your goal is not to hit a winner, but to force your opponent to move. To succeed your down-the-line switch must possess two qualities:

- **Depth:** you must hit your shot deeper than the 9-foot depth line
- **Recovery Time**: you must hit your shot in such a way that you have time to recover to the tactical center before your opponent strikes the ball

To meet these requirements often calls for hitting shots with less pace, a higher trajectory, and more spin. The deep loop and absorbing slice are excellent choices for this situation.

Option # 2 The Vertical Attack: Most aggressive baseliners are very comfortable in the back- and midcourt zones; however, this often changes when they approach the frontcourt and are forced to hit volleys. If their volley is suspect, bringing them to the net is a great option since you are forcing them to play with one of their weaker shots. To move your opponent forward and back requires two essential shots.

- The chip slice
- The deep topspin loop

To make this play work, you must first chip the ball down the line to bring your opponent forward, and then loop the ball deep crosscourt to move them back. Most aggressive players do not want to run, especially on the vertical plane from the service line to baseline. If you can follow your chip shot with a deep topspin loop, it is even better. Do this a few times in a point, and you will quickly wear them down, and a tired player is more apt to start making errors by going for too much too early in the point.

Situation # 3: Escaping the Backhand Cage

Key Thought: *Develop your down-the-line backhand, it is your most important weapon for dealing with the inside-out forehand barrage.*

The inside-out forehand barrage is the most potent force in today's game of tennis. Players who possess big forehands, will shift the rally to the *3 to 3 (backhand or ad court)* angle and then start running around their backhand to pound inside-out forehands into your backhand corner. Their goal is to keep you locked in a backhand cage until you either commit an error or send them a ball that is weak, short, or opens the court. When you open the door, they drive their inside pull-shot through your open court for an easy winner. Every successful player knows how to employ the forehand barrage; however, the most successful players also know how to counterattack it. When you feel trapped in the corner, what you need is an escape hatch.

The Down-the-Line Backhand Switch

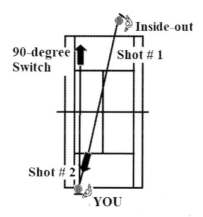

Diagram 9-3

When your opponent is employing the inside-out forehand barrage, they shift out toward their backhand side making them vulnerable to the down-the-line backhand *(Shot # 2 in diagram 9-3)*. You can often see the opening, but it is a tough one to hit. Every time you try to go down the line, your backhand is in danger of drifting wide. The success of the inside-out forehand barrage is rooted in just that, your inability to redirect their powerful shots into the down-the-line opening.

To hit a successful backhand down-the-line switch against a powerful inside-out forehand barrage requires three crucial qualities.

- **Hit it early:** go down-the-line at the beginning of the rally before your opponent has time to get their inside-out forehand grooved.
- **Avoid going for the kill shot**: to hit a winner does not require power, it requires placement.
- **Employ a 90-degree change of direction shot**: avoid aiming for the line or away from your opponent.

The Two-Shot Escape: If you have a solid backhand chip that you can angle through your opponent's backhand sideline, you have the perfect one-two punch that will make your backhand down the line highly successful. First, chip your backhand sharply crosscourt so that the ball crosses your opponent's sideline before crossing the baseline. This will force your opponent to use their backhand. Then when your opponent uses their backhand to send the ball back crosscourt, you immediately attack with a down-the-line counter.

Tactical Key: To defeat the inside-out forehand barrage, you must work hard in practice, so you can develop the kind of backhand that will hold up against this all-out assault.

Like the crosscourt counter, the down-the-line options are based on both the quality of your opponent's attack and your shot-making ability. When employing the down-the-line counter, there are five basic options:

- Deep Topspin Loop.
- Deep Absorbing Slice.
- Short chip.
- Move inside the midcourt taking the ball early and on the rise.
- Drop Shot.

The first option is defensive. It is used to move your opponent laterally while giving yourself time to recover back to the tactical center. The next two options are neutralizing shots. Again, you are forcing your opponent to move laterally across the court, but by changing the spin, depth, and pace of the rally, you are also disrupting the flow of your opponent's attack. The fourth and fifth options are aggressive. You will use these shots when your opponent sends you a ball that is weak or short drawing you inside the baseline.

Tactical Key: The down-the-line shot will always drift toward the near sideline; therefore, you must hit this shot using a 90-degree change of direction. Aim the ball straight up the court. Do not aim for the sideline, and do not aim the ball away from your opponent. Just hit this shot straight up the court. *(see tips for hitting down the line in chapter 3)*

Option # 1 The Deep Loop: Whenever you hit the ball down the line, you are choosing a low-percentage shot option. However, that does not eliminate the fact that sometimes sending the ball down the line might be the only way you can stay in the point. The deep loop is used when the pace or consistency of your opponent's shots have caged you in the corner of the court. To escape from the cage, you must change the rally angle.

The deep loop is a topspin shot hit on a high trajectory that will ensure net clearance and carry the ball deep past the 9-foot depth line. It eliminates much of the low-percentage risk from the down-the-line counter. It also gives you time to recover to the tactical center which is now located on the opposite side of the center hash mark. Changing the diagonal rally angle can often stall or put a halt to your opponent's momentum in the rally.

Tactical Key: The deep loop is especially effective against an opponent who is pounding you with a powerful crosscourt groundstroke attack. In this case, you need a switch that will create enough time for you to recover to the tactical center. The deep loop will slow the pace of the rally, buying you the time you need.

Option # 2 The Deep Absorbing Slice: The absorbing slice is probably more of a backhand option; however, there is no reason it cannot be just as effective from the forehand side. The purpose of the absorbing slice is two-fold:

- **Change-of-pace**: the slice will absorb the pace of your opponent's shot and slow down the speed of the rally
- **Nothing Ball**: if hit deep this ball will bounce almost straight up giving your opponent absolutely no pace to work with and forcing them to supply all the power to their shot. The nothing ball often throws off your opponent's timing and causing weaker shots and sometimes unforced errors.

Tactical Key: Deep balls are hard to slice; therefore, you should only use the absorbing slice on short to medium depth balls. If you are a step or two behind the baseline, a deep topspin loop would be a better change-of-pace shot.

Option # 3 The Short Chip: The down-the-line chip shot is used most often on the backhand side. The chip is hit low over the net using heavy slice *(underspin)* and aimed at the opponent's service line. You should hit the chip with moderate pace using a high to low knifing swing. The sharp knifing action creates a heavy, biting underspin that causes the ball to travel on a flat, laser-like trajectory. When struck correctly, this biting slice will cross low over the net and skid low on the bounce often rising no more than a few inches above the court surface.

Tactical Key: The slice is a front foot shot. You should "step on the ball" which is my way of saying get your front foot down and lean into this shot.

Because this shot uses a combination of sidespin and underspin, when hit down-the-line, the chip will also tend to break toward the near sideline and away from your opponent. This low, breaking action forces your opponent to hit from their lower strike zone, between the ankle and the knee. The combination of backspin and a lower bounce will challenge your opponent to hit any kind of aggressive return. This often leads to balls hit long or into the net. These kinds of errors will frustrate your opponent and sometimes even cause them to abandon their game plan.

Tactical Key: Your opponent must chase this ball on a forward diagonal. Since you forced your opponent to move both forward and toward the sideline to reach this ball, you can often hit your next shot past them for a clean winner long before they have time to recover.

Option # 4: Taking the Ball Early and on the Rise: When you can move forward to meet the ball early you are positioning yourself to attack. Contacting the ball from inside the baseline gives your opponent less time to recover. Even more importantly, it will often cause them to reach your shot late and without enough balance to continue their attack.

How aggressively you can hit this shot is dependent on the relationship of the ball to the top of the net. Balls above the net can be contacted with a flatter and more powerful swing. Whereas, balls that are below the level of the net should be hit with controlled topspin with an emphasis on control.

Tactical Key: The further into the midcourt you can advance before contacting the ball, the more aggressive your shot. Be sure to use the 90-degree change of direction guideline on this shot. Resist the temptation to aim for the corner and drive this ball through the baseline.

Option # 5 The Drop Shot: I list the drop shot last because it is the highest-risk switch shot.

- **The drop shot is the ultimate touch shot,** which means it takes more fine motor skills than any other shot
- **If the drop shot is hit too deep**, it sets up an easy finishing shot for your opponent
- **Because most players tend to use it at the wrong time** leading to lost points and lost opportunities

The goal of the drop shot is to pressure your opponent by hitting a short ball that is nearly, if not completely, out of their reach. If you force your opponent to run hard and to contact the ball below the level of the net, you have succeeded. Your opponent's shot will be weak, and they will be in a very vulnerable position up close to the net. Now you can choose to pass them with a shot into the open court or to lob the ball back over their head.

The Two Keys to a Successful Drop Shot

- **The right time:** because the drop shot is the most precise touch shot, you should never attempt a drop shot when you are feeling tense as you are less likely to control your shot
- **The right position**: you should only use the drop shot when you are well inside the baseline, the closer to the net the better.

Tactical Key: Move in after your shot. If you stay back, you are vulnerable to the opponent winning the point by returning your drop shot with a drop shot winner.

Set-up Options:

If you are still having trouble escaping from the backhand cage, try the following two-shot plays.

- **Hit your backhand deep crosscourt with pace.** This will push your opponent back and into the corner where they will either be forced to hit a backhand or go for an outright winner with their inside-out forehand. In either case, you will have opened the court to hit your next shot down-the-line.
- **Hit a backhand chip on a short crosscourt angle.** This will push your opponent wide and bring them forward forcing them to hit a backhand from the lower strike zone. If you see

them stretched out and reaching, you should move in and look to volley their weak shot for a winner. Otherwise stay back and hit your next shot into the open court away from them.

- **Adjust your position and start hitting your own inside-out forehands.** Then if they send you an inside ball, hit a forehand pull-shot into the open court.

Chapter 9 Summary: Counterattacking

When players think of a counterattack, they most often think of hitting into the open court, which requires a change-of-direction shot. However, some of the most important counterattacking shots require no change of direction. Instead, they call for a change in the shot characteristics. I teach my players to counterattack with three variables:

- **Pace:** how hard or soft they hit the ball.
- **Spin:** switching between topspin and slice.
- **Trajectory:** varying the arc of the shot.
- **Depth:** varying the depth of their shot.
- **Angle:** hitting shots through the sideline instead of the baseline.

Tactical Key: The first goal of the counterattack is to halt your opponent's point momentum by switching the rally angle or by altering the shot pattern, i.e., don't be a ball machine.

See you on the court.

Chapter 10
Baseline-Rally Drills

Key Thought: *Practice the way you want to play, and you won't be disappointed.*

The purpose of the **Base-X** drills is to teach you to play effectively from the baseline. The drills build upon the Base-X tactics helping you gain consistency and control over the three basic shots: **1)** *The Outside Crosscourt Shot;* **2)** *The Inside Pull-shot,* and **3)** *The Outside Switch.* Each drill repetition begins with a second serve which helps build consistency and flow from the first-exchange into the baseline rally. It is always my goal to make the drills as match-like as possible. The following list defines my drill theory.

Shot Accountability
- **Definition:** You are responsible for where your shot lands in the opponent's court.
- **Intent:** The biggest key to success in a tennis match will be your ability to hit the ball into a specific target area. Accuracy is critical to building a point with your strength *(offense)* as well as neutralizing the strength of your opponent *(defense)*.
- **Purpose:** You learn shot accountability in practice; however, this lesson will only be useful if you are held accountable for where you send the ball. Not just sometimes, but all the time. The first line of accountability is yourself, so refuse to make excuses and take responsibility for where you send the ball. The second line of accountability is your coach, and you must realize that sometimes your coach will use consequences to ensure mastery.

Shot Tolerance
- **Definition:** The number of consecutive shots you can hit before becoming uncomfortable and either going too big looking for a winner or by growing too tentative and playing it too safe.
- **Intent:** To be successful in the baseline rally, you must continuously seek to improve your shot tolerance.
- **Practice:** To increase shot tolerance you will often be asked to meet a specific standard for the number of consecutive shots you can hit.

Cooperative Drills

- **Definition:** Two players are working together to meet a set standard of shots.
- **Intent:** To develop control and consistency in the baseline rally. To build a sense of teamwork, trust, and support between teammates as they strive to reach a mutual goal.
- **Purpose:** Practice must be as match-like as possible. You will face pressure in a match, so you must face pressure in practice. Competing against a standard creates pressure.

Competitive Drills

- **Definition:** Two players competing against each other in a game situation. Usually, there will be stipulations for the direction of the shot.
- **Intent:** To develop control and consistency under match-like conditions.
- **Purpose:** Practice must be as match-like as possible. Therefore, since keeping score is part of match play, I use drills where scoring is essential. These drills replicate specific parts of a tennis point.

Short-Court Rally Game

Key Thought: *To win tennis points you must be able to cover the open court.*

Intent: This is a competitive drill. The purpose is to develop shot-direction and court-coverage in a highly competitive situation. I use this game every day at the beginning of practice. It teaches players to control the ball and cover the court while warming them up for the rest of a highly competitive practice.

Time: Each Game last five minutes.

Set-up: On a short singles court, two players play competitively using only the service boxes as boundaries. In this drill, the back-service line becomes the baseline.

Feed: Each point begins with a diagonal feed. Each player will alternate feeding one point to the deuce court and one point to the ad court sides. Players cannot lose points on the feed; however, once the feed is in play, the point is live.

Directions: Play points using the following stipulations. There are no volleys. Every shot must bounce inside one of the service boxes. The goal of this drill is to attack open court with control. Players may hit shots using slice or topspin.

Scoring: A player scores each time they hit a winning shot, or their opponent makes an error.

Practice Key: Learn to cover the court by anticipating your opponent's next shot.

Baseline Control Drills

Key Thought: *Consistency builds confidence.*

I use ten competitive drills to teach my players control and consistency in the **Base-X**

Rally patterns. Each drill has a different set of stipulations or restrictions on shot direction, depth, and or type of shot to be employed. However, each of the ten drills will use the same system for scoring. This system is listed below.

Five-Lives Scoring: Each player begins the drill with five lives. Every time they make an error or in some cases lose a point, they lose a life. The player who loses all five of their lives first is the loser. To keep players from becoming confused, I demand that they each call out their own score at the start of every point.

Winner: The coach will record the winner of each drill on their practice score pad. These totals are used to keep track of the strengths and weaknesses of each player's game. I have learned to use them as a tool in setting line-up positions between players with similar match records.

Standard: Throughout the season, a player should win a minimum of 40% of all Competitive Drills.

Basic Directions

Feed: Each rally begins with a second-serve feed. Missed serves count as an error for the serving player. This makes the players focus on getting a second serve into play.

Directions: Once the rally begins, it does not stop unless an error is committed. When a player commits an error, they subtract one life from their score. When a player loses all five lives, they lose the game.

Practice Key: When you are confident that you can keep your shots in play, you will be confident you can win points in a match.

Drill # 1: Stay Alive for Five.

Intent: This is a competitive drill. The purpose is to develop control and consistency in a competitive situation.

Set-up: On a singles court, two players play competitively.

Feed: Each rally begins a second serve feed. Each player will alternate serving one point to the deuce court and one point to the ad court sides. Missed serves *(feeds)* count as an error.

Directions: Players rally the ball. The goal of this drill is consistency. Each player starts with five lives. Every time they make an error, they lose a life. The first player to lose all five lives is the loser. This is a groundstroke rally so anytime you are forced to cross inside the service line to hit a ball, it counts as a miss for your opponent. **Note:** you cannot purposely run across the service line if you could have hit the ball from behind the service line.

Scoring: Each player starts the drill with five lives. Players lose a life each time they make an error. After each point, players call out their score. The first player to make five errors is the loser.

Note: Winners do not count as errors for the opponent.

Drill # 2: 4 to 4 Depth Rally

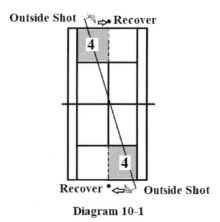

Diagram 10-1

Intent: This is a competitive drill. The purpose is to develop control and consistency when using the 4-to-4 rally angle.

Set-up: On a singles court, two players compete on a diagonal angle between the 4-targets. *(see diagram 10-1)*

Feed: Each rally begins on the deuce-court side with a second serve. The player who made the error feeds to start the next rally. Missed serves *(feeds)* count as an error.

Directions: After the serve, the two players rally on the 4-to-4 angle. Each player starts with five lives. Players lose a life every time they make an error. Each player calls out their score after every point. This is a groundstroke rally so anytime you are forced to cross inside the service line to hit a ball, it counts as a miss for your opponent. **Note:** you cannot purposely run across the service line if you could have hit the ball from behind the service line.

Scoring: Each player starts the drill with five lives. Players lose a life each time they make an error. After each point, players call out their score. The first player to make five errors is the loser.

Note: Winners do not count as errors for the opponent.

Practice Key: Practice must be challenging requiring you to train at the top of your playing range. If you hold back and seek comfort in practice, you will never reach your potential.

Drill # 3: 3 to 3 Depth Rally

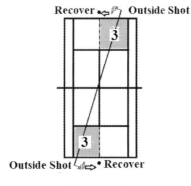

Diagram 10-2

Intent: This is a competitive drill. The purpose is to develop control and consistency when using the 3-to-3 rally angle.

Set-up: On a singles court, two players compete on a diagonal angle between the 3-targets. *(see diagram 10-2)*

Feed: Each rally begins on the ad-court side with a second serve. The player who made the error feeds to start the next rally. Missed serves *(feeds)* count as errors.

Directions: After the serve, the two players rally on the 3-to-3 angle. Each player starts with five lives. Players lose a life every time they make an error. Each player calls out their score after every point. This is a groundstroke rally so anytime you are forced to cross inside the service line to hit a ball, it counts as a miss for your opponent. **Note:** you cannot purposely run across the service line if you could have hit the ball from behind the service line.

Scoring: Each player starts the drill with five lives. Players lose a life each time they make an error. After each point, players call out their score. The first player to make five errors is the loser.

Note: Winners do not count as errors for the opponent.

Practice Key: Tennis is a game of technique and willpower. Are you willing to do what must be done, even if it might be uncomfortable? When you can adopt a positive attitude in response to a stressful situation you are building willpower.

Drill # 4: Depth Rally

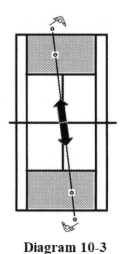

Diagram 10-3

Intent: This is a competitive drill. The purpose is to develop control, consistency, and depth in the baseline rally.

Set-up: On a singles court, two players compete on a full singles court. *(see diagram 10-3)*

Feed: Each rally begins with a second serve. Player's alternate with each serving one point to the deuce court followed by one point to the ad court. Missed serves *(feeds)* count as errors.

Directions: After the serve, players rally keeping the ball deeper than the service line. The rally stops when an error is committed. Each player starts with five lives. Players lose a life every time they make an error. Each player calls out their score after every point. **Note:** you cannot purposely run across the service line if you could have hit the ball from behind the service line.

Scoring: Each player starts the drill with five lives. Players lose a life each time they make an error. After each point, players call out their score. The first player to make five errors is the loser.

Note: Winners do not count as errors for the opponent. Balls that land inside the service line are out and count as errors.

Practice Key: Keeping the ball deep puts pressure on your opponent without risking the chance of hitting a ball wide.

Drill # 5: Ad Court Serve Inside-out Forehand 3 to 3 Rally

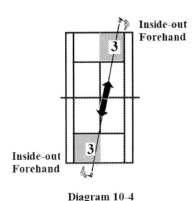

Diagram 10-4

Intent: This is a competitive drill. The purpose is to develop control and consistency when using the inside-out forehand in the 3-to-3 rally angle.

Set-up: On a singles court, two players compete using their inside-out forehands on a diagonal angle between the 3-targets. *(see diagram 10-4)*

Feed: Each rally begins on the ad-court side with a second serve. The player who made the error feeds to start the next rally. Missed serves *(feeds)* count as errors.

Directions: Players rally on the 3-to-3 angle using their inside-out forehand. The rally stops when an error is committed. Each player starts with five lives. Players lose a life every time they make an error. Each player calls out their score after every point. This is a groundstroke rally so anytime you are forced to cross inside the service line to hit a ball, it counts as a miss for your opponent. **Note:** you cannot purposely run across the service line if you could have hit the ball from behind the service line.

Scoring: Each player starts the drill with five lives. Players lose a life each time they make an error. After each point, players call out their score. The first player to make five errors is the loser.

Note: Winners do not count as errors for the opponent.

Drill Theory: I use restrictions and stipulations to mold my drills so that they simulate specific game situations. Then I demand my players perform within these parameters. Requiring players to stay within the stipulations teaches them discipline, aggressiveness, and patient consistency, otherwise known as willpower.

Drill # 6: The Base-X Rally Pattern

Intent: This is a competitive drill. The purpose is to develop control and consistency when using the Base-X Rally Pattern.

Set-up: Two players compete on a full singles court.

Time: Two five-minute rounds. **Round # 1:** Player # 1 uses the Base-X Rally Pattern against Player # 2 who is free to hit the ball anywhere. **Round # 2:** Player # 2 uses the Base-X Rally Pattern against Player # 1 who is free to hit the ball anywhere.

Feed: The player using the Base-X Rally Pattern will begin each point with a second serve. Points will alternate between deuce and ad court serves. Missed serves *(feeds)* count as errors.

Directions: Two players compete with Player # 1 using the Base-X Rally pattern against Player # 2 who can hit anywhere in the court. The two players will rally using the stipulated pattern until an opportunity ball is sent. The player receiving the opportunity ball will then attack, and the point is played out.

Scoring: Players score a point when they hit a winning shot, or their opponent makes an error.

Note: When playing from on or behind the baseline, the players will follow their baseline stipulation. However, when they move inside the baseline to hit the ball, they are free to attack.

Practice Key: Player using the Base-X Pattern will emphasize the crosscourt shot by implementing the following rule: **Always send your shot crosscourt. 1)** When your opponent hits crosscourt, you will hit crosscourt, and **2)** When your opponent hits down-the-line, you will hit crosscourt.

Drill # 7: The Mirror Pattern

Intent: This is a competitive drill. The purpose is to develop control and consistency when using the Mirror Rally Pattern.

Set-up: Two players compete on a full singles court.

Time: Two five-minute rounds. **Round # 1:** Player # 1 uses the Mirror Rally Pattern against Player # 2 who is free to hit the ball anywhere. **Round # 2:** Player # 2 uses the Mirror Rally Pattern against Player # 1 who is free to hit the ball anywhere.

Feed: The player using the Mirror Rally Pattern will begin each point with a second serve. Points will alternate between deuce and ad court serves. Missed serves *(feeds)* count as errors.

Directions: Two players compete with Player # 1 using the Mirror Rally pattern against Player # 2 who can hit anywhere in the court. The two players will rally using the stipulated pattern until an opportunity ball is sent. The player receiving the opportunity ball will then attack, and the point is played out.

Scoring: Players score a point when they hit a winning shot, or their opponent makes an error.

Note: When playing from on or behind the baseline, the players will follow their baseline stipulation. However, when they move inside the baseline to hit the ball, they are free to attack.

Practice Key: For the first two or three shots of every point, the player implementing the Mirror Pattern will use the following rule: **Hold the rally angle. 1)** If your opponent hits crosscourt, you hit crosscourt, and **2)** If your opponent hits down the line, you will hit down the line. Then on the third or fourth shot, they will break the pattern using the following rule: **Switch the rally angle. 1)** If your opponent hits crosscourt, you will hit down the line and **2)** If your opponent hits down the line, you will hit crosscourt.

Drill # 8: The 3-X Mirror Pattern

Intent: This is a competitive drill. The purpose is to develop control and consistency when using the 3-X Mirror Rally Pattern.

Set-up: Two players compete on a full singles court.

Time: Two five-minute rounds. **Round # 1:** Player # 1 uses the 3-X Mirror Rally Pattern against Player # 2 who is free to hit the ball anywhere. **Round # 2:** Player # 2 uses the 3-X Mirror Rally Pattern against Player # 1 who is free to hit the ball anywhere.

Feed: The player using the 3-X Mirror Rally Pattern will begin each point with a second serve. Points will alternate between deuce and ad court serves. Missed serves *(feeds)* count as errors.

Directions: Two players compete with Player # 1 using the 3-X Mirror Rally pattern against Player # 2 who can hit anywhere in the court. The serving player must set up the 3-X Mirror Rally pattern by hitting their second shot into the deep 3-target. From there the players will rally using the stipulated pattern until an opportunity ball is sent. The player receiving the opportunity ball will then attack, and the point is played out.

Note: Whenever possible, right-handed players should send the ball to the 3-target by using their inside-out forehand to attack a right-handed opponent's backhand.

Scoring: Players score a point when they hit a winning shot, or their opponent makes an error.

Note: When playing from on or behind the baseline, the players will follow their baseline stipulation. However, when they move inside the baseline to hit the ball, they are free to attack.

Practice Key: The server must set up the 3-X Mirror pattern by hitting their second shot into the deep 3-Target. Then they will hold the rally angle by using the following rule: **Send your shots into the deep 3-Target. 1)** If your opponent hits crosscourt to your 3-target, you hit crosscourt to your opponent's 3-target, and **2)** If your opponent hits down the line to your 4-target, you hit back down-the-line to your opponent's 3-target. However, once your opponent hits short or opens the court, you can attack with a shot into your opponent's open court, i.e., the 4-target.

Drill # 9: The 4-X Mirror Pattern

Intent: This is a competitive drill. The purpose is to develop control and consistency when using the 4-X Mirror Rally Pattern.

Set-up: Two players compete on a full singles court.

Time: Two five-minute rounds. **Round # 1:** Player # 1 uses the 4-X Mirror Rally Pattern against Player # 2 who is free to hit the ball anywhere. **Round # 2:** Player # 2 uses the 4-X Mirror Rally Pattern against Player # 1 who is free to hit the ball anywhere.

Feed: The player using the 4-X Mirror Rally Pattern will begin each point with a second serve. Points will alternate between deuce and ad court serves. Missed serves *(feeds)* count as errors.

Directions: Two players compete with Player # 1 using the 4-X Mirror Rally pattern against Player # 2 who can hit anywhere in the court. The serving player must set up the 4-X Mirror Rally pattern by hitting their second shot into the deep 4-target. From there the players will rally using the stipulated pattern until an opportunity ball is sent. The player receiving the opportunity ball will then attack, and the point is played out.

Note: Whenever possible, left-handed players should send the ball to the 4-target by using their inside-out forehand to attack a left-handed opponent's backhand.

Scoring: Players score a point when they hit a winning shot, or their opponent makes an error.

Note: When playing from on or behind the baseline, the players will follow their baseline stipulation. However, when they move inside the baseline to hit the ball, they are free to attack.

Practice Key: The server must set up the 4-X Mirror pattern by hitting their second shot into the deep 4-Target. Then they will hold the rally angle by using the following rule: **Send your shots into the deep 4-Target. 1)** If your opponent hits crosscourt to your 4-target, you hit crosscourt to your opponent's 4-target, and **2)** If your opponent hits down the line to your 3-target, you hit back down-the-line to your opponent's 4-Target. However, once your opponent hits short or opens the court, you can attack with a shot into your opponent's open court, i.e., the 3-target.

Drill # 10: The Tick-Tock Pattern

Intent: This is a competitive drill. The purpose is to develop control and consistency when using the Tick-Tock Rally Pattern.

Set-up: Two players compete on a full singles court.

Time: Two five-minute rounds. **Round # 1:** Player # 1 uses the Tick-Tock Rally Pattern against Player # 2 who is free to hit the ball anywhere. **Round # 2:** Player # 2 uses the Tick-Tock Rally Pattern against Player # 1 who is free to hit the ball anywhere.

Feed: The player using the Tick-Tock Rally Pattern will begin each point with a second serve into the outside service target. Points will alternate between deuce and ad court serves. Missed serves *(feeds)* count as errors.

Directions: Two players compete with Player # 1 using the Tick-Tock Rally pattern against Player # 2 who can hit anywhere in the court. The serving player must set up the Tick-Tock Rally pattern by using an outside serve followed by a second shot into their opponent's open court. From there the players will rally using the stipulated pattern until an opportunity ball is sent. The player receiving the opportunity ball will then attack, and the point is played out.

Scoring: Players score a point when they hit a winning shot, or their opponent makes an error.

Note: When playing from on or behind the baseline, the players will follow their baseline stipulation. However, when they move inside the baseline to hit the ball, they are free to attack.

Practice Key: The server must set up the Tick-Tock pattern by using an outside serve followed by a second shot into the open court. Then they will use the following rule: **Send your shots into the open court away from your opponent. 1)** If your opponent hits crosscourt, you hit down the line into the open court, and **2)** If your opponent hits down the line, you hit crosscourt into the open court.

Singles Stations Games
Key Thought: *Three in a row starts the flow.*

All singles stations games use the same format listed below.

Purpose: 1) To teach players to start points with their second serve. **2)** To motivate players to hold their serve; **3)** To teach players the importance of breaking serve. **4)** To show the interconnection and significance of the first-exchange and the baseline-rally phases. **5)** To illustrate the importance of accurate shot placement; depth; and consistency in the baseline rally.

Set-up: Two players compete against each other using various stipulations on a full singles court.

Feed: Spin a racket before the game to decide who will feed *(serve)* first. The feed is always a second serve. After the first station, the server *(feeder)* is always the player who has won the last station, i.e., to serve you must win a station.

Basic Directions: Each singles station game is composed of three stations; however, the game only advances to station three when the server wins at station two. If the returner wins station two, the game starts over at station one with the winner of station two serving. A player must win three stations in a row to get the point.

Note: The returner can win station one and still advance the point to stage two. However, the server must win station two for the point to advance to station three, and the server must again win in station three to score a point. If the returner succeeds in either station two or station three, the game returns to station one with no points awarded.

Station One: The serve will be in the deuce court. Only one serve *(second)* is allowed. After the serve, the station is played out using the stipulations for that particular game.

Station Two: The winner of the station one will serve to start station two. The serve will be from the ad side. After the serve, the station is played out using the stipulations for that specific game.

Advancement Rule for Station Three: To advance to station three, the player serving in station two must win. If the returner wins, the game returns to station one with no points awarded. However, the returner will now be the server in station one.

Station Three: When the server wins station two, the game advances to station three. The server can now choose to serve to either the deuce or the ad court. The station is again played out using the stipulations for the particular game being played.

Scoring: When the server wins station three, i.e., has won three stations in a row, they are awarded a point. Games are played until one player scores seven points, or for a specified length of time, usually five or six minutes.

Standard: Players should win a minimum of 40 percent of the station games they play

Singles Stations Game # 1: Groundstroke Depth The Baseline Game

Purpose: This game will teach you how to play through the first-exchange and baseline-rally phases. The game begins with a second serve and emphasizes groundstroke depth.

Depth Stipulation: After the serve, every shot must land deeper than the service line. Any shot landing inside the service line is considered out.

Set-up: Two players compete on a full singles court.

Time Limit: 7 points or five minutes.

Directions: See Basic Rules.

Practice Key: Use the **Base-X guidelines** for this drill. Hit your outside shots crosscourt and switch the angle on inside shots by using an inside pull-shot. Go down the line when your opponent's outside shot draws you inside the baseline. *(See chapter 7 for guidelines)*

Singles Stations Game # 2: The Crosscourt Rally

Purpose: This game will teach you to initiate the point with a second serve and then to play out the point on the designated angle. The focus of this drill is on depth, direction, and consistency.

Rally Stipulation: In this drill, all points start on the angle of the serve. For example: If the serve is to the deuce court, the point begins on the **4-to-4 angle** *(deuce court angle),* and if the serve is to the ad court, the point begins on the **3-to-3 angle** *(ad court angle).*

Attack Stipulation: The rally will stay on the initial rally angle until one of the following conditions is met.

- You receive a short crosscourt ball that brings you inside the baseline to strike the ball. When this occurs, you can attack with an outside groundstroke down the line.
- You receive a ball from your opponent that does not land on your side of the service sideline. When this occurs, you can attack with an inside pull-shot away from your opponent.
- Your opponent uses an inside-out groundstroke. When this occurs, you can attack down the line.

Point Finish: Once an attack is initiated the point can be played out using any shots or shot angles.

Set-up: Two players are playing competitively on a full singles court.

Time Limit: 7 points or 5 minutes.

Directions: See basic rules for stations singles games.

Singles Stations Game # 3: Down-the-Line Rallies

Purpose: To teach players to initiate and control a down-the-line rally.

Rally Stipulation: After the serve, the return is hit down the line. The return can be hit with either a forehand or a backhand. After the return, the point is played out down the line.

Attack Stipulation: The rally will stay on the initial rally angle until one of the following conditions is met.

- If your opponent hits an inside pull-shot down the line, you can immediately hit your next shot crosscourt.
- If your opponent sends you a short ball that draws you inside the baseline, you can attack crosscourt.

Point Finish: After an attack is initiated, the point is played out using any shots or shot angles.

Practice Key: When your opponent hits an inside pull-shot down-the-line it opens the opposite side of the court for your next shot. This is especially true when your opponent hits the inside pull-shot with their backhand. You should always be watching for this situation to occur. Take advantage of it!

Set-up: Two players are playing competitively on a full singles court.

Time Limit: 7 points or 5 minutes.

Directions: See basic rules.

SPIN DRILLS
Key thought: *When in doubt, spin it in.*

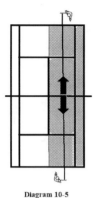

Diagram 10-5

Purpose: To teach you how to use a wide variety of spin shots, *i.e., the drive, topspin loop, and slice.* You will use this skill to keep the ball out of your opponent's ideal strike zone.

Set-up: All spin drills are played on half a tennis court. The doubles sideline forms the outside boundary, and the center service line forms the inside boundary. *(see diagram 10-5)*

Standard: Throughout the season, a player should win a minimum of 40% of all competitive Drills.

Drill # 1: Drive vs. Loop

Intent: The purpose of this drill is to develop control and consistency in a competitive situation. **1)** To practice hitting driving groundstrokes off looping groundstrokes. **2)** To practice hitting looping groundstrokes off driving groundstrokes. **3)** To hit swinging volleys and approach the net. **4)** To pass an opponent who comes to the net.

Practice Key: To pin your opponent behind the baseline, you need to apply heavy topspin to your shot. Heavy topspin causes the ball to kick up and back on the bounce making it difficult for your opponent to step in and take it on the rise. The best loops cross the baseline at shoulder level or higher. Great ones push their opponent back to the fence.

Set-up: On half a singles court, two players play competitively.

Time: 4 minutes divided into two 2-minute segments. Each player will have the opportunity to drive and loop.

Feed: The player hitting the drive is always the feeder. The feed is a groundstroke.

Directions: Players rally the ball with the feeder hitting topspin drives and the player receiving the feed hitting topspin loops. Both players will try to keep the ball deep. However, the driver can come forward to take short loops out of the air with a swinging volley and the looper can hit an approach shot when the driver sends their shot short. When a swinging volley or approach shot occurs, the point is played out with the attacker moving forward to the net. The point is played out on the half court without any other stipulations.

Scoring: Players score a point every time their opponent makes an error, or they hit a winner. Play mini-games of two out of three points. Each time a player wins a mini-game, they get the point. Keep the same score when starting the second segment.

Practice Key: The driver should learn to take the ball early. This means stepping inside the baseline and taking the ball on the rise. When possible, the driver should move forward and take the looping ball out of the air. The looper should look for the driver to hit short giving them the opportunity to attack the net.

Drill # 2: Drive vs. Slice

Intent: This is a competitive drill. The purpose is to develop control and consistency in a competitive situation. **1)** To practice hitting driving groundstrokes off slice groundstrokes. **2)** To practice hitting slice groundstrokes off driving groundstrokes, and **3)** To teach players that the most effective slice shot is hit so that the ball will skid and stay low on the bounce.

Practice Key: To execute a skidding slice shot, you must hit off your front foot, i.e., step into the ball, and you should be leaning forward into the shot. *(step on the ball)*

Set-up: On half a singles court, two players play competitively

Time: 4 minutes divided into two 2-minute segments. Each player will have the opportunity to drive and slice.

Directions: The feeder is the player hitting topspin drives. Players rally the ball with the feeder hitting topspin drives and the player receiving the feed slice. Both players will attempt to keep the ball deep. However, when a short ball occurs, the receiver should hit an approach shot and attack the net. After an attack, the point is played out on the half court without any other restrictions.

Scoring: Players score a point every time their opponent makes an error, or they hit a winner. Play mini-games of two out of three points. Each time a player wins a mini-game, they get the point. Keep the same score when starting the second segment.

Practice Key: It is difficult to drive a low ball. When the slice skids you should emphasize the upward swing of the racket and attempt to place the ball deep

Drill # 3: Slice vs. Slice

Intent: This is a competitive drill. The purpose is to develop control and consistency in a competitive situation. **1)** To practice hitting slice groundstrokes off slice groundstrokes. **2)** To practice hitting both offensive and defensive slice.

Practice Key: To execute a skidding slice shot, you must hit off your front foot, i.e., step into the ball, and you should be leaning forward into the shot. *(step on the ball)*

Set-up: On half a singles court, two players play competitively

Time: 4 minutes divided into two 2-minute segments. Both players will use slice.

Directions: Each player feeds one segment of the drill. Players rally the ball hitting skidding slice drives, slice loops, slice lobs, or drops shots. When a player is brought into the net, they can hit volleys or overheads, and the point is played out on the half court with no other restrictions.

Scoring: Players score a point every time their opponent makes an error, or they hit a winner. Players play best out of three points. Keep the same score when starting the second segment.

Practice Key: It is difficult to hit a deep skidding slice off a really low ball. When the slice skids you should emphasize the upward swing of the racket and attempt to place the ball deep. The same is true of a high deep ball that bounces up to shoulder height.

Chapter 10 Summary

Key Thought: *We are what we repeatedly do. Excellence is therefore not an act, but a habit.* – Aristotle, Greek Philosopher

If you want to play high-quality tennis, you must have high-quality practices. If you are not careful during your practice sessions, you can do as much damage to your game as you can do to improve it. Easy, mindless hitting, lack of hustle to reach difficult balls, and ineffective drills will not prepare you for the demands of high-performance tennis. If you work hard at the wrong things, you will not get better. Only optimum practice will create optimum results.

To make the most out of your practice sessions, you must simulate the demands of competition. You must work on technique, tactics, emotions, mental toughness, willpower, and physical conditioning. That is why you need to train in a competitive environment. The competition will take your practice sessions to a new level making them challenging and stimulating. You need practices that stretch your limits and that propel you forward to the next level.

The drills that make up the **Tactical Point Control System** are effective in teaching you how to perform in each of the five phases of point-building. However, it is up to you to take them out on the court and make them work. Find a practice partner that is at or above your current performance level. Make sure they also want to improve and are willing to sweat on the court with you. Then get out there and drill. Keep a record of how each of you performs in the different drills. This will help you find your strengths and identify your weaknesses. Over time, it will also help you measure your improvement.

See you on the court.

Chapter 11
Approach-and-Volley Phase

Key Thought: *Read... React... Attack!*

Approach and Volley Attack
Key Thought: *Play decisive and finish strong!*

The approach-and-volley game demands an aggressive mindset. You must be alert and ready to approach into the frontcourt at every opportunity. When you approach, you must be confident in your ability to put the next ball away with either a volley or an overhead. If you fail to put away your volleys and overheads in the frontcourt, you will have trouble reaching your full tennis potential.

The ability to hit winning volleys and overheads takes hours of repetitive practice. It also takes the right mindset. First, you must prepare yourself to recognize every short-ball opportunity. Then, during a match, you must constantly remind yourself to approach. Finally, when that chance comes, you must play without fear.

Tactical Key: If you learn to play bravely in the frontcourt, you will see rapid improvement in your game.

The Approach-and-Volley Attack
Key Thought: *Play from your strength.*

Besides opening the court or forcing your opponent to make an error, a significant goal of the baseline rally is to create opportunities to advance into the frontcourt where you can end points with your volley or overhead smash. There are three types of Approach-and-Volley situations.

- **The short-ball approach:** This is the most common situation and occurs when your opponent sends you a ball that lands short in your court. I tell my players to hit approach shots whenever you can contact the ball inside the 9-foot depth line. *(see diagram 11-1)*
- **The sneak approach:** This is the second most common situation and occurs when you send your opponent an attacking shot that forces them into a vulnerable or defensive position.

- **The planned approach:** This is the third and least common situation. It is a deliberate approach such as a serve and volley, return and volley, or second-shot and volley attack. The planned approach is rarely used in today's game. However, if volleys and overheads are the strengths of your game, the planned approach should become an important part of your game plan.

Tactical Key: To reach your full tennis potential, you must be able to win points at the net. How you get to the net will often depend on the style of point you prefer to play.

When to Launch an Approach-and-Volley Attack
Key Thought: *He who hesitates is lost.*

Approach opportunities come in two varieties. Either your opponent sends you a short ball allowing you to hit an approach shot, or you hit an attacking shot that forced your opponent into an awkward or vulnerable position. For example, you force your opponent deep behind the baseline, out wide of the doubles sideline, or into an awkward hitting position.

When you pressure your opponent to either stretch for the ball or force them to hit shots from outside their ideal strike zone, they will make errors. You must jump on this opportunity by following your shot forward into the frontcourt where you can end the point with a volley or overhead winner. To help you launch both fearless and decisive approach-and-volley attacks, use diagram 11-1 and the following six premises as your guide.

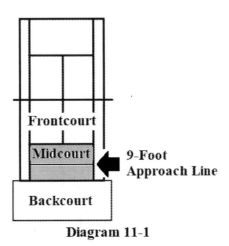

Diagram 11-1

Premise # 1: To attack effectively, you must be positioned inside the baseline in what I refer to as the midcourt zone *(see diagram 11-1).* Unleashing an attack from behind the baseline is risky and opens the door for your opponent to launch an effective counterattack. The planned approach would be the one exception to this premise.

Premise # 2: If you contact the ball behind the 9-foot approach line, you should hit a pressuring shot and drop back to a position just in front of the baseline hash mark. As you drop back, you will read the effectiveness of your shot. If your opponent has been placed in an awkward or uncomfortable position, you can launch a sneak approach. *(see diagram 11-1)*

Premise # 3: If you contact the ball inside the 9-foot approach line, you should hit an approach shot and then advance behind your shot into the frontcourt zone ready to end the point with a volley or overhead winner. *(see diagram 11-1)*

Premise # 4: The frontcourt zone is the easiest place to finish a point, so you must always be willing to move forward aggressively when the situation calls for the approach-and-volley attack. The key for most players is the approach shot. A good approach leads to a winning volley.

Premise # 5: You must attack with your strength. Therefore, if your strength is your net game, you should launch an approach and volley attack whenever possible.

Premise # 6: You must always think of the approach and volley as a two-shot play. Never underestimate the skill or tenacity of your opponent. Expect them to get your approach shot back over the net. Resist the temptation to celebrate early; as your opponent may reach any shot, even one you think is a winner. Constantly remind yourself to follow every approach shot aggressively to the net. When you do, even your staunchest opponent will feel the pressure and will often send you a weak shot that you can put away with a volley.

From the frontcourt, you do not have to be a great net player or hit fantastic volleys. You can win from this position, by just getting your next shot into play. However, when you are tentative and fail to approach, you give your opponent an opportunity to neutralize your advantage forcing you to start building the point all over again. Even worse, your opponent might win the point on a short ball you could have easily reached, had you only followed your approach shot into the frontcourt. Tentative players often lose points they could have easily won.

The Short Ball Opportunity
Key Thought: *Strike quick, strike decisively, no fear!*

A primary goal of the first-exchange and baseline rally is to induce a short ball from your opponent. When you do, it marks the beginning of the approach-and-volley phase. There are three kinds of short balls:

- **The Attack ball** that bounces high allowing you to make contact above waist level.
- **The Approach ball** that you can contact in a strike zone that is between your knee and your waist.
- **The Neutral ball** that is below knee level. To succeed in the approach-and-volley phase, you must have a plan to deal with each of these situations.

Tactical Key: The ideal short ball will be above waist level, pull you inside the 9-foot approach line, and leave open court for your approach shot.

When you receive a short ball, your tactics shift from building the point to attacking the situation. With this change in tactics, there is an immediate acceleration in the intensity of the point. You have gained the advantage, and the end of the point is now in sight. This transition of mindset often comes with the temptation to finish the point with one shot. However, yielding to this temptation often leads to the sin of over-hitting and at this juncture in the point, over-hitting is the fatal downfall of many players. When you let points you could have won slip away, your confidence starts to drain which often results in tentative play.

The Approach Shot
Key Thought: *The right shot for the right situation.*

You cannot win in the approach and volley phase with a tentative mindset. To help you avoid overhitting while still maintaining an aggressive mindset, I suggest you always think of the approach and volley phase for precisely what it is, a two-shot play. The approach shot occurs when you receive a short ball that you can contact from inside the 9-foot, approach line *(see diagram 11-2)*. When you can anticipate short balls, you will move forward quickly and hit more effective approach shots.

Tactical Key: For some reason reacting quickly and hitting hard are synonymous in the minds of many players. Do not become one of them.

Approach Shot Options

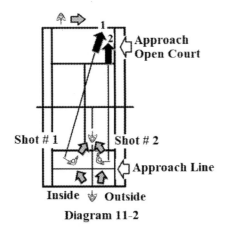

Diagram 11-2

Inside Approach: The inside approach occurs when your opponent sends you a ball that does not cross the front of your body and is on the inside of the court. You will hit inside approach shots into the open court away from your opponent *(Shot 1 in Diagram 11-2)*.

Outside Approach: The outside approach occurs when your opponent sends you a ball that crosses the front of your body and is headed toward the outside of the court. You will hit an outside approach shot down the line *(Shot 2 in Diagram 11-2)*.

Shot Selection: Your approach shot selection will depend on the type of shot you receive. Do not over-hit your approach shot. The most important thing is to get the ball in play. Often your opponent will feel the pressure of your court position and commit an error.

- **Attack Ball** *(high bounce),* you will hit an aggressive shot through the baseline. This shot is hit flat and with pace. Since pace is your weapon, aim this shot into a big target, i.e., the middle of the deep target box.
- **Approach Ball** *(medium bounce),* you will hit an approach shot. This shot can be chipped with slice *(often on your backhand side)* or with controlled topspin. Placement is key to this shot. If you hit with topspin, you must keep this ball deep forcing your opponent to hit a passing shot

from behind the baseline; however, if you use a chipped slice with a low bounce, depth is not as important. In this case, you are forcing your opponent to hit from the lower strike zone.

- **Neutral Ball** *(low bounce),* you will usually use slice, especially on the backhand side. Placement is critical to this shot. You need to keep this ball deep so that your opponent is forced to hit their passing shot from behind the baseline.

Tactical Key: Avoid giving your opponent a free point by missing your approach shots.

The Volley Finish

Key Thought: *When you can hit a winner, you must choose an aggressive shot with a decisive attitude.*

Once you have worked your way into a position to end the point, you must play decisive volleys with a confident mental attitude, or you will lose. How aggressively you hit your volley will be determined by the height of the ball at contact, your court position, and your playing style.

The Height of the Ball at Contact

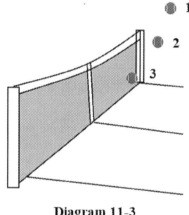

Diagram 11-3

- **Above the net:** *Ball # 1 in diagram 11-3.* You must move forward and go for the winner. When contacting the ball above the net you should use a crisp, volley that is angled away from your opponent.
  - **Level with the net tape:** *Ball # 2 in diagram 11-3.* You must pressure your opponent with placement. This volley should also be angled away from your opponent; however, with less pace than the high volley.
  - **Below the net:** *Ball # 3 in diagram 11-3.* You must play with control. You should slice this volley. On this shot you have two choices: **1)** angle the volley short and away from your opponent; or **2)** send the ball deep down the line or at your opponent's feet. When you go deep, keep the ball in front of you treating this volley as a second approach shot

When in the frontcourt always move forward to the ball. You should never wait for the ball to come to you. I tell my players to attack the ball with their feet, not with their swing. When you move forward you will get to more balls while they are still above the net; thus, giving yourself more chances to finish points. If you wait for the ball, you must have excellent hands with the ability to place this shot low and slow into the open court or back deep at your opponent's feet.

When you aim for your opponent's feet, it makes no difference if they are in the backcourt, midcourt, or frontcourt, they must play defensively. However, if you float your shot high, your opponent will attack and often win the point.

Tactical Key: Trying to hit the ball hard when it is at or below the level of the net tape, will only lead to errors. Usually, this results in a ball hit into the net, or a shot hit on an upward trajectory that will go wide or long. Sending a low-ball deep at your opponent's feet or into the open court forces your opponent to lift the ball, giving you the opportunity to cut off a floating ball with an easy put-away volley.

Frontcourt Positioning

Key Thought: *Pressure your opponent with aggressive positioning!*

In tennis, positioning creates pressure. The closer you are to the net, the more pressure you apply to your opponent. When you are at the net, your opponent cannot make a mistake, or you will end the point with a winner. However, just as you must balance pace and control on your shots, you must also balance aggressive positioning with court coverage as well. Too close to the net, and you make it easy for your opponent to lob the ball over your head. Too far back and they can angle their passing shots out of your reach. You must seek a position where you can spring forward to hit a volley and yet have enough space to retreat for an overhead.

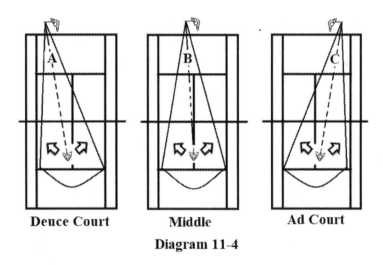

Deuce Court	Middle	Ad Court

Diagram 11-4

Ball at A: When the ball is at position A in the deuce court, you will position just left of the center service line.

Ball at B: When the ball is at position B in the middle, you will position on the center service line.

Ball at C: When the ball is at position C in the ad court, you will position just right of the center service line.

In general, if you are tall, you can play closer to the net because it is harder to lob over you. Whereas, if you are short, you must play a little further back because of your shortened vertical reach. Does this mean that tall players are better net players? Not necessarily. Shorter players are often quicker than their taller counterparts, so their agility can make up for their lack of height. The key is knowing where you must position, and that skill can only be learned on the practice court. In practice, you must focus on finding the depth at which you play your best; because the best net players are the ones who can position in ways that take advantage of their strengths.

How to Finish in the Frontcourt

Key Thought: *In the frontcourt, tentative play is not an option!*

Attacking the net requires an aggressive nature coupled with the ability to execute effective approach shots, well-placed volleys, and aggressive overheads. To succeed at the net, you must be able to put your volleys and overheads away. You cannot come to the net hoping your opponent will make an error. You must expect them to return the ball, and you must react instinctively to your opponent's shot. At the net, tentative play is never a winning option.

How do you develop instinctual reactions at the net? One way only. You must be willing to get up to the net and practice. Most players fail to work on this phase of their game. In practice, they prefer to rally from the baseline. Just watch players warm-up. They might hit a few volleys, but they spend most of their time rallying from the baseline. You cannot develop the instincts for net play unless you are willing to spend countless hours in practice working on the complete net game package. Working on your approach shots, volleys, and overheads must become a part of your daily practice routine. Just hitting volleys or overheads as part of your warm-up will never be enough.

In practice, you must look for short balls you can attack. Not just with your aggressive groundstrokes, but also with approach shots you can follow to the net. To win points at the net, you must first know how to get there. Play live-ball games that force you to move forward. Practice getting to the net where you can learn to react to passing shots or lobs. Make your practice sessions feel more like match play by keeping score. You will never become a net player in matches unless you first become a net player in practice. If you discipline yourself to work on your net game for twenty minutes every day, you will begin to feel comfortable in the frontcourt. Once you feel comfortable, you will start to win points. When you start winning points, the net attack will become an important part of your game plan. Maybe the approach-and-volley will never become your primary option, but it can become an option that you use effectively whenever the situation arises.

The Split-Step

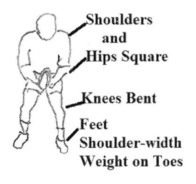

Shoulders
and
Hips Square

Knees Bent

Feet
Shoulder-width
Weight on Toes

Diagram 11-5

The split-step is a fundamental movement in the game of tennis. Except for the serve, it is a vital part of every single tennis shot, whether on the baseline, in the midcourt, or at the net. The split-step allows you to get your body balanced and ready to spring quickly in any direction to reach the ball.

The split-step is nothing more than a straddle stop with both feet landing slightly wider than your shoulders. You must land with your knees bent, your weight on your toes, and your body in a balanced athletic position. From the split-step, you are ready to explode toward the ball in any direction. The split-step is used in almost every sport. Watch any infielder in baseball, defender in basketball, or linebacker in football, and you will have a good idea of how the split-step position is supposed to look.

The key to the split-step is in its timing. Since you are shortening the distance to the ball, the timing of the split-step is crucial when approaching the net. To ensure you have time to split-step, you must start your split-step with the bounce of your approach shot in your opponent's court. Timing is crucial because it will take a split second for you to stop your forward momentum and gain your balance before your opponent strikes the ball. In my experience, it is better to execute your split-step too early and have your feet under you, then to split-step late with your feet in the air as the ball is headed toward your position.

Tactical Key: The split-step is not a permanent position. In other words, you don't land and stop. You land and then shuffle your feet as you ready yourself to spring forward in the direction of the ball. The instant you see where the ball is going, push off the opposite leg and take a step toward the ball with your ball side leg. It may take more than one step to reach the ball; however, it should end with a volley step.

The Volley Step

Step toward ball with opposite foot

Diagram 11-6

I tell my players to volley first with their feet, and then with their hands. After the split step and your initial step toward the ball, you will use one or more small adjustment steps to position yourself for the volley. However, your last step must be the volley step. *(see diagram 11-6 and note the opposite foot stepping toward the ball)* The volley step should occur as you are hitting the volley. However, on a reaction volley, it might occur slightly after the hit, but in any case, the volley step must happen.

In my experience, when your mind is thinking of making this step, your shoulders will turn, and your arm will travel on the necessary path to execute a successful volley. Failing to take this step often results in reaching for the ball with your chest facing the net. The result, you dump what should have been an easy volley into the net. *(This is especially true on the forehand side where your hitting arm is behind your shoulders.)*

Tactical Key: To help my players understand the volley step, I use the teaching phrase: **"step on the ball."** I believe this gives my players both a verbal and visual cue that helps to get the opposite foot moving toward the ball.

The Inside Volley

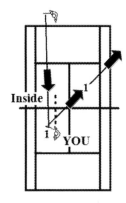

Diagram 11-7

Definition: An inside volley is hit off an opponent's passing shot that does not cross the front of your body *(dotted line in diagram 11-7)*. Inside volleys occur when your opponent sends you a down-the-line passing shot.

In *diagram 11-7* your opponent has hit a down-the-line pass, and you respond with an inside volley hit crosscourt through target-box 1. Placement is key. High volleys can be struck crisply, but low volleys must be hit low and slow.

Shot Selection: Always hit this volley into the open court away from your opponent. I tell my players to aim for the opposite short target box *(1-Target in diagram 11-7)*. The inside volley must be angled through the sideline.

Tactical Key: Remember to always follow the flight path of your volley. This will put you in position to hit a second volley should your opponent be able to run down the ball.

The Outside Volley

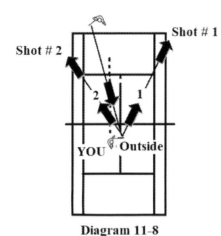

Diagram 11-8

Definition: An outside volley is hit off an opponent's passing shot that crosses the front of your body. *(dotted line in diagram 11-8)*

Shot Selection: I have two rules for this volley:

• **If the ball is above the net**, hit an aggressive inside-out volley into the open court away from your opponent. Hit the ball through the center of the diagonal short target box, *(1-Target in diagram 11-8)*.

• **If the ball is below the net,** you cannot hit an aggressive volley. Instead, hit an outside volley low and slow back toward your opponent. This shot can be angled through the short target box *(2-Target in diagram 11-8)* or back into the corner. Another good place to hit this volley is right at your opponent's feet.

In *diagram 11-8,* your opponent has hit a crosscourt passing shot. If the ball is above the net, you will respond with an aggressive volley into short Target-1. This volley is angled away from your opponent and through the singles sideline *(shot # 1 in diagram 11-8)*. However, if the ball drops below the net, you will hit a crosscourt volley low and slow with no change of direction. Aim this ball into short target-2 and through the singles sideline *(shot # 2 in diagram 11-8)*.

Tactical Key: Remember to always follow the flight path of your volley. This will put you in position to hit a second volley should your opponent be able to run down the ball.

The Overhead

An overhead opportunity occurs when your opponent throws up a lob. Usually, this means that you have placed them in a precarious position, and they are just trying to keep the point alive. That said, you must always take advantage of your opponent's short lobs by finishing the point with your overhead smash.

Tactical Key: Whenever you hit an overhead, be sure to finish the point.

To win points, you must run around your backhand to make sure you are taking advantage of the situation with a true overhead shot, i.e., from your forehand side. The overhead is struck much like your serve; however, since you are not restricted to hitting the ball into the service box, you have a much bigger target. Also, since you are closer to the net, it does not present nearly the obstacle that it does on your serve.

Tactical Key: Failing to use your overhead smash will give your opponent an easy out whenever they feel pressure. They know they can neutralize your attack by simply throwing up a lob. Do not let them off the hook.

Overhead Rules

- **Rule # 1: If you are close to the net,** aim your overhead midway through the service box and angled through the sideline.
- **Rule # 2: If you are back near the service line,** aim your overhead into your opponent's backhand corner.
- **Rule # 3: If the lob is deep, or there is a problem with wind or sun,** let the ball bounce and then aim your overhead into the center of one of the deep target boxes.

If you follow the three rules and hit your overheads aggressively, you will discourage your opponent from simply throwing up lobs. This will then increase your chances of using your volley at the net.

The Sneak Approach: *Creating Approach Opportunities*
Key Thought: *Force your opponent into a weak or awkward position.*

Unlike the short-ball approach, in which your opponent has sent you a ball that lands short in your court, the sneak approach, is dependent on the quality of your last shot. You will not approach unless your shot has forced your opponent into an uncomfortable or awkward position. When employing a sneak approach, it is not as crucial that you be inside the 9-foot approach line. However, your approach will always be more effective from a position inside the baseline.

Tactical key: When you hit an attacking shot move forward one or two steps taking up a position just inside the baseline hash mark. Hold this position as you read the quality of your shot. Then, as soon as you recognize that your opponent is in trouble, sneak quickly forward into the frontcourt ready to put a volley or overhead away.

Tactical Key: To succeed in using the sneak approach, you must know the five situations where the sneak approach is most likely to occur. These situations are explained in the following sections.

Sneak Approach # 1: Topspin Angle: The topspin angle is hit so that the ball will cross the singles sideline before it crosses the baseline. This shot will force your opponent out wide of the singles sideline. The sharper the angle, the further your opponent will be forced to move, and the more likely a weak reply will occur. The topspin angle also forces your opponent to move on a forward diagonal which will often carry them outside the doubles sideline opening the opposite side of the court for your next shot.

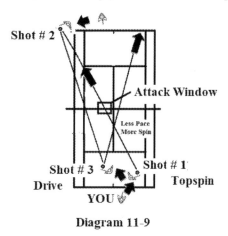

Diagram 11-9

When you see your opponent pushed wide, you should step forward inside the baseline looking for a short or weak return. However, if you see your opponent on the run or stretching to reach this ball, expect a weak floating reply. As soon as you read this situation, move forward well into the midcourt zone putting yourself in position to attack the weak return with either an aggressive groundstroke or a put-away volley. In either case, your opponent will have very little time to react, and you can often send your shot past them for a clean winner. Be sure to follow your attacking shot to the net so you can put the next ball away with a volley. *(Diagram 11-9)*

Tactical Key: When hitting the topspin angle, spin is more important than power, so brush sharply up the back of the ball. Aim your shot about one-foot over the center net strap and into the short corner of the diagonal service box.

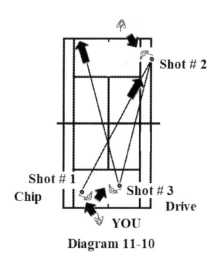

Diagram 11-10

Sneak Approach # 2: Chipped Angle: The chipped angle is a sliced shot hit so that the ball will cross the singles sideline before crossing the baseline. Like the topspin angle, this shot will force your opponent out wide of the singles sideline. However, the low trajectory of the slicing shot will also cause this ball to skid and stay low on the bounce. Now, your opponent is both stretching to reach this ball and hitting from their lower strike zone. When you hit the sliced angle to your opponent's backhand side, you are almost always guaranteed a weak reply.

If stretched wide, the low skidding bounce will force your opponent to hit their backhand from their lower strike zone. Hitting a running backhand from the lower strike zone usually forces your opponent to respond with a floating slice. A ball you can easily put away.

When you see your opponent stretching for this low ball, move in and prepare to volley your opponent's floating return into the open court. Since you have forced your opponent both forward and wide of the sideline, they will have very little time to react to your second shot which can be hit past them for an easy winner. On this volley, placement is critical. Avoid the temptation to overhit this ball.

Tactical Key: The chipped slice should be used on short balls that give you a better angle through the sideline. Like the topspin angle, spin is more important than pace. Use a short slicing action comparable with a backhand volley, but with a slightly longer follow through. Aim this shot just above the center strap and into the short corner of the diagonal service box.

Sneak Approach # 3: Deep Loop: The Deep loop is hit with heavy topspin and aimed to land

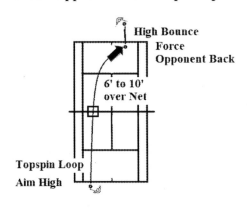

Diagram 11-11

beyond the 9-foot depth line. When hit deep, the loop will force your opponent to move back several steps behind the baseline. Many players have trouble hitting high-bouncing balls, especially on their backhand side. So, when you send the loop deep into your opponent's backhand corner, you should always be ready to move forward. The high bounce of the deep loop will force your opponent to either move back and take the ball as it descends from the bounce or move forward to take it early and on the rise. Both options create difficult situations that can lead to opponent errors or short balls you can attack. Often, your opponent will return your deep loop with a loop of their own. Hence, when you push your opponent back well behind the baseline, move forward into the midcourt ready to hit a volley, a swinging volley, or even an overhead from near the service line.

Tactical Key: The loop should be hit with heavy topspin and aimed six to ten feet over the top of the net. It should be aimed deeper than the imaginary 9-foot, depth line. The heavy topspin will cause the ball to bounce up and kick back toward the rear fence which will challenge your opponent's timing and almost always result in a looped return.

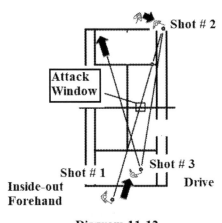

Diagram 11-12

Sneak Approach # 4: Inside-out Forehand Drive: Against a right-handed opponent, you will hit your inside-out forehand into your opponent's backhand corner. When your shot forces your opponent back behind the baseline or out wide of the singles sideline, you will have placed them in a vulnerable position. Whenever the pace of your inside-out forehand overpowers your opponent's backhand, you can expect the return to be struck late and to drift to the inside of your court. If you anticipate a short or inside return, you should move forward into the midcourt where you can send the next ball crosscourt into a wide-open court *(see diagram 11-12)*. When driving your inside-out forehand, always make sure you balance the power of your shot with the need for control. Although you are trying to overpower your opponent's backhand, you cannot win points if you are making errors.

Tactical Key: The inside-out forehand is essentially a topspin shot. When hitting through the baseline aim your shot about 3-feet over the net. If you are hitting an angled shot through the sideline, aim your shot about 1-foot over the center net strap and about halfway between the back service-line and the baseline. Do not aim for the short corner on this shot. The key to this shot is net clearance, so make sure you use enough topspin to both lift the ball over the net and to bring the ball down into the court.

Sneak Approach # 5: Drop Shot: The drop shot is hit with slice. Do not hit your drop shot flat and low over the net. Instead, hit it up with a low arc. The peak of the arc should occur well before the ball crosses the net. You know you have hit a good drop shot whenever the ball is on its downward path as it crosses the net. The backspin *(slice)* will cause the ball to bounce nearly straight up making it a difficult shot for your opponent to reach.

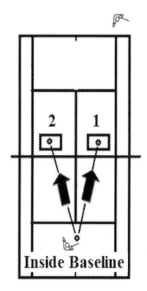

Inside Baseline

Diagram 11-13

Tactical Key: When practicing your drop shot, it should land in the service box and bounce two to three times before it crosses the service line.

It is critical that you follow your drop shot forward into the midcourt. As you move forward, read the effectiveness of your shot. If you see that your opponent will have trouble even reaching the ball, you should move forward quickly. In desperation, your opponent will often try to drop shot you back. However, if you are moving forward, you will be positioned to hit your next shot into the open court away from your opponent. If you shot lands too deep, no problem. You have just brought your opponent to the net, so now you must ready yourself to counterattack with either a passing shot or a lob *(see chapter 12 for details)*.

Tactical Key: Only hit the drop shot from on or inside the 9-foot approach line. This shot is the ultimate touch shot, so your arms and hands must be relaxed. Do not attempt the drop shot when you are feeling tense or under pressure as it will be too difficult to control. Use a slice motion but cut under the ball on contact. This ball should reach the peak of its trajectory before crossing the net. Aim for a spot about halfway between the net and the center of the service box. Never aim for the sideline as your objective is to keep this ball in the court.

The Planned Approach
Key Thought: *Your opponent is never completely prepared for a surprise attack!*

The planned approach is used most often by players who employ the net rushing playing style. The net rusher is comfortable playing in the frontcourt. They also possess both the aggressive mentality and the shot-making tools needed to succeed with the planned approach.

   The net-rusher wants to get to the net as quickly as possible. When serving, a true net-rusher often employs a serve-and-volley attack, and when returning, they will follow most second-serve returns to the net. They have programmed their mind to get to the frontcourt as quickly as possible making the planned approach an essential part of their basic game plan. However, for players who prefer to attack from the baseline, the planned approach is more often employed as a surprise tactic used for winning an occasional point or for getting inside of their opponent's head.

   You must be alert for situations when your opponent has become comfortable with just getting the point started. When you see your opponent sending weak serves or merely floating their returns into play, it is an excellent time to attack. Running a serve-and-volley or return-and-volley play in this situation is a good option. Even if you lose the point, you leave your opponent wondering when or if you will do it again. The planned attack will put more pressure on your opponent which can force them to be more precise with their serves and returns. This added stress can cause an opponent to double fault or make careless errors on their return.

Planned Approach # 1: The Serve-and-Volley

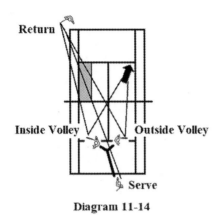

Diagram 11-14

The serve-and-volley attack is an advanced tactic. For it to work, you must be able to hit a pressuring serve. Although the perception of pressure is often equated with power, a power serve is not always the best choice for this style of play. When you hit your serve hard, you have less time to move forward into proper position near the back edge of the frontcourt zone *(see diagram 11-14)*. Serves that are hit with precise placement, moderate pace, and heavy spin work better and with much less risk. When you serve and volley, you must follow the angle of your serve forward toward the frontcourt zone. Get in as close to the service line as possible executing a split-step just before your opponent contacts the ball. Then move forward toward the incoming ball and follow the volley guidelines.

Keys to an Attacking Serve

- **Get your first serve in**: you cannot serve-and-volley as effectively behind a second serve.
- **Placement Advantage**: The outside serve forces your opponent wide and opens the opposite side of the court for your volley; Body serves often result in a weak blocked return into the middle of the court; Inside serves hit with power and placement force weak returns while at the same time moving the returner into the middle of the court. With the returner in the middle of the court, you can hit your volley effectively into either corner.
- **Attack a weakness** – In the return game, most players will be weaker on one side than the other. As often as possible, attack with your best serve into your opponent's weaker return. Often this weakness is your opponent's backhand. Thus, a high-bouncing kick serve hit deep into your opponent's backhand side is often the best serve to follow to the net.

Planned Approach # 2: Return-and-Volley

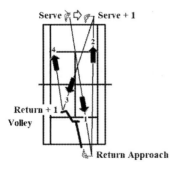

Diagram 11-15

Attacking on the return is high-risk tennis, but if you can pull it off the rewards are plentiful. Taking advantage of an opponent's weak second serve is often the key to breaking serve. Thus, for the net rusher, a return-and-volley attack is an excellent option for pressuring their opponent into making a mistake. To make this attack effective, take up a return position a step or two inside the baseline. Then move forward and chip your return down-the-line. Follow your return forward into the frontcourt executing a split step just before your opponent strikes the ball. Then spring immediately forward toward the oncoming ball and hit your volley using the volley guidelines.

Keys to the Attacking Return

- **Vary your return position:** Move in on second serves. The weaker the serve, the more you move in. Use the Bait and switch by setting up in your normal position and then moving forward to the attack position on the server's toss.
- **Get your return in play:** Avoid giving points away with reckless errors.
- **Modify your swing:** Shorten your backswing and chip or slice your return. Meet the ball square and in the center of your strings. Be sure to follow through.

Planned Approach # 3: Second-shot-and-Volley

When facing a strong server or returner, you may not want to risk the approach on the serve or return. Instead, follow your second shot to the net. Again, it is crucial to split-step just before your opponent contacts the ball. Then spring forward toward the ball and hit your volley using the volley guidelines. The second-shot-and-volley attack is not as aggressive as the first two planned approaches. First, because it does not require a powerful serve or return, and second because it gives you the opportunity to start the point before launching the attack. This approach will take the pressure off your serve and your return. If you are a net rusher, this is important on those days when either your serve or return is a little bit off.

Keys to the Second-shot Attack

- **Take the ball early and on the rise:** Taking the ball near or inside the baseline shortens the distance you must travel to reach the frontcourt. You do not have to hit this shot hard, just get it deep into one of the corners.
- **Use the inside-out forehand as often as possible:** Push your opponent out wide and force them to pass you with their backhand. Often you will get an easy ball to put away.
- **Use the backhand chip:** The chip will give you time to get inside the frontcourt. It will also skid and stay low on the bounce making it hard for your opponent to hit an attacking passing shot.

Chapter 11 Summary

Key Thought: *Act without hesitation and play to win!*

The Scenario

You made it through the first-exchange. Now, you are battling against a very good opponent in the baseline-rally. You are hitting deep crosscourt shots at each other and then running each other ragged with well-timed directional switches. Finally, it happens. Your opponent sends you a ball that lands short in your court. You read it early and move forward into the midcourt preparing to launch your attack. You know you have an opportunity to win this point, but, there are so many options available that you are feeling a bit indecisive about which one you should choose. You get to the ball, you swing, and the ball crashes into the net. Your shoulders slump as you turn back toward your baseline. That little voice inside your head is telling you how stupid it was to blow such an easy shot.

The Problem
What just happened? In my estimation, this error was caused because you had no real game plan for how you are going to attack a short ball. You are not alone. Wide open attacking shots are some of the most-often missed shots in tennis. Why? There are three reasons.

- **Timing:** Even though the short ball is an invitation to attack, it also requires you to adjust to a ball that has changed the pace, the rhythm, and the timing of the rally.
- **Shot-angle adjustments:** Furthermore, the short ball attack usually calls for you to change the direction of the rally. On outside balls, this requires the use of the lower-percentage down-the-line switch, which is hit over a higher part of the net and into a shorter length of the court. Thus, although attacking the short ball can bring an immediate reward, to capitalize on the short ball often requires the use of a lower-percentage shot.
- **Overhitting:** Trying to end the point with a single shot is often the cause of this problem. This kill-shot mentality makes it difficult to adjust both the timing and the technical requirements necessary to execute an attacking shot.

The Cure
Key Thought: *When you receive a short ball always think two shots, the approach and volley.*

Have a set plan for how you are going to attack the short ball. This plan can have some variation depending on the depth and type of ball you receive. For example, you can have a different plan of attack for a short ball that lands behind the 9-foot approach line, for a short ball that lands inside the 9-foot approach line, and for a short ball that opens the court. Having a short-ball plan eliminates indecision and allows you to attack decisively.

Tactical Key: When you can instantly recognize and react to a short ball, you position yourself to dominate your opponent. Where do you learn this? Practice… you have got to drill it, if you want to own it!

The approach-and-volley phase begins when you decide to advance into your frontcourt zone. Now, the pressure intensifies. You are in close to the net where things happen fast. In the frontcourt, points can be won or lost with but a single swing of the racket. As the attacker, you have the advantage, but only if you play with intensity. There are three types of approach-and-volley attacks.

- **The planned approach:** where before the point begins, you have already determined to move forward into the midcourt, for example, a serve-and-volley or return-and-volley attack.
- **The short-ball approach:** where you move forward when your opponent sends you a ball that lands short in your court.
- **The sneak approach:** where you decide to move forward after you see that you have pressured your opponent into an awkward or defensive position.

The volley or finishing shot is the most rewarding part of a tennis point. It occurs when you can win the point with a single shot. This winning shot is most often achieved by placement, although in some cases there is an element of power. Always remember that there will be no additional reward for hitting the ball hard. I tell my players hit hard enough to win but not hard enough to miss.

Tactical Key: The exception to the power rule is the overhead. I tell my players that they must learn to punish lobs by blasting their overheads. So I have my players practice overhead smashes until every player on the team is confident putting this shot away.

When you are finishing points in the frontcourt, you are playing perfect points. By that, I mean that you are advancing the point through the point-building phases without error and are putting yourself in a position from which you can dominate your opponent.

Tactical Key: When most of your points are perfect points, you are building points like a tennis champion. That means you are starting to reach your full potential as a player.

See you on the court.

Chapter 12
Passing Shot or Lob Phase

Key Thought: *Counterattack – an attack in reply to an attack.* – Webster's Dictionary

During every tennis match, there will be times when your opponent moves forward into the frontcourt to take up an attacking position at the net. If you show your opponent that this rattles you; that you cannot pass them or lob over them without making errors, a smart opponent will keep coming to the net. However, once you prove to your opponent that you can pass them or at least make them hit volleys, many players will become discouraged and venture to the net only when you force them to move forward.

Tactical Key: When your opponent is weak at the net, hitting short chip shots and drop shots to bring them to the net can be a great tactic. Whenever possible, you must force your opponent to play from a weakness.

The Three Stages of a Counterattack

Stage One: Recognize when your opponent has an opportunity to attack. This attacking opportunity will present itself in two situations. The first situation occurs when your opponent has forced you into a defensive position. When this happens, your opponent will move forward looking to take your next shot early and, on the rise. Often they will send their attacking shot into the open court on your side of the net.

The second situation occurs when you send your opponent an opportunity ball. I define an opportunity ball as a shot that is weak, lands short in your opponent's court, or that leaves open court into which your opponent can hit their next shot. If you recognize when you are in a defensive position, you increase your chances to either neutralize your opponent's advantage or in some cases to counterattack effectively into the weakness in your opponent's attack.

Tactical Key: The earlier you prepare, the more effectively you can either neutralize or counterattack.

Stage Two: Read the quality of your opponent's attack, i.e., how well they have struck the ball. You must instantly read whether you are in immediate danger of losing the point or if you can still hit an effective passing shot or lob. In the first instance, you must scramble and defend; whereas, in the second situation, you can go on the offensive by launching a counterattack of your own.

Tactical key: When defending, your goal is always to make your opponent hit one more ball. In doing so, you give your opponent one more opportunity to make an error.

Stage Three: React with a preplanned response to your read of the situation. When you know what to do, you eliminate one step in the preparation process, and since net points are bang-bang plays, the time you save will make a huge difference in the effectiveness of your response. When you follow the three-stage plan for counterattacking, even when you choose the wrong option, the quality of your shot may still win the point.

Tactical Key: Wrong choice and strong shot are always better than the right choice followed by a weak shot or an error.

The Attacker

To effectively counter a net attack, you must first stop giving the net rusher so much credit. To win points at the net, net rushers are depending on your missing a large percentage of your passing shots. Without your errors, they cannot win consistently. Therefore, the most important thing you can do with your passing shot is to get the ball in play. It takes a put-away volley to win the point at the net and put-away volleys are not easy to hit. There are four relevant facts that you must understand about most net players.

- **Most net rushers fail to reach a correct coverage position at the net.** So, you almost always have at least one big target for your passing shot.
- **Most net rushers have a very limited range and little anticipation at the net.** So, you should avoid aiming for the lines with your passing shots.
- **Net rushers who are great volleyers are very rare.** So, they have trouble putting their volleys away.
- **Many net rushers cannot react effectively to a lob.** So, you may find that all you must do to neutralize them is throw up a lob.

Tactical Key: Make your opponent hit volleys, and you will force many of them into making errors. You will be surprised by how many of them stop coming to the net.

Counterattacking the Net Player

Key Thought: *Stay calm. You can win in this situation.*

When counterattacking against a net player, you must always think two-shot play. You will make too many errors if you go for outright winners with your first passing shot. Instead, the goal is to keep your first passing shot low forcing your opponent to volley from below the net. From below the net, it is almost impossible to hit an aggressive volley; hence, your second passing shot will always make for an easier pass.

Tactical Key: Always get your first passing shot in play!

Six Steps to a Successful Passing Shot

- **Move forward:** Always meet the approach shot early and on-the-rise, never wait for the ball.
- **Relax:** If your hands are tight, you cannot control your shot.
- **Watch the ball:** Know where to look. Play the ball, not the volleyer.
- **Pick a side:** Always go for a clear opening; however, when in doubt go crosscourt.
- **Let the racket do the work:** Use a smooth, flowing swing. Avoid muscling up and trying to jerk the ball past the net player.
- **Follow your shot forward:** Take two to three steps forward and get inside the baseline. Your opponent will probably respond to your pass with an angle or drop volley. So, by moving in you put yourself into position to get to the ball. Take at least one step forward after each passing shot.

Tactical Key: To hit a good passing shot, you must make a conscious effort to relax. The passing shot is more about placement and touch than it is about power. If you are tight, your hands cannot work freely making it challenging to hit the low accurate passing shot that is necessary for this situation.

The Passing Shot
Key Thought: *Always aim your passing shot into the largest opening available.*

Remember, the counterattack is a two-shot play. This means: Every time you hit a passing shot, you must expect the ball to come back and must be prepared to hit another passing shot. A huge part of this preparation is to move forward a step or two after each passing shot. Since your opponent will almost always volley into the open court, mentally you should be leaning in that direction.

Pass or Lob
Deciding whether to hit a passing shot or a lob is dependent on how you read the court position of both you and your opponent.

- **The first read is your court position.** If you are pushed wide of the singles sideline or deeper than the baseline, hit a lob. If you are on or inside the baseline, hit a passing shot. Base this decision on the trajectory, pace, and angle of the approach shot. With practice, you should be able to make this read quickly, even before the ball has passed over the net.
- **The second read is your opponent's court position.** If they are hugging the net, hit a lob. However, if they are hovering on or just inside the service line, hit a passing shot. Never try to win the point on your first pass. Your goal is to get your first passing shot in play. Always make your opponent prove they can volley.

The Down-the-Line Passing Shot

Early in the match, it is best not to change the direction of the ball with your passing shot. Why, because most errors occur when changing the direction of a ball, and you always want to get your first passing shot in play. Thus, if your opponent approaches down the line, hit your passing shot back down the line with no change of direction. When hit one-foot over the net, the down-the-line passing shot possesses two clear advantages:

- **First,** the down-the-line pass will cross the net before the crosscourt pass. Thus, the ball will get past your opponent faster than when you hit the crosscourt pass.
- **Second**, unlike a baseline groundstroke, the down-the-line distance to the baseline is longer than the length of the short angle crosscourt to the sideline. Thus, there is more court for the ball to land.

However, there are also two significant disadvantages:

- **First,** the net is six inches higher on the sideline. Thus, the crosscourt shot passes over the lowest part of the net.
- **Second,** if the passing shot is hit too high over the net, the volleyer has a sizeable crosscourt opening into which they can hit a finishing volley.

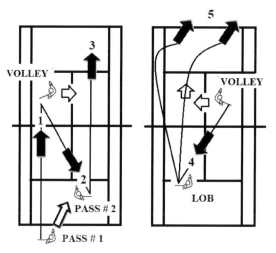

Diagram 12-1

1st Passing Shot: When passing down the line hit with topspin aiming your shot about 1 foot above the top of the net. Relax your hands and swing smoothly. Avoid trying to power this ball past the volleyer. Let the topspin do its work by dipping the ball low and forcing your opponent to hit their first volley from below the net. Although they have a great angle, they will need to use touch which gives you the chance to run down the ball.

2nd Passing Shot: If your first pass is low, your opponent will almost always volley softly crosscourt. From your position inside the midcourt, you can move forward and hit your second passing shot down the opposite sideline. The volleyer will have little time to recover, so your second passing shot will often be hit into a wide-open court.

Lob: If your opponent is speedy and can cover this second pass, they will be extremely vulnerable lob toward the open court. It is almost impossible to race laterally across the court to your volley and then reverse back in the opposite direction to cover a lob.

Tactical Key: After each passing shot, take a couple of steps forward into the midcourt zone. Following your passing shot shortens the distance between you and your opponent increasing the effectiveness of your next passing shot.

The Crosscourt Passing Shot

If your opponent approaches crosscourt, hit your passing shot back crosscourt with no change of direction. Hitting crosscourt may at first seem like you are hitting the ball back to your opponent; however, since they are racing forward and across the court to cover a possible down-the-line pass, you are actually hitting behind them. The crosscourt passing shot has two distinct advantages over the down-the-line pass:

- **First**, the crosscourt pass is hit over the lowest part of the net. Thus, it is easier to lift the ball up and over the net.
- **Second,** the volleyer does not have an immediate put-away angle for their first volley.

Unlike the down-the-line pass, the crosscourt passing shot has only one real disadvantage. There is less court space to land your shot inside of the singles sideline.

Tactical Key: There is one exception to the crosscourt pass. If your opponent hits a crosscourt approach but is out of position, the down-the-line pass will be wide open. Always hit your passing shot into the biggest target available.

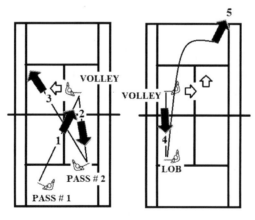

Diagram 12-2

1ˢᵗ Passing Shot: When passing crosscourt hit with heavy topspin aiming your shot one foot over the top of the net strap. You should hit this shot on a short angle into the back corner of the diagonal service box. On the crosscourt passing shot, spin is more important than pace. Topspin will make this ball dip and force the volleyer to contact the ball from below the net. Some players use slice on this pass; however, remember that slice is a touch shot, and placement is critical. Not only that, a sliced passing shot must be hit on a much lower trajectory using just a six-inch clearance over the center net strap. Nevertheless, for players with exceptional backhand touch, the slice shot though tantalizingly slow can make for a deadly passing shot.

Tactical Key: Because a sliced ball will tend to rise, I tell my players to aim the slice passing shot at the net tape.

2nd Passing Shot: When your first passing shot is low, your opponent is forced to volley from below the net. The low pass often results in a touch volley directed into the open court directly in front of your opponent. After hitting a passing shot, you should be moving forward into the midcourt, so that you can reach this touch volley which will often land short in the court. When you reach your opponent's first volley, you can hit your second passing shot back crosscourt using the opposite diagonal. Because the net player is now positioned near the singles sideline, there will be a large opening for your second crosscourt shot.

Tactical Key: Always follow your crosscourt passing shot forward into the midcourt zone.

Lob: If after the first or second volley, you see the net player smothering the net, lob the ball straight down the line *(90-degree switch).* The down the line lob presents a problematic angle for your opponent to run down and when it is deep and gets past them, it will often become a clear winner.

Tactical Key: If your opponent hovers near the service line, hit your passing shot low and crosscourt. If they don't move forward on a diagonal to cut off your passing shot, then continue to bring them to the net and pick them apart!

The Lob Pass

If you are well behind the baseline, wide of the singles sideline or your opponent is smothering the net; your best passing shot will be the topspin lob. Depending on the situation, you can use the lob as either your first or second passing shot. However, since the net rusher is further from the net on the first volley, a low passing shot is often the best response. Then if your opponent continues to close toward the net, you can use the lob as your second pass. When your opponent likes to smother the net, the lob will almost always win as your third pass. Awareness of court positioning is critical. Once you have drawn your opponent into a position close to the net, you have an excellent opportunity to lob the ball over their head for a winner.

Tactical Key: Some opponents will react so poorly to lobs that they never get into position to hit an overhead smash. Against these players, you can neutralize almost every net attack by simply throwing up a lob. This is especially true if you can lob the ball over their backhand shoulder.

Dodge Ball

There is one additional option. Hit your passing shot right at your opponent. Aim your shot for your opponent's racket-side hip, i.e., right hip for right-handers and left hip for left-handers. A hard-hit passing shot into this location is almost impossible to return. *(Avoid this tactic in social tennis)* Also, be aware that hitting a ball at your opponent is an open invitation for them to hit the ball back at you. So, as the saying goes, "If you can't take the heat, stay out of the kitchen."

Chapter 12 Summary
Key Thought: *Avoid giving the volleyer too much credit.*

Do not panic when your opponent comes to the net. You are still in a very winnable situation. Most volleyers fail to get into the correct frontcourt position and are limited in the range of shots they can cover. They are counting on you making an error, so get your passing shot in play. Make them prove they can beat you with a volley. If they fail, they will get discouraged, and most will give up the net attack.

When to Lob?
First, read your court position. If you are wide of the sideline or behind the baseline, hit a lob. If you are on or inside the baseline, go for a passing shot. Your second read is your opponent's court position. If they are hugging the net, throw up a lob; however, if they are hovering back by the service line, send them a passing shot.

Think Two-Shot Pass
Avoid over hitting the first passing shot. Instead, send it low forcing your opponent to contact their volley from below the net. Then move in and finish off your opponent with your second passing shot into the open court.

If you pass down the line, your opponent will volley crosscourt giving you a down-the-line opening on the other side of the court. If you pass crosscourt, your opponent will often volley straight ahead into the open court in front of them. This down-the-line volley leaves the court open for a second crosscourt passing shot to the opposite side.

See you on the court.

Chapter 13
Net-Play Drills

Purpose: The following drills will develop both your ability to attack your opponent from the frontcourt zone with the approach and volley, and to counterattack with passing shots or lobs when your opponent attacks you from the frontcourt zone.

Drill Principles: Before I delve into the net play drills, I need to review the four fundamental principles that govern all my drills: **1)** Drill Theory; **2)** Pressure Training; **3)** Shot Accountability; and **4)** Shot Tolerance.

Drill Theory: The point-phase drills are games in which players compete against either another teammate *(keeping score)* or against a set standard *(required number of consecutive shots into a target)*. Each drill simulates the approach and volley *(attack)* and the passing shot or lob *(counterattack)* phases of the tennis point. You will be taught to play within a tactical framework where you must problem-solve each shot. You will learn to hit each shot with a purpose. I use *restrictions* and *stipulations* to mold the drills in a way that will simulate specific net play situations. By playing within the defined parameters of each drill, you will learn discipline, increase your willpower, and be forced to problem-solve in game-like situations. Each drill is timed, has a certain number of repetitions, or ends when the desired score is achieved. Every drill uses recordable results allowing you to see how well you are performing in each practice and to measure your improvement from week to week.

Pressure Training: The real test of your tennis ability will be demonstrated by how well you compete under the pressure of an actual tennis match. Practice should be challenging requiring you to train at the top of your playing range. During a tennis match, you will face four kinds of pressure: tactical pressure, mental/emotional pressure, momentum pressure, and physical pressure. In practice, you must prepare yourself to succeed under the same kinds of pressures you will face in an actual match.

Shot Accountability: You are responsible for where your shot lands on the opponent's side of the court. Shot Accountability is the most significant key to success in tennis. To win a match against an equally skilled opponent, you must be able to hit the ball into a specific target area. Accuracy is critical to building a point with your strength *(offense)* as well as neutralizing the strength of your opponent *(defense)*. Practice is where shot accountability is learned; however, it can only be mastered if you hold yourself accountable for where you send the ball. Not just sometimes, but all the time.

Shot Tolerance: I define shot tolerance as the number of consecutive shots you can keep in play? Points end quickly in the net play scenario; therefore, shot tolerance takes on a different emphasis than in the baseline rally. When using either the approach and volley attack or the passing shot or lob counterattack, you must be able to use a two- or three-shot combination without committing an error. Thus, shot tolerance is short but must be consistent. For example, It does you little good to hit the right approach shot and then miss your volley. Thus, the focus of each net play drill is on developing your ability to complete the specific shot combinations with both accuracy and consistency.

Developmental Drills

Key Thought: *In the pressure-packed net-play scenario, you must have dependable attacking and counterattacking shot combinations on which you can rely.*

I develop the net-play scenario with five developmental drills. Each drill develops one or two of the critical components necessary to attack or counterattack in this situation. A fourth element, competitive success, is an integral part of each of the developmental drills.

- **Consistency:** I expect my players to execute the 3-shot scenarios successfully 80-percent of the time. *(shot tolerance)*.
- **Accuracy:** I expect my players to direct a minimum of sixty percent of their approach shots into the correct target area. *(shot accountability)*
- **Competitive Success:** I expect players to win between forty and sixty percent of the competitive drills. *(shot tolerance and accountability)*.

Drill # 1: Short-Court Rally Game

Key Thought: *To win at the net, you must learn to anticipate.*

Purpose: This is a competitive drill. The purpose is to develop shot-direction and court-coverage in a highly competitive situation. I use this game every day at the beginning of practice. It teaches players to control the ball and cover the court while warming them up for the rest of a highly competitive practice.

Time: Each Game last five minutes.

Set-up: On a short singles court, two players play competitively using only the service boxes as boundaries. In this drill, the back-service line becomes the baseline.

Feed: Each point begins with a diagonal feed. Each player will alternate feeding one point to the deuce court and one point to the ad court sides. Players cannot lose points on the feed; however, once the feed is in play, the point is live.

Directions: Play points using the following stipulations. The feed and next shot must bounce. After the second shot *(feed return),* players can hit volleys. The goal of this drill is to attack open court with controlled volleys and passing shots. Emphasis is on touch and control. Players may hit shots using slice or topspin.

Scoring: A player scores each time they hit a winning shot, or their opponent makes an error.

Practice Key: Learn to cover the court by anticipating your opponent's next shot.

Drill # 2: Half-Court Approach-and-Volley Points

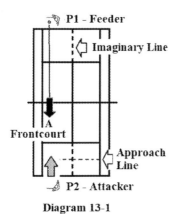

Diagram 13-1

Purpose: This drill has both an attacking and a counterattacking objective: **1)** First, it will teach players to recognize and attack short balls with an approach and volley attack; and **2)** Second, it will teach players to counterattack using low, well-placed passing shots. By using only half the tennis court, it guarantees that more volleys are hit than on a full tennis court.

Set-Up: Divide the tennis court into two halves by extending either an imaginary or a visible rope line from the center service line to the baseline hash mark on each end of the court. Two players will then compete on half the court using the doubles sideline and the center service line as the side boundaries. *See diagram 13-1.*

Procedure: Both players will begin behind the baseline. Player # 1 *(P1 in the diagram)* will feed a ball to player # 2 *(P2 in the diagram)* so that the ball lands in the service box *(A in diagram 13-1).* P2 will move forward quickly attempting to contact the ball early inside the approach line. *(See diagram 13-1)* Then, P2 will follow their shot forward into the frontcourt to volley the next shot from P1. P1 and P2 will play out the point on the half-court with P2 in the frontcourt hitting volleys and P2 in the midcourt hitting passing shots.

Stipulation: No lobs are allowed in this drill.

Time: 10 minutes – Player # 1 will feed for 5 minutes. Then, player # 2 will feed for 5 minutes.

Scoring: Each player will keep a separate score of the number of points won while on offense and defense. This will help the player to recognize both their attacking and counterattacking strengths and weaknesses. It will also help them to track improvement throughout the season. The score is reported to the coach who then records it on the practice score sheet.

Drill # 2: Full Court Approach and Volley Points

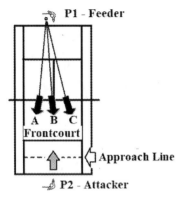

P1 - Feeder

A B C
Frontcourt

Approach Line

P2 - Attacker

Diagram 13-2

Purpose: This drill has both an attacking and a counterattacking objective: **1)** First, it will teach players to recognize and attack short balls with an approach and volley attack; and **2)** Second, it will teach players to counterattack using low, well-placed passing shots.

Set up: Two players compete on a full singles court.

Procedure: Both players will begin behind the baseline. Player # 1 *(P1 in the diagram)* will feed a ball to player # 2 *(P2 in the diagram)* so that the ball lands in target A, B, or C. P2 will move in quickly attempting to contact the ball early inside the approach line. *(See diagram 13-2)* Then, P2 will follow their shot forward into the frontcourt to volley the passing shot from P1. P1 and P2 will then play out the point on the full singles court with P2 in the frontcourt hitting volleys and P2 in the midcourt hitting passing shots.

Stipulation: No lobs are allowed in this drill.

Time: 10 minutes – Player # 1 will feed for 5 minutes. Then, player # 2 will feed for 5 minutes.

Scoring: Each player will keep a separate score of the number of points won while on offense and defense. This will help the player to recognize both their attacking and counterattacking strengths and weaknesses. It will also help them track improvement throughout the season. The score is reported to the coach who then records it on the practice score sheet.

Tactical Key: 1) Keep passing shots low by using topspin. **2)** Try to force the net player to volley from below the net. **3)** Move inside the baseline two steps after each passing shot. **4)** Get approach shot in and deep. **5)** Volley through sideline when possible, and **6)** Put high volleys away.

Drill # 3: Half-Court Lob/Overhead Drill

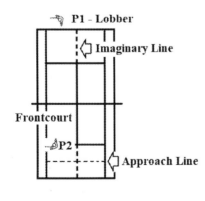

P1 - Lobber

Imaginary Line

Frontcourt

P2

Approach Line

Diagram 13-3

Purpose: The purpose of this drill is two-fold: **1)** To teach the baseline player to hit lobs over the head of the net player, and **2)** To teach the net player to put overheads away off short lobs.

Set up: The court is divided into two halves by adding an imaginary line that runs from the center service line to the center hash mark on the baseline. *(see diagram 13-3 for court division)*

Procedure: Player # 1 (P1) begins behind the baseline. Player # 2 (P2) starts on the service line. P1 starts with a feed to P2 who volleys the ball back to P1. P1 then hits a lob over P2's head. P2 hits an overhead if possible. If not, P2 runs down the ball and returns it with a lob. The point is played out on half of the tennis court. *(see diagram 13-3)*

Stipulations: A player cannot win a point on the feed or the first volley.

Scoring: Players score one point for winning the rally. The score is reported to the coach who then records it on the practice score sheet.

Drill # 4: Full Court Lob/Overhead Drill

Purpose: The purpose of this drill is two-fold: **1)** To teach the baseline player to hit lobs over the head of the net player, and **2)** To prepare the net player to put overheads away off short lobs.

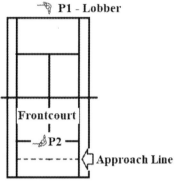

P1 - Lobber

Frontcourt

P2

Approach Line

Diagram 13-4

Set up: Two players compete on a full singles court.

Procedure: Player # 1 (P1) begins behind the baseline. Player # 2 (P2) starts on the service line. P1 starts with a feed to P2 who volleys the ball back to P1. P1 then hits a lob over P2's head. P2 hits an overhead if possible. If not, P2 runs down the ball and returns it with a lob. The point is played out on a full singles tennis court. *(see diagram 13-4)*

Stipulations: A player cannot win a point on the feed or the first volley.

Scoring: Players score one point for winning the rally. The score is reported to the coach who then records it on the practice score sheet.

Tactical Keys: 1) Think, lift the lob aiming for the length of the court. Do not just try to get the ball over the net player's head. **2)** When possible, lob over your opponent's backhand shoulder. **3)** Avoid hitting a backhand overhead by running around the lob when possible. **4)** On overheads inside the service line, angle the ball through the sideline; however, on overheads beyond the service line, aim deep for the middle of the deep target box.

Drill # 5: Singles Stations Drill

Purpose: The purpose of this drill is two-fold: **1)** To teach players to get to the net and finish points, and **2)** To prepare players to counterattack against a net player.

Set up: Two players compete on a full singles court.

Stations: There are three stations:

- **Station One:** Baseline

- **Station Two:** Service Line
- **Station Three:** Halfway between the service line and net.

Stations mark the players starting position for a rally, i.e., position from which the feed is made. After the feed takes place, players can move anywhere on the court.

Stipulation: A point is composed of a series of rallies. The winner of each rally will feed to begin the next rally. The point ends when a player wins a rally after feeding from station 3. *See procedure for description.*

Procedure: Play begins with both players at **station one** *(Baseline)*. Player # 1 feeds, and the two players play out a rally. Winner of the rally moves to **station two** *(Service line)* and becomes the feeder. Loser remains at **station one** *(Baseline)*. From this juncture, the winner will always move up one station and the loser will move back one station *(If loser started the rally at station one, they remain on station one for the next rally)*.

For example: If player # 1 feeds from **station two** and wins, they move up to **station three**; however, if player # 1 lost, they would move back to **station one** and player # 2 would move up to **station two** and become the feeder for the next rally. Play continues in this fashion until the player who feeds the ball from **station three** wins the rally. The winner from station three then scores a point. Then a new point begins with both players again on the baseline at **station one**.

Time: 5 minutes

Scoring: To score a point, a player feeding from **station three** must win the rally. Until a player wins a rally from **station three**, the game continues with winners moving up one station and losers moving back one station. Remember, you cannot move further back than **station one**. So, if you lose at **station one**, you stay at **station one** for the next rally. When the drill ends, the score is reported to the coach who then records it on the practice score sheet.

Chapter 13 Summary

Both attacking the net and counterattacking a net player require an aggressive nature coupled with the ability to execute effective approach shots, well-placed volleys, and aggressive overheads as well as effective passing shots and aggressive lobs. You cannot be successful at net play by hoping your opponent will make an error. You must expect them to return the ball, and you must react instinctively to your opponent's shot. Whether you are attacking or counterattacking at the net, a tentative play is never an option.

How do you develop instinctual reactions at the net? Only one way, you must practice playing points at the net. Most players fail to work on this phase of their game. In practice, they prefer to rally from the baseline. Just watch players warm-up. They might hit a few volleys, but they spend most of their time rallying from the baseline. You cannot develop the instincts to play the net unless you are willing to spend countless hours in practice working on the complete net attack and counterattack package. Working on attacking and counterattacking at the net must become a part of your daily practice routine. Just hitting a few volleys or overheads as part of your warm-up is not enough.

You must learn to play the net game using live ball situations. You must keep score to make it feel like a match. Do this twenty minutes every day, and then even if you are a diehard baseliner, you will begin to feel comfortable when you come to the net. Once you feel comfortable, you will start to win points. When you start winning points, you will start making the net attack a part of your game plan. Maybe not the primary option, but an option that you can use effectively when the situation arises.

See you on the practice court.

Chapter 14
The Four Playing-Styles

Key Thought: *Know thine own self.*

Before you can effectively counterattack your opponent, you must first examine your own game. This means understanding your personality, your physical traits, and your shot-making skills. After a thorough examination of your strengths and weaknesses, you can then develop your playing style. Then after you understand how you play best, you can begin to build a game plan for counterattacking the playing style of your opponent.

Tactical Key: If under pressure you fail to recognize your strengths and choose to play from your weaknesses, you will never reach your tennis potential.

The Consistent Baseliner

Definition: The consistent baseliner reacts to their opponent's shots. They are content to let their opponent dictate play while they counterattack into the openings and weaknesses created by the court position and shot-making of their opponent.

Personality: To be successful, the consistent baseliner must be mentally tough. Consistent baseliners must possess an I can run-down-every-ball-you-hit mentality. The phrases *'give up'* and *'I can't'* are not in their vocabulary. They are patient and seldom force shots unless there is an obvious opening. Their game is cautions, but tenacious. They create pressure with their consistent optimism and can-do personality.

Physical Traits: The consistent baseliner is physically fit. They possess the aerobic endurance that is necessary to play long grinding points, games, and matches. They are unafraid to play a third set because they always know that they can go the distance. They also possess excellent anaerobic power for speed and quickness. They move well, especially side to side. They possess quick reflexes and excellent footwork.

Shot-making: The consistent baseliner has consistent groundstrokes and good shot control. They know how to use spin, especially slice. They have excellent passing shots, good lobs, and can hit with consistency and accuracy when on the run.

Game Plan: They often play several steps behind the baseline and hit their groundstrokes with more net-clearance and trajectory than the aggressive baseliner. Their game is built on consistency, depth, and control. They rely on quickness and strong footwork patterns to run down every ball. Rarely are they out of position as they recover relentlessly to the tactical center after every shot.

Intent: To turn every point, every game, and every match into a physical and mental struggle. Consistent baseliners make it a point to stay positive, no matter what is happening on the court. While at the same time forcing their opponent into a negative mindset, and then turning their opponent's frustration into anger.

Countering the Consistent Baseliner

When playing a consistent baseliner, you must expect long physical and sometimes mentally excruciating points and matches. You must be patient and wait for opportunities to attack. In doing so, it is crucial that you stay focused on finishing points, but you must also expect to hit more shots.

Here lies the trap that the consistent baseliner has set for you. Their shots are consistent and deep, but not necessarily overpowering. At first, they may seem ripe and vulnerable for an attack. However, trying to shorten the rallies by going for quick winners in the face of their stifling defense will lead to more errors. When you start making more errors, you are playing right into the consistent baseliner's game plan. They know they cannot hit winners and are counting on your errors to win the match.

Guard your emotions. Because, the consistent baseliner wants to force you into a negative mindset, which will lead to you making even more errors. When they see your frustration turning to anger, their confidence goes way up because they are controlling the match, and they know it.

The first step in beating the consistent baseliner is to understand they want to get into a stone throwing contest. Their most significant weapon is consistency, so if you are satisfied with a stone-throwing competition, the consistent baseliner is happy. However, to beat the best consistent baseliners, what you need is a big weapon. By that, I mean at least one big shot, that you can hit consistently. So, take that big weapon and go to work. Below you will find a helpful list of key tactics that will allow you to defeat the consistent baseliner using your more powerful weapons.

- **Use your patterns but be patient.** Don't go for a quick kill. Wait for an opportunity to attack, i.e., Base-X, Mirror, or the inside-out forehand barrage.
- **Attack when an opportunity presents itself, but understand that you are facing a rabbit, so the ball will most likely come back.** Expect to hit two or three high-quality finishing shots before you can put the ball away.
- **When you are out of position, hit a neutralizing shot.** The consistent baseliner will pick you apart whenever they see an open court. Remember, their shots may not be powerful, but they are consistent and accurate. They also enjoy making you run. Remember, one of their goals is to win the physical battle by wearing you down.

- **Be careful hitting down the line.** The consistent baseliner moves well and can hit on the run. What might look like a winning shot will often come back and be well-placed into the court that you just left open by hitting down the line.
- **Do find the crosscourt pattern that gives you the most advantage.** Then force the rally to that angle as often as possible. Use the 3-X or 4-X patterns to take advantage of your opponent's weaker side. Remember, the consistent baseliner has based their game on high-percentage shots. Their strength is the crosscourt groundstroke, so force them to go down the line.
- **Do bring them to the net.** This is especially true if you discover they are weak net players. Don't give up too early on this plan. Even if they can volley, it is not the style they prefer. You might not be able to beat their option # 1, but over the course of a match, you might be able to beat their option # 2.
- **Do go to the net.** Make them pass or lob you. If this isn't your style, you don't have to do it every time. Just often enough to put doubt in your opponent's mind. However, if you are a net rusher, you must get there as often as possible, which means stick with your game plan.

Tactical Key: Don't fall into the trap of playing the consistent baseliner's style; unless you are better at it than your opponent

The Aggressive Baseliner

Definition: The aggressive baseliner also relies on their groundstrokes. However, they play much closer to the baseline where they can take the ball on the rise and dictate the point with their powerful shots. The aggressive baseliner will have at least one groundstroke weapon that they can use to pressure or finish off points. Often this weapon will be their forehand, and they will try to use it as often as possible. Usually, the aggressive baseliner will be quick and agile with a solid return or an attacking serve.

Personality: The aggressive baseliner wants to be in charge. They want to dictate play with powerful groundstrokes. They are often fearless and when an opportunity presents itself, will go for winners from nearly any part of the court. They are risk-takers who are unafraid to throw caution to the wind. Many aggressive baseliners are impatient. They want to do more than just win; they want to crush their opponent.

Physical Traits: Aggressive baseliners come in many different sizes, tall or short, heavy or thin, but they all possess excellent power on their groundstroke shots. It is a decided advantage if they are quick and agile, but not a necessity. They must have good footwork, balance, and solid shot-making skills.

Shot-making: The aggressive baseliner must have at least one groundstroke weapon, usually their forehand which they often employ using the inside-out attack. They hug the baseline and take balls early and on the rise. Most have a powerful serve that allows them to set-up their forehand for their second shot. Usually, they have a solid return game which enables them to attack successfully, especially off their opponent's second serve.

Game Plan: The aggressive baseliner's goal is to dictate the point. They often play first-strike points *(points that last five shots or less)*. The aggressive baseliner uses their powerful serve and attacking return to set up their big forehand. Their game plan does not call for extended rallies. Two of their favorite patterns are the inside-out forehand attack into their opponent's backhand *(forehand barrage)* or an aggressive groundstroke attack that drives their opponent back deep behind the baseline allowing them to step in and use angles to open the court for a change of direction attack *(Tick-Tock Pattern)*.

Intent: To overwhelm and dominate their opponent with their powerful attack.

Countering the Aggressive Baseliner

- **Try to strike first by focusing on hitting a quality first shot.**
- **Keep your shots deep.** Depth cuts down the angles and gives you more time to react.
- **Avoid becoming their ball machine.** Destroy their timing by varying the speed, location, depth, and spin of your shots. If you allow them to hit with rhythm and timing, they will blow you off the court.
- **Keep the ball out of their power zone.** Send slice to make them hit from their lower strike zone and deep heavy topspin to either force them back or make them hit from their upper strike zone.
- **Send the aggressive baseliner out wide on the side of their strength.** Then move them across the court to hit on their weaker side.
- **Use the crosscourt counter.** The aggressive baseliner will attack down the line, so be ready to step into the court and attack when you can, and when you cannot attack, merely loop the ball back crosscourt and deep.
- **Keep them off-balance and on the move.** Most aggressive players hit best when they can get their feet set. So, use the change of direction shots, not to win points, but to keep your opponent on the move by running them corner to corner.
- **Use the short angle shot to force an aggressive baseliner to move both forward and on diagonal angles to reach the ball.** Once you have moved them forward and out wide, it will make it easier to hit the ball past them into the open court.
- **Take their legs.** Once the aggressive baseliner is fatigued, their shots lose their sting.
- **Avoid getting pinned in the backhand corner.** Hit a ball deep crosscourt toward their backhand corner and then take the next one down the line forcing them to prove they can hit a running forehand.

The Net Rusher

Definition: The net rusher wants to finish points at the net. They prefer short, first-strike points with the intent of getting to the net within their first two or three shots. They know playing long points from the baseline places them at a disadvantage. Although it is difficult in today's game, most net rushers would prefer to advance the point straight from the first exchange into the approach and volley phase.

Personality: The net rusher has an aggressive nature. They are risk-takers that play with high intensity and concentration but have little patience for rallying the ball from the baseline. The best net rushers are persistent in the pursuit of their goals. They are not discouraged by passing shots or lobs. They play to the tune of a single drummer advance, advance, advance.

Physical Traits: The net rusher is athletic with soft hands and a great touch. They are blessed with anaerobic power that gives them both speed and agility. Height helps as it often gives them a more powerful serve and greater reach at the net; however, athleticism is the key to their success. Only great athletes can become successful in this style of play.

Shot-making: The net rusher often possesses an exceptional serve, a big weapon that they can hit with control, variety, power, and disguise. Outstanding hand-eye coordination is a must. The successful net player has excellent approach shots, volleys, and overheads. Although it may not be how they win points, if the net rusher possesses quality groundstrokes it will make them even more dangerous.

Game Plan: The net rusher's game plan is to get to the frontcourt as quickly as possible. They use first-strike plays like the serve and volley, the return and volley, and the second shot approach to entirely bypass the baseline rally. However, when they must rally, they are continually looking for the slightest opportunity to advance to the net. Once in the frontcourt, the net rusher will use their excellent anticipation skills to end points quickly with accurate volleys and powerful overheads.

Intent: Get to the net quickly and end the point with a volley or an overhead.

Countering the Net-Rusher

- **Get your first serves in play.** This makes it difficult for your opponent to run a return and volley attack.
- **Return serve at the feet of serve and volley players.** The low volley is difficult for them to put away.
- **Use the lob early in the match.** Let net-rushers know the lob is a part of your counterattack plan.
- **Focus on two-shot passing plays.** Hit the first passing shot low, and then attack the open court with the second.
- **Get your first passing shot in play.** You must make your opponent prove they can volley consistently.
- **Go to the net first.** Net players have good approach shots, volleys, and overheads; however, they may have very weak passing shots. Even if you are weak at the net, you may still be able to put the ball away.
- **Attack your opponent's second serve.** Use this opportunity to take charge and dictate the kind of point you want to play.

The All-Court Player

The all-court player is an exceptional athlete. They have the physical characteristics, mental strength, and shot-making ability to employ at least two of the three playing styles. Of course, the most dangerous all-court player is the one who can use all three.

Countering the All-Court Player

- **Determine which of the three playing styles is their strength.** Since the all-court player can use all three playing-styles, this is a difficult task. However, every player is stronger in one area than another. To find their strength, look for the style they most often employ, especially on crucial points or when they are behind. This style is usually their strength.
- **Determine which of the three playing styles is their weakness.** Most of the time it is difficult to spot the weakness of the all-court player immediately. So, start by forcing them to play outside of their strength. Then, if you notice that they are making more errors in a particular point style or even avoiding it all together, try exploiting that style to see if it is indeed the chink in their armor.
- **Bring them to the net**. In today's game, most players, even all-court players are stronger on the baseline than at the net. So, bring them forward. Even if their net skills are considerable, and they can hit volleys and overheads, bringing them to the net may make them less comfortable. Sometimes, this is enough to take the sting out of their net game.

Chapter 14 Summary
Key Thought: *Play from your strength.*

Always remember that every opponent, no matter how good they might be, is fully capable of committing errors. So, never give up. Throughout the match keep probing to find their weakness. Sometimes you will discover it early in the match. Sometimes you will find it late. The key is this: **the match is never over until it is over**. Even if you are down a set or match point, if you discover a weakness, it is never too late to turn the match around.

Tactical Key: Errors most often come, not as single spies, but in battalions. Once your opponent starts making errors, keep them off balance and keep playing hard. Any player can melt down. In fact, just as many players meltdown when ahead as meltdown when they are behind. Keep fighting!

See you on the court!

Chapter 15
Mental Toughness

Key Thought: *"Being able to perform at one's best when one's best is needed."* Coach John Wooden

One of the indescribable joys of tennis is that feeling of complete satisfaction as you walk off the court knowing you defeated a tough opponent by playing at the top of your game. Money cannot buy that feeling. It can only be purchased with sweat, hard work, and determination. Your technical skills *(stroking ability)* and your tactical plan are only two-thirds of that equation. The final third is your mental and emotional toughness. If you fail to train your mind, it will be difficult to play your very best tennis on a consistent basis.

The key to tennis success is to love the game. A love that comes from learning to leave your losses on the court while taking your victories with you wherever you go. Sometimes your game will be spot-on, sometimes it will be sporadic, and at other times you may wonder if you have ever picked up a racket. However, if even on your worst day, you still love the game, your chances of becoming a successful tennis player are better than average.

Tactical Key: Learn to use your brain as your biggest weapon.

During matches and practice, a large part of your time will be spent between points and between repetitions. What you think about and how you focus during these breaks will affect how you perform during the next point or next repetition. Most players fail to realize that they can control what they think. Instead, they dwell on whatever thoughts come into their mind with absolutely no idea of the connection between thinking and success. This random thinking is a massive mistake because thoughts and feelings will have a direct impact on how they will perform. Do not become one of those players.

Even if what you are thinking is false, it will feel real to you. For example: Have you ever found yourself in tears, or angry at something you read in a novel. The story you read is fiction, yet the emotions you feel are real. Your thoughts are no different. They have a direct impact on your emotions, your confidence, and your performance. If your thoughts are negative, your performance will suffer. If they are positive, your performance will be enhanced. Thus, to reach your tennis potential, you must train yourself to think performance-enhancing thoughts, not performance-destroying thoughts. Otherwise, you will always be fighting against two opponents. First, the player across the net from you and second, that little voice inside your head that is constantly reminding you of how inept you are playing.

If you find this hard to believe, try this little experiment. Next time you are playing poorly, take some time to recognize what you are thinking. Do the same thing the next time you are playing well. If you begin to examine and become aware of what you are thinking, you will start to discover how your mind is either working for you or against you. Learning to think correctly is a huge part of the mental battle. A battle that you must understand because it will ultimately determine whether you win or lose.

When you learn to control and perfect your thinking between repetitions in practice, it will start to become automatic during your matches. Very quickly you will notice a significant improvement in your game. First, your performance during practice will improve, and second, you will see substantial improvement in how you perform during match play.

Confidence and Self-Talk *(Internal Thinking)*
Key Thought: *"You can't climb uphill with downhill thinking."* – Zig Ziglar

Your confidence will be determined by how you talk to yourself. If you are negative, your confidence will be low. If you are positive, your confidence will remain high. It is also essential to make sure your self-talk is centered on what you want to have happened, not on what you want to avoid. Your mind does not recognize the word not. For example: Try to stop thinking about something by constantly telling yourself not to think about it.

Although tennis is just a sport, it can teach you many essential life skills. The importance of controlling your words is one of them. This skill is vital in two distinct ways: **1) Self-talk:** what you say to yourself; and **2) Conversation:** what you say to others.

The adage that, "sticks and stones can break my bones, but words will never hurt me," is far from accurate. Words hurt! What you say to others and what others say to you carries more weight than you realize. Every day, careless words destroy marriages, friendships, and work relationships. In sports, the words you communicate with your teammates will either build-up or tear-down your team. Likewise, what you tell yourself will have an immediate impact on your performance.

Tactical Key: "Put your mind into motion before you put your mouth into gear."

Without words, communication would be impossible. Words are tools that build teamwork and enhance performance. Words power relationships. Words are also weapons, that cut and destroy. With words comes great responsibility.

Whether you like it or not, you are responsible for the effect of your words. Ignorance of their impact can ruin relationships, tear teams apart, and ultimately destroy your dreams. What you will become will in large part be shaped by the words you decide to use, or more importantly, the words you choose to believe.

As important as words are to your relationships, what you tell yourself will determine your self-esteem, self-confidence, and performance. Why, because what you say to yourself is a clue to what you think of yourself. If you call yourself stupid, what are you saying? If you tell yourself that you can't win, what image do you hold in your mind? If you say to yourself, I don't stand a chance. What do you think will happen?

How would you feel if your coach voiced those same thoughts to you? Quite possibly, you would start looking for a new coach. However, guess what, no matter where you go, you will be there, and those same thoughts and words will still be there too. Since you can't get away from yourself, maybe it would be better to get away from your words. Proverbs 21:23 tells us, *"Watch your tongue and keep your mouth shut, and you will stay out of trouble.* (NLT)

Tactical Key: Words can cause damage or words can build up. How you choose to use words is up to you!

How Mentally Strong are You?

Key Thought: *"Learning to think positively in a negative situation is one of the best things you can ever do for yourself."* Joyce Meyer

How mentally tough you are is an important question that you must answer for yourself. The answer to this question is crucial to your success as a tennis player, and I would submit that it is also essential to your success in any endeavor in life.

The Mental/Emotional Battle is the first and ultimately the most important of the four battles. Why, because the Mental/Emotional Battle is the only battle over which you can have complete control. This battle is composed of three distinct parts:

- **The way you think.**
- **The image you project.**
- **The rituals you have established.**

The Mental/Emotional battle takes place between points. Since the ball is not in play, your opponent has no control over this situation. That is unless you give them control by letting them get inside your head. You decide how you are going to use this time, and how you choose to use this time will be vital to your success as a tennis player.

Tactical Key: You need to understand the effects of pressure if you hope to play your best tennis.

To win the Mental/Emotional Battle, you must employ a two-pronged attack. First, you must find a way to impose your will upon your opponent, and second, you must resist every attempt by your opponent to impose their will upon you. Ultimately, this battle becomes the underlying theme in each of the other battles, and it often becomes the force that decides the course of a tennis match.

If you are to understand mental toughness, you must first dispel the myth that being mentally tough means the absence of pressure or nerves. Players who pursue this myth are doomed to failure. Why? Because every player faces pressure to perform; in fact, winning players face even greater pressure because their expectations of performance are much higher than the expectations of the average tennis player.

To understand pressure, you must first recognize that the root of all pressure is fear. Although a tennis match is not an actual life or death proposition, your brain cannot detect that difference. To your brain, fear is merely a chemical reaction. In tennis, your brain responds to pressure as if your life was on the line. This response can manifest itself in three ways.

- **Anger:** You feel threatened, so the fight syndrome takes over. Sometimes this anger is directed at your opponent, but most often it is directed at yourself. In either case, it is destructive to your ability to succeed.
- **Panic:** This happens when your perception of threat has triggered the flight syndrome, you want to run away. Since you can't physically run away from this situation, you may choose the next best option, to give up. Giving up is really a flight response as it allows you to distance yourself from the pressure. Giving up often evidences itself in the form of excuse making as your brain tries to convince you that although you could win, today just isn't your day.
- **Choke:** In this case, you want to fight, but your body seems to be immobilized. You know what to do, but you just cannot make yourself do it. Choking is often the most painful of the three reactions because you care about the result but feel helpless to do anything about it.

Tactical Key: *"Courage is being scared to death and saddling up anyway."* John Wayne

The first step to becoming mentally tough is to recognize that your nerves, your composure, and your mental toughness are all directly connected to your ability to identify and manage situational fear. The good news is this: You can learn to control fear. Think about soldiers, especially soldiers in combat. Their situational fear is real. It is intense. It is life-threatening. However, they learn to push back that fear, which allows them to function and accomplish their mission even under the most life-threatening of situations. If a soldier can learn to manage fear on the battlefield, certainly you can learn to control your anxiety on a tennis court.

Controlling What You Think
Key thought: *For as he thinketh in his heart, so is he* Proverbs 23:7 (KJV)

You are what you think. The very first key to mental toughness is mind control, and the best way to control your mind is to manage your self-talk, i.e., what you say to yourself. The first step to controlling your thoughts is to recognize what you are saying to yourself. Most people become so accustomed to that little voice inside their head that they hardly realize what that voice is saying. They just blindly agree with it as if it were speaking the truth. Even more dangerous is the fact that they are utterly unaware of the consequences of accepting what that little voice has to say.

Words are powerful. Words can cause damage; however, words can also build. How you choose to use words is entirely up to you! When I researched the power of self-talk, I was reminded over and over that thoughts become words, and then words become actions. So, the question becomes, how do I harness the power of my words?

Programming your mind: As stated earlier, changing your self-talk is the key to controlling what you think. Often the mind is compared to a computer, and you know that a computer is only as good as its program. A programmer uses code to program a computer; however, the root of that code is the programmer's words or the word picture of what they want that computer to accomplish. In the same way, you program your mind with the words or word pictures that describe what you want your body to do.

A foundational element of the Tactical Point Control System is the reprogramming of the mind so that it can remain focused and confident between points, games, sets, and even matches. However, this reprogramming does not happen overnight. It must be worked on continually during practice and in matches. Unlike a computer, it takes time to reprogram your thoughts. Research implies this reprogramming can take up to thirty days. However, a conscious decision to control your self-talk is the first step toward success in the Mental Battle.

Control the Image You Project

Key thought: *Actions prove who someone is, words show who they want to be.*

What you see is what you get. The second key to mental toughness is the image or body posture you present to yourself and your opponent. Your body posture, your voice, and your willingness to make eye contact will broadcast either an image of power and confidence or an image of weakness and defeat. If your opponent sees strength and unshakeable confidence, they know that no matter how far they might be ahead, they are still in for a battle. However, if they see frustration, lack of composure, uncontrolled anger or negative gestures, it reaffirms their assumption that they are in control and are on track to win the match.

Win an Academy Award: Projecting a powerful image is often a matter of role-playing. Your objective or goal for every match should be to win an academy award for the image of confidence you portray to your opponent. However, the image you project is more important for you than it is for your opponent. This image will have a direct influence on your performance. When you act confident, you will learn to be confident.

Establishing Rituals for Every Tennis Situation

Key Thought: *"You have power over your mind – not outside events. Realize this, and you will find strength."* – Marcus Aurelius, Philosopher and Roman Emperor, 121-180 A.D.

Make success a habit. The third key to mental toughness is the reliance on rituals. You should have a ritual that you use before every serve and before every return. You should have a ritual for the time between points, between games, and between sets. You should have a ritual for your pre-match warm-up. To succeed, you need a ritual for every component of a tennis match.

Why, because rituals keep you focused and motivated. They also project an image of strength to your opponent. One of the easiest ways to know that you are giving up is when you begin to rush. When you just want to get the match over. Your opponent can sense this too. Know too, that when an opponent's rituals start to break down, it is also a good sign that they are on the verge of giving up. It is a good indication that they have lost the will to fight and are just going through the motions.

Mentality Traps

Players often fall into one of the eight mentality traps listed below.

- **Trap # 1: Over analysis:** I call this paralysis by analysis.

- **Trap # 2: Blaming or excuse making:** You will never improve your game unless you take responsibility for your results.
- **Trap # 3: Confusion:** It is easier to claim you don't know what is happening than it is to stop and think about it. This is another indication that you are not taking responsibility for your results.
- **Trap # 4: Helplessness:** If you tell yourself you are helpless to change the situation you can avoid responsibility for the situation.
- **Trap # 5: Daydreaming:** This is merely refusing to focus on what is happening and allowing your thoughts to drift to more pleasant things that are unrelated to the tennis match.
- **Trap # 6: I can't:** If you stop expecting to win, it will not hurt when you lose.
- **Trap # 7: Hopelessness:** It is easier to give up if the problem seems insurmountable even if there is hope.
- **Trap # 8: Giving up**: If you stop caring, there is no pain in losing.

The mentality traps are sometimes hard to recognize. However, once you understand them and recognize how destructive they can be, you can teach yourself to avoid them. In almost every mentality trap, the real problem is a failure to take responsibility for what is happening on the court. Responsibility demands action; unfortunately, it is more comfortable to make excuses then it is to battle on for a victory. Champions are those players who refuse to accept excuses for their poor play. Instead, they continue searching for a way to win even when winning appears hopeless.

Tactical Key: You must think performance-enhancing thoughts not performance-destroying thoughts if you hope to reach your tennis playing potential.

Performance Checkpoints

To better understand the role of the brain in successful tennis, I have developed a system of performance checkpoints. Using the performance checkpoints will give you a method of measuring your mental focus and concentration in five critical elements of your tennis game. Each checkpoint is in the form of a question that will help you think through the mental aspect of what is happening on the court. The performance checkpoints will help remind you to stay positive and think performance-enhancing thoughts.

- **Technical Checkpoint:** Am I using proper shot selection strategies that balance risk with the situation at hand?
- **Tactical Checkpoint:** Am I controlling my court position by recovering to the tactical center after every shot?
- **Momentum Checkpoint:** Am I choosing the correct point style for the game score and momentum situation?
- **Mental/Emotional Checkpoint:** Am I controlling my self-talk and following a between point routine.
- **Physical Checkpoint:** Am I using positive body language?

Process vs. Outcome Thinking

As you enter a tennis match you will find your thoughts focused on either the outcome of the match, i.e., will you win or lose; or on the process of playing the match, i.e., your rituals and game plan. Outcome thinking focuses on the future, on what you want. It places a significant emphasis on the score, the result, and on perfection. Process thinking focuses on the present, on how to get what you want. It emphasizes enjoying the game, keeping a quiet and peaceful mind, and accepting adversity as a challenge. It reminds you to stay relaxed and focused on a one-shot-at-a-time mentality. Both types of thinking are essential, but each plays a different role in the development of your mental game.

Outcome thinking helps you set goals and can keep you motivated during practice as you push yourself toward your goals. However, it is of very little value in the actual playing of the match. Since you can win while playing bad and lose while playing well, when your focus is solely on results, you will see very little progress in your game.

Process thinking keeps you focused on the task at hand allowing you to channel all your energy, both mental and physical, into the actual playing of the point. By focusing on your rituals and the game plan that you have auto-programed, you can limit your negative self-talk allowing you to focus on your game plan as you negotiate your way successfully from one point to the next. Having a process-thinking focus and using a between-point ritual are two critical elements necessary to your tennis success

The Between-Point Ritual

Key Thought: *Failing to plan is planning to fail.*

One of the keys to mental toughness is to have a mental/emotional game plan. Most players place too much emphasis on shot-making and tactics; thus, they completely omit any planning and preparation for the mental/emotional aspect of the game. When you exclude the mental/emotional part of tennis, it is a huge mistake. In a close match, the winning player is often the one who forces their opponent into a negative frame of mind. Once a player becomes negative, the next step will be either frustration or anger. You do not want to be the first player to break. When you lose your mental focus, you are standing on the edge of the canyon called defeat. Let me assure you of this: it is dark and dreary at the bottom of that pit.

If you can force your opponent to focus on failure rather than on coaching themselves back into the game, you are well on your way to winning the match. In the heat of the battle, you must never allow your mental focus to crack. The best way to prevent a mental breakdown is to remain focused on your mental/emotional game plan. Having a plan will help you stay focused, confident, and in complete control of your emotions. With a well-practiced plan, you can address all five of the performance checkpoints in the short 20-second span between points. Admittedly, twenty seconds goes by very quickly, so when a point ends, you have absolutely no time to waste.

The Tactical Point Control System is all about playing with a plan. Just as you have a plan for how you will build points, you must also have a plan for what you will do between points. When you neglect to use the time between points productively, your play will eventually suffer. To simplify things, I dived the time between points into four stages. Stage one begins as soon as the point is finished and stage four ends when the next point begins.

Stage One: Release *(2 to 5 seconds)*

Purpose: Tennis is a very emotional game, so the first goal of stage one is to release the built-up emotion of the last point. The second goal is to remain positive or at the very least neutral to the situation that just occurred. To accomplish this, you must exert immediate control over your self-talk, i.e., the internal dialogue that runs inside your head.

Tactical Key: The emotional state of each player determines momentum.

There are only four ways that a point can end: **1)** You hit a winner; **2)** You make an error; **3)** Your opponent hits a winner; **4)** Your opponent makes an error. Each situation requires a slightly different response; therefore, you must have a specific plan for each situation. This emotional-release plan should include two parts.

- **A verbal key** that sets the tone for your internal dialogue
- **A physical gesture** that establishes positive body language by sending an image of confidence to your opponent.

Emotional-Release Plan

- **Situation # 1: You hit a winner:** Use a verbal trigger such as "Yes," or "Come on," accompanied with a physical gesture like a fist pump. The goal is to stay in a positive emotional flow.
- **Situation # 2: You make an error:** Use a verbal trigger such as "no problem," and a physical gesture of correcting your shot mechanics or turning away from the error. The goal is to keep a neutral emotional flow.
- **Situation # 3: Your opponent makes an error:** Use a verbal trigger like, "Yes," accompanied with a physical gesture like a fist pump. The goal is to stay in a positive mental flow.
- **Situation # 4: Your opponent hits a winner:** Use a verbal trigger such as "nice shot," and clap the strings of your racket. The goal is to keep a neutral emotional flow.

The verbal response does not need to be loud, but it must be verbalized. Likewise, the physical gesture does not have to be extreme, but it must be enacted. Between points, you are on a stage, and like an actor, you have a role to play. First, you are defining your role to yourself, and second, you are portraying a story to your opponent. That tale will influence how much momentum your opponent gains from playing a good point, and how much energy they lose when they make a mistake.

Tactical Key: When you have made an error, self-talk can be useful in correcting your mistake. However, you must focus on the outcome you desire and not on the result you are trying to avoid. For example: If you hit the ball into the net, tell yourself something like "lift the ball" and then mimic the stroke you want using your racket as you visualize the ball passing over the top of the net. Avoid saying something like, "don't hit the ball into the net," as this is the outcome you wish to eliminate. The subconscious mind will focus and is drawn toward the image you present, so make sure your words and visualizations present a picture of the outcome you desire.

Stage Two: Refocus *(4 to 8 seconds)*

Purpose: In stage two, your goal is to continue to manage your emotions with positive self-talk while maintaining a confident body image. At this moment, you are on center stage, so it is crucial that you control your eyes, your posture, and your breathing. Your eyes control your focus, so don't let them wander. Keep them in your court. An excellent technique is to hold the racket in your non-hitting hand and focus on the strings as you walk toward the back fence.

Posture: Your posture will mirror your confidence. When down, your shoulders will want to slump, and your arms will tend to droop at your sides. Instead, make a conscious effort to keep your shoulders up, and let your arms relax. Hold the throat of your racket in your non-hitting hand as you focus your gaze on the strings tracing the pattern with your eyes. Sometimes it even helps to touch the strings with your hitting hand.

As you walk, your breathing controls your energy and exerts control over tension, anger, impatience, or nervousness. As you refocus your thoughts and emotions, breath in through your nose letting the air inflate your stomach like a balloon, then blow the breath out through your mouth. As you cross the baseline and move toward the back fence, take three to four deep abdominal breaths, to balance your energy and stabilize your emotions.

Stage two represents a significant part of your recovery. Until your emotions are under control, it will be impossible to analyze the match situation objectively and to come up with a tactical plan for the next point. During stage-two, it is crucial to keep your feet moving. Don't rush this stage. The more stressful the last point, the more time you should take. However, do not exceed the twenty-second time limit. As you train yourself in the recovery process, you will soon learn to recover more quickly, which gives you more time to reset your game plan in stage three.

Tactical Key: When your self-talk is positive, it enhances your self-worth and lifts the level of your performance. Positive self-talk helps you stay focused and in-the-present, not dwelling on the past or drifting into the future. Controlling your self-talk enables you to maintain your positive emotions by dispelling the negative ones.

Motivation Level

At the beginning of stage two, you must take a quick inventory of your mental/emotional level. By consciously monitoring and controlling your self-talk between points, you will develop a sense of how you must feel to play your best tennis. If your self-talk is negative or distracting, you are not in the proper emotional state. It is at this moment that you must take immediate action to get yourself ready to perform at your best.

Motivation too low: When you are down, discouraged, or lack energy, you must use positive words to bolster your sagging emotions. Use energy producing phrases like "come on!" "right now!" or "rev up!" At the same time, take a few short rapid breaths coupled with aggressively bouncing on your feet.

Tactical Key: Building positive energy increases your heart rate energizing you and preparing you to raise the level of your performance.

Motivation too high: When you feel nerved up and tight. When the skin on your face feels tight, and your heart is pounding, when you feel overly excited and want to rush, it is time to slow down. The key is to calm your body, which will then ease your mind. Use gentle, calming phrases like "no problem," "hold the course," rock solid," or "stay strong." At the same time focus on slow deep breathing. Inhale a long 4-count breath through your nose, hold it for 4-counts, and then exhale forcefully for a 4-count. Stay focused on your breathing until you feel the tension flowing out of your body. If a negative thought tries to creep back into your mind, take another deep breath and repeat this process.

Tactical Key: Deep breathing and reassuring phrases will steady your nerves and get you ready to perform at your best on the next point.

Stage Three: Reset *(5 to 10 seconds)*

Purpose: In stage three, you must objectively evaluate your situation. However, your evaluation will only be valid when your emotions are under control, and you are mentally prepared to fight through the next point. As you assess the situation, you will also be forming your plan for how you will play the next point. In stage three you have two decisions to make:

- What two-shot combination will you use in the first exchange?
- What rally pattern you will employ in the baseline rally?

When you have decided how you will play the next point, it is time to shift your focus to your pre-planned and well-rehearsed pre-point rituals. Take a deep breath and let it out slowly. Use a positive affirmation as you step up to serve or return. At this moment, you must place your complete trust in the rituals you use every day in practice. As the point begins, you are on automatic pilot ready to execute and react instinctively with your preprogrammed game plan to each shot your opponent sends your way.

Tactical Key: To play your best tennis, you must plan how to play and then play out your plan.

Stage Four: Rituals *(2 to 5 seconds)*

Purpose: In stage four, you must block out all distractions and focus your complete attention on executing a perfect first shot. Rituals deepen your concentration allowing you to focus your conscious mind on the present. Using a planned sequence prepares the mind and body to react with an instinctual and automatic form of play.

Sample Serving Ritual

- Stop behind the baseline and show your opponent a positive image – fake it if you must.
- Call out the score using a calm, confident voice – again fake it if you must.
- Bounce the ball – have a set number of bounces that you use every time.

- Pause after the last bounce and see your target. Avoid thinking about technique, grips, or strategy. Keep the target in your mind and eliminate all self-talk.
- Visualize – see a successful two-shot sequence in your mind
- Breath in, pause and then make your toss
- Use a 1-2-3 rhythm exhaling as you contact the ball
- Hold the picture of your serving target in your mind until you have finished your follow through.

Sample Return Ritual

- Take up your return position
- Remind yourself where you will hit your return should you receive an outside, inside, or body serve.
- Show your opponent a confident image – fake it if you must.
- Keep your feet moving even as you assume the ready position
- Keep your eyes on the ball – see it bounce and see the toss
- Split step as your opponent strikes the ball and spring forward into the return.
- At this point, your focus is entirely on the ball. You have relegated the return to your preplanned game plan and trust your instincts to carry out your plan.

Tactical Key: Using consistent rituals is the best way to stay process-oriented and to remain focused in the present.

Consistency

You must use the between-point ritual after every point in a match. Your primary match goal should be to play a perfect between-point match. To help you evaluate your performance between points, I have included three evaluation tools in *Appendix B* at the end of this book. The first is a form that either a teammate, parent, or coach can fill out as they evaluate how you perform between points. The second is a self-evaluation that you can fill out after every match. This form will help you evaluate how stress is affecting your play.

Understand the Importance of Stress

It is important to realize that physiological stress is an expenditure of energy in response to an external or an internal stimulus. Although you cannot eliminate all stress from a match, the good news is this: like any energy expenditure. Stress can be trained for, managed, and controlled. However, to manage stress, you must first understand the four sources of stress.

Physical Stress: This type of stress is the most obvious. It involves your heart, lungs, muscular strength, muscular endurance, and muscular coordination. The more skilled your opponent, the more physical stress you will feel. Physical stress can lead to fatigue. Fatigue leads to a breakdown of skills. A decline in skills leads to a collapse in confidence, and a failure in confidence leads to defeat in the match. However, since it is physical, you can train yourself to meet the demands of physical stress. You prepare to overcome physical stress through physical conditioning.

Mental Stress: Mental stress comes from the enemy within. That little voice that criticizes and judges your performance. The voice that informs you whenever you make a mistake and then belittles you for making it. It is the same voice that tells you there is no way you can beat this opponent and urges you to give up, or at best to accept the moral victory of staying close. It is the voice that starts making excuses and starts looking for a way to lose with comfort. How can you defeat the enemy inside your head? The answer is mental training. Mental training is not a fantasy. It is learning to control that inner voice. It is real training and some of the toughest you will ever undertake. However, if you learn to control that inner voice, you will be able to manage your emotions. When you can manage your emotions, you will be able to play your best tennis.

Situational Stress: This is the stress that the match creates. The tougher your opponent or, the more important the match, the greater the situational stress. However, situational stress goes far beyond your opponent or the importance of the match. It is multiplied by what happens during each successive point. Once again, it involves that inner voice that continually monitors your play. Self-inflicted situational stress can defeat you before you ever step on the court. What to do? Create a routine in which you treat every match with the same amount of respect. Where does this start? It begins by respecting your opponent. It is the only way to program yourself for success no matter the skill of the opponent or the importance of the match.

Life Stress: What you carry onto the court from your off-court life will have a significant influence on how well you can perform. How do you overcome life stress? This one is a little more difficult; however, it begins with your management skills. Life stress can be reduced when you live a balanced life. Which means taking the time to work on all the essential issues that you face, i.e., family, friendships, jobs, school, nutrition, and sleep. Of course, there are more issues than these, and the amount of stress will vary from individual to individual. However, you must continuously work to minimize these off-court distractions through scheduling, meeting deadlines, and always remembering to put 'first things first.' When you take care of the most important areas of your life, you will automatically feel a lowering of your inner stress level. For many players, this is where stress management should begin.

The Importance of Goals

Your thoughts control the direction of your life. Therefore, having goals gives your life focus. Goals provide direction. They help you make the right decisions by allowing you to evaluate your choices based on where you want to go in life. Poor choices make attaining your goals more difficult. Make enough poor choices, and your goals can become unattainable. Whereas, sound choices bring you one step closer to the realization of not only your goals but also your dreams and ultimately the vision for your life.

Long-term Goals: These goals are the ones that control your destiny. They are the vision you have for your future. They are the targets for which you aim. They are your hopes and your dreams. You should have long-term goals for every area of your life: relationships, education, employment, as well as tennis. Whatever you set as your long-term goals, they will be the instrument with which you can measure where you are against where you want to be.

Mid-term Goals: Mid-term goals focus on where you want to be in four to six weeks. What skills do you want to improve? What friendships do you want to build? What projects do you need to complete? Mid-term goals help you establish and maintain your short-term goals. You will see tremendous progress in your life when you can make the two sets of goals work together.

Short-term Goals: The short-term goals are your focus for the day. These are the goals that ultimately lead to success. They are not based on winning or losing, but on tangible things that will make winning a possibility. If you are a student, some of these goals would be attending class, studying the material, and breaking projects down into manageable steps. In tennis, they might include arriving at practice early, listening carefully to instruction, and focusing on executing skills correctly. You must write down these goals. You must verbalize them often. You must focus on them during your day. Your short-term goals help you to avoid procrastination, help you to make wiser choices, and ultimately will help to reduce the stress in your life.

Working Together

When all your goals *(short-term, mid-term, and long-term)* are in line, your life can take off like a rocket ship. However, you cannot limit your goals to tennis. Why, because you are much more than a tennis player. They must encompass all areas of your life. Your life is much more complicated than any single component. You can train hard on the court, but the life you live off the court can sabotage all your hard work. For example: If you want to get a tennis scholarship, you must also be a good student. Without good grades, it will not matter how well you can play. You must also be a good person. No coach wants to recruit trouble onto their team. Above all, you are going to need a support group. If you neglect your relationships with family, friends, coaches, and teachers, you will be facing life all on your own. When trouble comes, we all need someone to lean on. How will you know that your life is a success? When you not only have family and friends you can lean on, but you also have family and friends who can lean on you. Life is about helping others. If you are just living for yourself, someday you will be all that you have, and that makes for a very lonely life.

Chapter 15 Summary

To win the Mental/Emotional Battle, you must first understand that it is composed of two major components. First, you must find a way to impose your will upon your opponent; and second, you must resist every attempt by your opponent to impose their will upon you. To succeed, you must understand that this two-pronged battle takes place inside your head. The Mental/Emotional battle is won by controlling your thoughts. It might seem like one big battle, but it is so much more. Ultimately, the mental/emotional struggle often becomes the underlying theme in each of the other battles, i.e., physical, tactical, and technical. I believe that the mental/emotional battle is the battle that often changes the course of an entire tennis match.

What is pressure? Match pressure is a combination of two critical factors: **1)** your performance expectations, and **2)** the importance you place on any specific match. This is dangerous because the pressure to not lose to a weaker opponent can be even greater than the pressure to win against a better one. Pressure will always create a level of anxiety. Too much stress will limit your ability to reach your peak performance, and too little will cause you to lack the motivation to perform at your highest level. Maintaining a balance between an anxiety level that is either too high or too low is one of the essential elements of mental toughness.

What is anxiety? Anxiety is your feelings of worry, uneasiness, or nervousness caused by an event where the outcome is uncertain. Every player will experience anxiety. Butterflies and nervous jitters are merely the body's way of preparing for competition. Rather than fearing them, you should recognize and embrace them as a sign of the intensity you will need to perform at your best. The best response to anxiety is to learn to respond to it with confidence, focus, and mental composure. Maintaining the right level of tension is the key to peak performance.

What is mental toughness? Most players will tell you that mental toughness is simply being able to win under difficult circumstances. However, I believe that mental toughness has nothing to do with winning or losing. Instead, I define mental toughness as your ability to perform at your best when your best is needed. I firmly believe that you can walk away from either a loss or a victory knowing you have played your very best. If your only goal is to win, you will create too much situational pressure, which then leads to anxiety, which in turn leads to a poor performance. However, when you focus on playing your best, whether you win or lose the match, you can find much encouragement and joy in the game of tennis.

The Verbal Vomit Blocker

If your self-talk is constant and distracting or even hints at self-doubt or anger – you must immediately terminate it. To help you stop the flow of negative words, use the following four-step plan:

- **Become aware of your self-talk** and recognize your negativity as personal puke**.**
- **Stay motivated to win** even when your inner voice is looking for an excuse to give up. For example, I can't hit a forehand. I'm tired. I can't play on this court or in the wind or in the sun or with people watching or when my opponent is cheating.
- **Interrupt the negative flow**. You must have a planned **word trigger** and **physical gesture** to remind yourself to stop the flow. This word trigger can be as simple as **"STOP!"** The physical gesture can be squeezing your fist or slapping your thigh. However, both the word and the gesture must get your attention, but without the chance of causing actual physical harm. You do not need to draw blood. Some of my players wear a loose rubber band around their wrist and then snap it when that little voice in their head turns negative.
- **Reverse the flow**, draw in a deep breath, and release it out slowly. Relax as you exhale. Substitute one of your pre-planned positive affirmations for the negative chatter. When no matter the circumstance, you can stay focused and energized, you will be playing with the confidence of a champion.

See you on the practice court!

Chapter 16
Momentum Control

Key Thought: *The confident player sees themselves as a constant and recognizes their opponent's ups and downs; the player who lacks confidence focuses on their ups and downs and sees their opponent as the constant.*

When it comes to controlling momentum, it is often confusing. Even advanced players find it difficult. If you rely purely on instinct, you might eventually figure out what to do. However, if you understand the characteristics of momentum, you will find the answer to momentum control more often and much earlier in the match. More importantly you will learn to use momentum in ways that will have a significant influence on the outcome of your match.

I teach my players six strategic factors that influence momentum control:

- Proper Respect for your opponent
- Understanding the flow of a match
- Remembering every point is important
- Avoiding mental lapses
- Controlling the tempo between points
- Developing a second wind

Respect Your Opponents
Key Thought: *Confidence is believing in yourself and respecting your opponent. Cockiness is believing in yourself and disrespecting your opponent.*

Pressure will affect how you play. Too little pressure and you will tend to back off resulting in a corresponding drop in your shot-making efficiency. Too much pressure, may at first lead to more focus and a higher level of play; however, when the burden of pressure becomes too great, most players cave in and give up as it is easier to lose than to fight through the pressure to victory. Believe it or not, a balanced respect for your opponent's abilities is the key to a consistent performance.

Lack of Respect *(Over Confidence)*

A lack of respect for your opponent will result in negative or neutral emotions. This is a dangerous trap. When things start off good, you might roll right through the match. However, when things go bad, frustration can completely overwhelm you as you begin to think thoughts like: How can I be losing to this player.

When you disrespect your opponent, you risk playing below your capabilities. It is hard to keep your edge if you don't think it is necessary. Rarely can anything good come out of this kind of attitude. Why? Because if you believe you are far superior to your opponent, you have placed yourself in an, I have everything-to-lose and a nothing-to-gain situation. When you believe you have everything to lose, you can freeze-up, or choke. This everything-to-lose attitude is often the cause of a tennis upset. You cannot play your best when you are playing from fear. That is why having something to gain is an essential ingredient for consistent play.

Too Much Respect *(Hopelessness)*

Too much respect for your opponent leads to up-and-down play. In this case, you have put yourself in a nothing-to-lose situation. You are not expecting much of yourself, so it becomes easy to excuse your way into defeat. It is challenging to win when you believe your opponent is far superior. When you feel inferior to your opponent, you may become complacent and just react to your opponent's shots. You stop believing in your ability to dictate points and end up just hitting the ball and hoping for the best.

Remember, winners always dictate the action, while losers react to the opponent's play. In this case, what fight you had at the beginning of the match, will be taken away by your reactions to what happens on the court. What usually happens is this: you play a good close match, but you never really had a chance of coming away with the win. Playing close is not a problem. However, being satisfied with playing close can become one.

Proper Respect *(Viewing your opponent as a competitor)*

A balanced respect for your opponent prevents the roller coaster ride of highs and lows that are typical of the first two positions. Emotional balance is the key to consistent play. If you are anxious or angry, you cannot perform at your best. Tennis is a game of fine-motor skills, and to efficiently execute those skills, your muscles must remain loose. It is impossible for your hands to control the racket when your muscles are tight. When you respect your opponent, it is easier to control your emotions and to react positively to what is happening on the court. Thus, it is easier to keep your hands functioning freely.

Emotional Control *(Staying balanced)*

Emotional-control occurs between points, which means that you must have a plan for what you will do from the moment a point ends to the moment the next point begins. In chapter 15, I gave you a detailed explanation of the between point routine that I give my players, but here is a summary.

The Between-Point Routine

- **Stage One: Release:** You must release the emotion of the last point. Stay positive, stay tough, and move on.

- **Stage Two: Recover:** You must ready your mind, emotions, and body for the next point. Control your self-talk, your eyes, and your breathing. Also, remember the importance of presenting a positive body image to your opponent. They must believe you will never retreat, never surrender, and never give up.
- **Stage Three: Refocus:** Analyze the score, the situation, and determine the point-style you will use. It is imperative that you know what you will do with the first two shots of the point *(first-exchange),* and how you will build points in the baseline rally.
- **Stage Four: Rituals:** Start your pre-planned rituals as you get ready to serve or return. Control your self-talk and enter a positive flow.

Tactical Key: What you do between points is just as important as what you do during points. In every match always strive for a perfect between point performance. Avoid making excuses!

Understanding the Flow in a Match
Key Thought: *Two points in a row starts the flow!*

Tennis momentum is built primarily on winning consecutive points. I call this the flow of the match. When you have won two or more points in a row, you are in a positive flow. However, when your opponent has won two or more points in a row, you are in a negative flow. Thus, one of the keys to controlling momentum is to be able to recognize the direction of flow in your match. In tennis, there are two principal streams of flow:

- **The serving flow:** The ability to consistently hold serve.
- **The returning flow:** The ability to consistently break your opponent's serve.

To win a tennis match, you must consistently maintain a positive flow in at least one of the two streams. Simply put, you must be winning your service games or winning your return games. When you established consistent control in one of the two streams of flow, that stream represents your strength and you must make it your biggest weapon. As long as you continue to maintain momentum in that stream, you are in a position to win the match. However, if you can maintain a positive flow in both streams, you are positioned to dominate the match.

It makes no difference which stream you control. What is crucial to momentum is your ability to maintain the flow in one stream while breaking your opponent's positive flow in the other. The player who establishes a positive flow and then is the first to break their opponent's positive flow has put themselves into a position to win.

For example: When both players have established a positive flow with their service game, the player who can first break their opponent's serve, *(breaks the negative momentum of their own return game)* will most likely win the set. Conversely, if both players have established a positive flow with their return game, the key to the set will become which of the players can hold their serve, i.e., break the negative flow of their serve stream.

When two players are unable to establish a positive flow in either stream, the first player to generate a positive flow will have the first chance to win the set. *(This most often occurs among young and inexperienced players who have not mastered their serving game.)*

As explained in Chapter 3, most points are decided in the first-exchange or within the first four shots of the tennis point. Thus, momentum can be gained or lost very early in the tennis point. The first four shots of every tennis point are extremely important. This is the reason you must have a solid game plan for the first-exchange, i.e., both a two-shot plan for when you are serving and returning. Otherwise, you are leaving too much to chance. If your only hope for winning is luck, you will not win many matches against top-level competition. Top-level competitors work hard to eliminate luck from their game plan. They play every point and hit every shot with a purpose. They place no faith in chance, so they develop a plan.

Tactical Key: Why choose to serve first? Because if you can establish a positive flow in your first service game, your opponent will continually be serving from behind. That means if both you and your opponent stay on serve throughout the set, your opponent will be forced to hold their serve at 4-5. When the set is on the line, it puts extra pressure on the final service game where the server must hold serve or lose the set. Just as importantly, if you fall behind, always try to win your last service game, as this will force your opponent to win the set on their serve. Not only does this increase the pressure on your opponent, but even if they win, you get to serve first in the next set. Whenever possible, try to force your opponent to serve from behind.

Adopt the Mindset that Every Point is Important
Key Thought: *A good competitor has an overwhelming desire to win.*

Your main momentum goal in every game is to make your opponent play from behind. Why, because playing from behind increases the pressure on your opponent. Winning the first point of each game forces your opponent to consistently play from behind, which over time, increases the pressure allowing you to establish the flow at the beginning of every game. Once you win the first point, your goal is to maintain a positive flow by winning the next point. When you take a 30-love lead, you can actually trade points with your opponent as you only need to win two of the next four points to win the game.

The next big goal is to reach a score of 40 before your opponent. Being the first player to 40 gives you the first chance to win the game. Do this often enough, and your opponent's match anxiety will begin to weigh heavy on their shoulders.

Score Pressure
Key Thought: *Make the game score work for you.*

Your goals as you head into each game are as follows:

- Make your opponent play from behind.
- Win the first point.
- Establish a positive flow by winning two in a row.
- Win two of the first three points. *(If you lose one of the first two points, your goal is to win the third).*
- Be the first player to reach the score of 40 *(this puts you one point away from winning the game).*
- If you are behind, you must stay within striking distance. *(stay within one point.)*

- Win your first game point.
- Never let your opponent win their first game point. *(make your opponent work to win games)*

The key to the every-point-is-important strategy is to play one point at a time. When you understand the importance of every single point, you become more focused and thus are less likely to give free points to your opponent. Like your mother told you, learn to shut the door. Every time you give away a free point, it is like leaving the door open for your opponent. A good competitor always closes the door.

Conversely, when things are going bad, be on the lookout for any doors left open by your opponent. When you find one, get your foot inside and shove it open. No matter how bad things are, this is your opportunity to change the momentum of the match. Big comebacks begin with a single point.

Comebacks are also great for your reputation. They put fear into the heart of every opponent you face later in the tournament or season. When your opponent knows you never give up and that you are always in the hunt, it increases the pressure for them to maintain their lead. Remember this; players crack just as often when they are in front as they do when they are behind. Learn never to give up.

Tactical Key: Don't be satisfied with a moral victory. Players sometimes become satisfied with just keeping the score close against a good player. They decide that this is victory enough. However, this is a trap. Once you learn to accept moral victories, it is hard to find the determination to fight for the real victory. When you are satisfied, you stop trying to dictate points and become little more than a hitting partner for your opponent. Just getting the ball over the net and keeping the point close is not enough. Do not become that kind of player.

When in the lead, you must avoid the temptation to relax and stop dictating points. The truth of the matter is this: Most players make their worst mistakes when they are ahead. If you let the intensity of your game drop off, you may not be able to get it back. Not only that, your opponent is looking for an opening, any opening that will give them even a sniff of hope. Once a real competitor finds hope, they are like a hound dog on the trail of a scent. It is hard to shake them off.

You must stay focused on winning every point. Refuse to play loose points when you have a 40-0 lead. In this situation, almost every comeback is the result of the leading player giving away a free point. Remember what mom said: and SHUT THE DOOR!

Avoiding Mental Lapses
Key Thought: *Mental strength is a combination of concentration and confidence.*

Concentration is focusing all your mental energy on a decisive goal. In tennis, this is a difficult task. To succeed, you must continuously monitor and control your self-talk during and between points, games, and sets. Staying positive will enable you to keep your intensity high which will help you to keep more of your shots in play. Negative thoughts will destroy your confidence and hinder your ability to concentrate. A proper focus will not only help you maintain a positive flow, but it will also give you many more opportunities to convert a negative flow into a positive one.

Even when this concept is understood, every player is going to experience mental lapses. The key is to recognize them quickly and then to take immediate action to end them well before they get out of hand. The first step in this process is to understand that you will face two kinds of mental lapses: **1)** Discouragement lapses which occur after a negative result, and **2)** Presumptuous lapses which happen after positive outcomes. The second step is to understand their differences.

Discouragement Lapses

Discouragement lapses are most likely to occur after you fail to capitalize on a great opportunity. For example, you make an error when you had the chance to end a game with a winner. Now the score is suddenly deuce, and your opponent has renewed hope. In this case, you know that you have left the door open for your opponent. Discouragement lapses are a natural response to a disappointment. However, if you have too many of them or you allow yourself to dwell on them too long, your game is going to suffer, and you will have trouble winning a match.

Tactical Key: The best way to avoid a discouragement lapse is to always follow a missed opportunity with the determination to win the next point. You can't change the missed opportunity, and if you dwell on it, you will probably lose the next point. The best thing you can do is switch the momentum or flow of the game by winning the next point.

Presumptuous Lapses

Presumptuous lapses occur when you allow yourself to feel too comfortable with your lead. You are counting a game or set as a win before you actually have it won. There are three situations where presumptuous lapses are likely to occur: **1)** when you reach a score of 40-0 in a game; **2)** when you lead in a set by more than one game; **3)** after you have won a break-point or a set. The first step to avoiding a presumptuous error is to know the situations in which they are most likely to occur.

However, presumptuous errors cannot be avoided entirely. So, when they occur, you must recognize them immediately and regain your focus immediately. Otherwise, your lead will quickly evaporate, and you will find yourself back in a battle against a player who now has renewed both their confidence and their will to fight.

Tactical Key: Shut the door. If when you get a lead, you can keep the mental image of shutting the door in your mind, you will find that you can focus on finishing the point. Whenever you find yourself out in front, remember to tell yourself to "shut the door."

Control the Between Point Tempo
Key Thought: *When ahead, hurry up but don't rush.*

Learn to play points at your tempo. You have twenty seconds from the time the last point finished to be ready to play the next point, i.e., to get yourself into position to serve or return. You should use as much of that twenty seconds as you need to prepare yourself for the next point. However, be careful not to exceed the twenty-second time limit. With the twenty-second time limit in mind, you should follow these basic guidelines.

- When you are ahead, you should try to shorten the time between points.

- When you are behind, your opponent has the momentum, or you are winded, you should use as much of the twenty-second time limit as possible. *(Be careful not to go over the twenty-second time limit as this is considered to be gamesmanship.)*

Slowing the Tempo

Slow down the point whenever you are behind. Why? Taking longer between points gives you more time to both recover and to decide how you want to play the next point. Slowing down might also cause your opponent to lose their concentration or patience. Either situation can affect your opponent's play. Taking a little more time between points will disrupt your opponent's ability to dictate the tempo of the match which can sometimes reverse the momentum of the match. However, remember the importance of sportsmanship. Even when your goal is to slow things down, you must be ready to play the next point within twenty seconds of the end of the last point played.

Increasing the Tempo

Speed up the time between points when you are ahead. When you are ahead, you need less time to recover or to decide on the tactic you are going to use. Your primary concern is to maintain the momentum necessary to continue to dictate the tempo of the match. Speeding up the between-point time gives your opponent less time to recover mentally and physically from the last point played. It also provides them with less time to decide how they want to play the next point. When you are ahead, your goal is to win as many points and games in as short a time as possible.

Tactical Key: Before a big point, you should almost always take extra time to plan your strategy. Do this whether you are behind or ahead. The only exception will be if your opponent is exceptionally fatigued or winded. In this case, shorten the time giving your opponent less time to recover physically.

Find Your Kick
Key Thought: *Make your opponent play from behind.*

In a distance race, runners often count on that last burst of energy that will propel them past their opponents and across the finish line. This same energy burst happens in tennis as well. When embroiled in a lengthy physical match, there will come an opportunity where you can begin to put distance between yourself and your opponent. Typically, the player who is out in front will find their kick first.

This kick might start with something as simple as jumping out in front by winning the first game, or it may come later after the first break of serve. Whatever the case, when it happens, the front-runner will catch their breath and begin to play with renewed energy. Because they are closer to the goal than their opponent, being ahead in the set often decreases the burden of fatigue.

Smart players know that once they are ahead and have the end in sight, their adrenalin will kick in enabling them to play at a much higher level than their opponent. Be alert for those moments when you have caught your second wind. Finding your kick is the hidden key to third set play. Almost always it is the player who takes the lead which receives this adrenalin boost. Once achieved, the player who is behind rarely finds enough energy to close the gap.

Ten Keys that Signal a Change in Momentum
Key Thought: *Often it is the little things that count the most.*

I believe ten simple keys can help you regain a belief in yourself. They are little signs, of which you must be constantly aware. For as small as they are, they often indicate that you are starting to play better.

- **Longer rallies.** When you hit more shots per point, you are starting to play better.
- **Hustling to more balls:** You can often jumpstart your offense by playing better defense.
- **Keeping the ball deep:** When you start keeping your shots deep, you are beginning to neutralize your opponent's attack.
- **Hitting shots from closer to the baseline:** When you start contacting the ball close to or inside the baseline, you are in a position to start dictating points. Usually, this occurs in conjunction with keeping the ball deep. When you hit deep, your opponent is more likely to hit short.
- **More Set-up shots:** When you are getting more opportunities to finish points, whether you end them or not, you are starting to play better.
- **Making passing shots:** They do not have to be winners; they just have to force your opponent to hit a volley.
- **Getting more first serves in play:** Your opponent cannot attack first serves as well as they can attack second serves. Even if you have to back off, it helps to get more first serves in play.
- **Getting more returns in play:** Make your opponent earn points. When you are getting your returns into play, you are getting closer to breaking serve.
- **Hitting some volleys:** When you start to get volley opportunities, you are starting to dictate play.
- **Staying within striking distance:** When you remain within one point of your opponent and are forcing more deuce games, you are starting to play better.

You should become aware of these ten little keys and use them to pump yourself up with words like "that's better," or "way to play." As these small keys begin to pile up, you should start to feel the flow of the match switching in your direction. Your confidence will increase as you begin to see improvement in your game. Keep on pressing. You are about to turn the match around.

Chapter 16 Summary

There are three hidden keys to momentum control. Fortunately for you, most players do not know what they are, so they never find them. However, when you know how to recognize them, you have positioned yourself to turn match momentum into a potent part of your game plan. In the following paragraphs, I will quickly review the three hidden keys to changing the dynamic of momentum. Learn them, watch for them, but most importantly, learn to use them every time you step out on the court.

Key # 1: The Mental/Emotional Temperature: There is one big difference between a thermometer and a thermostat. A thermometer can only measure the temperature; whereas, a thermostat can control it. Almost everyone is a thermometer. However, if you want to manage momentum control efficiently, you must teach yourself to become a thermostat. Becoming a momentum thermostat is the lynchpin to the mental tug-a-war between you and your opponent.

Thermometer Control

The thermometer can only tell you two things: First if you are feeling down your play will drop, while at the same time your opponent's game will pick up. Thus, momentum is shifting to your opponent. Second, if your opponent is feeling down, their play will drop while your game picks up. Therefore, it helps you see that the momentum is shifting in your direction.

Thermostat Control

The thermostat not only tells you what is happening. It will also show you how to force the momentum to change:

- **Maintain your rituals and stay focused on the process**. Remaining focused will help you avoid mental lapses, or even worse, an emotional melt-down;
- **If you feel pressured, tight, or tired, slow down between points.** Slowing down gives you time to regroup.
- **If you sense your opponent is feeling pressured or tight, speed up the time between points.** Speeding up gives your opponent less time to regroup. In either case, you must continue to follow your in-between point routine. Hurry, but do not rush. Slow down but stay positive.

Key # 2: The Situation: Using your thermometer, you must always remain vigilant of the four situational keys. When a point finishes take note of how the point ended. For example, did you just hit a winner or force an error? Did your opponent give you the point with a bad unforced error? Did you give your opponent the point by committing a bad unforced error? Did your opponent just hit a winner or force you into committing an error? Then based on the situation, use your thermostat, to regulate the kind of response you should make.

- **Situation # 1: You just hit a winner or forced an error** – Play the next point using your best point-building style. Do not press or try to repeat that same shot immediately. Why, because great shots are usually the result of your hard work to set them up. The natural tendency is to try to play better and better and better. Instead, your game collapses. Big shots are often high-risk shots hit on the very edge of your control. Although you always want to play at the upper limits of your game playing right on the razor edge of control can lead to missed shots and errors. These errors can result in a complete collapse in your confidence shifting the momentum back to your opponent. Remember always keep building the point!
- **Situation # 2: Your opponent just gave you the point with a bad unforced error** – Put immediate pressure on your opponent by playing a point from the attacking point-building style. If you are a big hitter or you are more than two points ahead, go with your best first-strike point. If not, use your most aggressive baseline pattern instead. Why attack? Because if this mistake came on a critical point, it might be the first sign your opponent is starting to crack. If possible, shorten the time between points and prepare yourself to attack right away. Win or lose, if your opponent responds with a good solid point, they are probably not cracking, and you still have more work to do. However, if they commit another terrible error, this just might be the start of the end.

- **Situation # 3: You just gave your opponent a free point with a bad error** – Regroup by playing a point using the Base-X point-building style. Whenever you make a critical error, it is time to slow down and regroup. However, the natural tendency is to speed things up trying to make up for your big mistake immediately. But beware, speeding up puts you in danger of piling up errors, and the momentum can quickly snowball against you. Do not let a series of throw-away points result because you panicked over one miscue, bad call, or lost opportunity. Slow down and think. Control your self-talk and do not let your emotions take over control of your game. It is not the bad error it is the point following the bad error that is critical to momentum control.

- **Situation # 4: Your opponent just hit a winner or a good shot that forced you into committing an error** – Avoid panic and do not retreat! Strike back with confidence by employing your best point option from within your point-building strength. Countering your opponent's good play with a good play of your own is an essential aspect of momentum control. It shows your opponent that you have not given up and you are unafraid. Not coming back strong may open the door for your opponent to gain confidence, and if it is late in the match, it might be that spark of confidence that launches them into their final kick. Never let your opponent believe that you are afraid of their game.

Key # 3: Every Point is Important: Too many players get wrapped up in the score. It's easy to do, because in tennis, the score is called out before every point, and when you are serving, you are the one calling it out. What would other sports look like if before every pitch or before every play, the team with the ball had to call out the score?

What do you do? First, keep score, because no one else will, and it is an essential aspect of the game. Most scoring problems occur between players who fail to call out the score before each point. However, rather than the score, what you are most concerned with is momentum, which I define as how many points have been won or lost in a row. The same thing is true of games. I have seen players utterly defeated when they lose the first set 5-7. However, if you go back and check the flow of the games, they just won four of the last five games. In this situation, which player really has the momentum going into the next set?

The thermometer will measure the momentum, i.e., who is winning consecutive points or games. Thus, the most critical point is always the point you are on. Why, because, on every point, you are either establishing, losing, or building the momentum in the match. Thus, the momentum goal is this: **1)** Establish your momentum or stop your opponent's momentum by winning the current point; **2)** Build your momentum by winning two or more points in a row; and **3)** Break your opponent's momentum by preventing them from winning two or more points in a row.

If you never lose two points in a row, it is impossible for you to lose the game. If you never lose two games in a row, it is rare that you lose a set. If you never lose two sets in a row, you will win more matches than you lose. However, this is all determined by your ability to stay focused and by learning to play each game one point at a time.

See you on the court!

Chapter 17
The Tactical Point Control System

Key Thought: *"Aristotle said that an unplanned life is not worth examining because it is one in which we do not know what we are trying to do or why, and one in which we do not know where we are trying to get or how to get there. It is also not worth living because it cannot be lived well."* Mortimer J. Adler author of Aristotle for Everybody. New York: Macmillan Publishing Company, 1978.

Every system of coaching has a foundational principle, and the heart and soul of the Tactical Point Control System is this concept: The mind leads, and the body follows. To control a point, you must know how to build a point, and to build a point, you need to have a blueprint. Like Aristotle, I believe that random unplanned point play is not beneficial because the player does not understand why they are failing or why they are succeeding. There is no purpose for each swing of their racket, and there is nothing that can be measured or replicated. I call this kind of random play "hit and hope tennis." In other words, a player just reacts to their opponent's shots by hitting the ball back over the net while hoping their opponent will make a mistake before they do.

The Tactical Point Control System will help you build a solid foundation upon which you can formulate a game plan that gives you the opportunity to win every time you step on the court. Foundations are not meant to be pretty. They are the below-the-surface bedrock that solidifies the structure which is visible from above. When you watch professional tennis, you are watching the final product of their game, i.e., the structure that rises above the surface. What you can not see is the years and years of foundational work upon which their game now stands.

Tactical Key: Learn to use your brain as your biggest weapon.

Everything in this world is created twice. First, as an idea in the mind, then materially as it comes into existence. For example, the house you live in didn't suddenly materialize; it first was a concept in the mind of the architect. Then it became a blueprint on a piece of paper. After that, it was translated into materials and organized for building by a contractor. Finally, the hands of the hard-working builders constructed it. This same concept carries over to your car, your computer, and even to what you had last night for supper. As you can readily see, without purposeful thought, nothing of real value in the physical world would ever be accomplished. The principle of winning tennis is no different. However, three steps are crucial to its successful implementation.

Step One: Be Positive
Key Thought: *Believe in Yourself.*

Playing your best tennis while striving to win a match raises your anxiety level. Why, because so much is at stake: the point, the game, the match, the team result, your tennis ranking, and more significantly your self-esteem as a tennis player. As a match progresses and these anxieties increase, you must do something positive to confront your fears. That something is to remain disciplined and in complete control of your thoughts and your emotions. If even in the direst situations, you can hold on to a sense of control, you will remain confident, and when you are confident you can make positive things happen.

However, staying positive in matches is only part of the battle. It is just as important that you learn to stay positive in your practice sessions. Learning new skills and new tactics can also raise your anxieties. It is never easy to learn something new. No one likes to fail, but failure is an essential part of the learning process.

Tactical Key: To master a new technique or tactic, you must be willing to play poorly while in the learning stages.

Barriers to Maintaining a Positive Attitude
Key Thought: *To remain positive throughout a match or practice session requires two fundamental principles: discipline and confidence.*

In the Tactical Point Control System, I define discipline as a sense of self-command or self-direction. Whether in match play or practice, a disciplined tennis player will have a plan that allows their thinking to remain organized as they explore all options, check for progress, and seek to excel in their performance. The result of a disciplined approach to managing your performance will be a sense of control over the variables associated with either match play or learning a new skill.

Successful tennis players are disciplined. They stick with their plan which in turn develops their confidence. This confidence eventually becomes a positive 'can do' attitude that is difficult to defeat, thus leading to success.

I define confidence as poise or self-reliance and self-assurance. Confidence increases over time as players mature in their role as a competitive tennis player. This maturing confidence coincides with the player's growing awareness of the strengths and limitations of their tennis game.

When you understand the strengths of your game, you can build on or play to those strengths. In the same way, when you know your limitations, you can avoid playing to your weaknesses. This growing understanding of your own game will increase your sense of control over every situation you face. When you believe you can exercise control over any situation, it becomes an essential ingredient for sustaining confidence throughout a match or practice session.

Tactical Key: When you are disciplined, you can maintain control over your thoughts and emotions. When you are in control, you can remain confident. When you can remain confident, you can keep a positive attitude. When you can stay positive, anything is possible.

Step Two: Be Reflective
Key Thought: *Step back and reflect before you step forward.*

To reflect is to think back over a situation or series of events to discover what has happened. Reflection allows you to see the relationship between what you know, what you think, and what options are available. Most importantly, it will enable you to learn from past situations and apply what you learned to the situation you are currently facing.

   The purpose of reflection is not to judge or second-guess your previous decisions or performance; but instead, to use what you learned to choose the best way forward in your tennis match or practice session. To be successful, you must strive to be both truthful and accurate during the reflective process. You must do more than just see what happened. You must also seek to understand why or how it happened. It is the why and the how of a situation that the Tactical Point Control System will teach you to control.

Tactical Key: To maintain control, the mind and the body cannot be separated.

Barriers to Effective Reflection
Key Thought: *Accept no excuses.*

The key to effective reflection is humility. You must have an honest perception of your capabilities. If you cannot admit your limitations, you will be unable to choose the wise course of action. To charge forward using skills you do not possess, only puts you on the fast track to failure. Honest reflection is the key. No two matches or situations are ever exactly alike. Sometimes your opponent may be able to neutralize one or more of your strengths. When this happens, you must be able to identify what you can and cannot do against this opponent. The key is to remember that there will always be something you can do. Having a positive attitude along with the correct reflective mindset will give you the ability to find and execute a plan that will lead to success.

Tactical Key: Arrogance will always interfere with your ability to maximize your potential.

Step Three: Be Inquisitive
Key Thought: *"It's what you learn after you know it all that counts."* – John Wooden

How often do you question or investigate new ways of doing things? Are words like what, where, when, how, and why a part of your vocabulary? As a tennis player, you must develop a curiosity for new tactics and technical skills. Without a desire to learn or delve deeper into the topic of tennis tactics, you will stagnate, and very soon you will find yourself losing to opponent's who are themselves continually learning and improving their game. If you want to continue winning, you must have a burning desire to improve.

Barriers to the Inquisitive Mind
Key Thought: *You must be willing to grow.*

To learn, you must have an open mind. The inquisitive mind is willing to consider a wide range of ideas, concepts, and opinions. Whereas, a closed mind has already decided that their way is the only way. Perseverance to continue along a chosen path despite difficulty and opposition is essential. However, to reach your full potential, this persistence must propel you forward on a path of progressive development and growth. Without growth, perseverance is nothing more than blind stubbornness that will stagnate your mind and lead to discouragement. This is the kind of discouragement that causes many players to abandon the game.

So, what keeps you on the path of growth and development? The answer is motivation. Motivation inspires and encourages you to act. Not just to play the game, but to experiment and find new ways to play it better. It prompts you to investigate new ways to do things. It gives you the enthusiasm to embark on a new journey using new tactics and new techniques designed to help you reach your full potential.

Tactical Key: "Are you green and growing or ripe and rotting?" – Ray Kroc

Chapter 17 Summary

The Tactical Point Control System is a complete plan for playing a tennis match. The difference between this book and many other books on tennis is merely this: Winning tennis involves much more than just tactics. The TPC system will develop your game on a tactical, mental, and emotional level. It will teach you to recognize and control the momentum of the match. It will show you how to build a tennis point from the first to the last shot of the point.

Most importantly, it provides you with a method for learning how to play your best tennis. And, when you play your best tennis, you are going to be much happier. I dare say, you are going to surprise yourself at how high you can raise the level of your game.

Parting Thoughts

Thank you for allowing me to share my tennis journey with you. I hope you use the ideas and drills presented in this book to perfect your tactics. Now get out there on the court and put them to practice. I know you will win more points and ultimately more matches. However, the most important thing is that you have fun playing this great game of tennis

See you on the court.

Appendix A
Tennis Skill Test

Serving Test
Set-Up

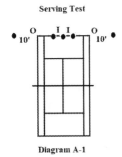

Serving Test

Diagram A-1

Using a full tennis court place five cones as shown in diagram A-1. *(dark circles represent the cones)* The first cone is placed ten feet outside of the deuce court doubles sideline and even with the baseline. The second cone is placed on the baseline halfway between the deuce court singles sideline and the center hash mark. The third cone is placed on the center hash mark. The fourth cone is placed halfway between center hash mark and the ad court singles sideline. Finally, the fifth cone is placed ten feet outside the ad court doubles sideline and even with the baseline.

Description

The serving test consists of a total of eighteen serves. Nine of these serves will be hit into the deuce court, and nine will be hit into the ad court. The eighteen serves will be divided as follows:

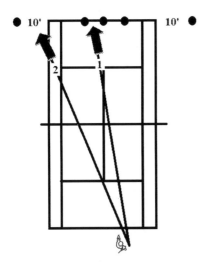

Diagram A-2

- **Slice Serve:** Each player will serve three slice serves into both the deuce and the ad courts. The right-handed player will aim their slice serve into the outside target in the deuce court and into the inside target in the ad court. Whereas, the left-handed server will aim their slice serve into the inside target in the deuce court and the outside target in the ad court. *(Diagram A-2 shows deuce court serves. Serve 1 to the inside Target and Serve 2 to the outside target)*
- **Topspin Serve:** Each player will serve three topspin serves into both the deuce and the ad courts. The right-handed player will aim their topspin serve into the inside target in the deuce court and into the outside target in the ad court. Whereas, the left-handed server will aim their topspin serve into the outside target in the deuce court and into the inside target in the ad

court. *(Diagram A-2 shows deuce court serves. Serve 1 to the inside Target and Serve 2 to the outside target)*

- **Power Serve:** Each player will serve three power serves into both the deuce and the ad courts. The power serve is not aimed into a specific target, but must be hit through the baseline. *(See Serve 1 in diagram A-2)*

Scoring

Inside Serves: If aiming into the inside target, the ball must pass through the baseline before crossing the singles sideline. Thus, depth is essential. Scoring is as follows:

- **Accuracy:**
    1-point if your serve lands in the service box.
    2-points for getting your serve in the inside target area. *(Serve 1 in Diagram A-2)*
- **Depth:**
    0-points if second bounce lands inside the baseline.
    1-point if second bounce lands beyond the baseline.
    2 points if the second bounce hits the back fence.

Outside Serves: If aiming into the outside target, the ball must pass through the singles sideline before crossing the baseline. Thus, the angle is critical. Scoring is as follows:

- **Accuracy:**
    1-point for getting your serve in the correct service box.
    2-points for getting your serve in the outside target area. *(Serve 2 in Diagram A-2)*
- **Angle:**
    1-point if second bounce lands outside the singles sideline.
    2-points if the second bounce is outside of the doubles sideline.

Power Serves: Power serves must pass through baseline before crossing the singles sideline. Thus, power is important. Scoring is as follows:

- **Accuracy:**
    1-point for getting your serve in the correct service box.
    2-points if serve passes through Inside target. *(Serve 1 in Diagram A-1)*
- **Power:**
    0-points if second bounce lands inside baseline.
    1-point if second bounce lands beyond baseline.
    2-points if second bounce hits back fence.

Note: Be aware that the distance to the back fence will vary from court to court. If there is a lot of space to your back fence, put down a rope line at a distance of fifteen feet behind the baseline. Then if the second bounce is beyond the 15-foot rope line, score them as a power point.

Groundstroke Test

Description

The groundstroke test consists of a total of thirty groundstrokes. Eighteen of these groundstrokes will be hit with your forehand and twelve will be hit with your backhand. The thirty groundstrokes will be divided as follows:

Note: All groundstroke tests will use the **four target boxes**. *(see chapter 3 diagram 3-2)*

Forehand Groundstrokes: Each player will hit three outside crosscourt shots using topspin, and three outside crosscourt shots using slice. Next, they will hit three outside down-the-line shots using topspin followed by three outside down-the-line shots using slice. Finally, they will hit three inside-out forehands using topspin and three inside pull-shots using topspin.

Backhand Groundstrokes: Each player will hit three outside crosscourt shots using topspin, and three outside crosscourt shots using slice. Next, they will hit three outside down-the-line shots using topspin followed by three outside down-the-line shots using slice.

Scoring

Crosscourt Shots: The crosscourt shot should be aimed into the center of the diagonal deep target box. *(4-to-4 or 3-to-3 rally angles)*. Both depth and angle are important.

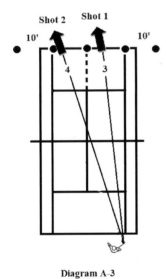

Diagram A-3

- **Accuracy:**
  1-point for getting your shot in the singles court. *(Shot 1 in Diagram A-3)*
  2-points for getting your shot crosscourt *(Shot 2 in Diagram A-3)*.
- **Depth/Angle:**
  0-points if the second bounce is inside the baseline.
  1-point if the second bounce is beyond the baseline or outside of the doubles sideline.
  2-points if the second bounce is hit into the back fence or outside 10-foot cone.

Down-the-Line Shots: The down-the-line shot should be aimed into the center of the deep target box that is perpendicular to your position *(3 to 4 or 4 to 3)*. Depth is essential on all down-the-line shots.

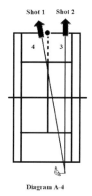

Diagram A-4

- **Accuracy:**
  1-point for getting your shot in the court. *(Shot 1 in Diagram A-4)*
  2-points for getting your shot down the line. *(Shot 2 in Diagram A-4)*
- **Depth:**
  0-points if the second bounce is inside the baseline.
  1-point if the second bounce is beyond the baseline.
  2-points if the second bounce is hit into back fence.

Net-Play Test

Description

The net-play test consists of a total of twenty shots. twelve of these shots are volleys and eight are overheads. The sixty shots will be divided as follows:

Note: All net-play tests will use the **four target boxes**. *(see chapter 3 diagram 3-2)*

Deuce Court Volleys: Player will position in the center of the 2 Target Box. The will then hit three *outside volleys* crosscourt into the diagonal 2 Target Box, followed by three *inside-out volleys* crosscourt into the diagonal 2 Target Box.

Ad Court Volleys: Players will position in the center of the 1 Target Box. They will then hit three *outside volleys* crosscourt into the 1 Target Box, followed by three *inside out volleys* crosscourt into the 1 Target Box.

Frontcourt Overheads: Each player will hit eight overheads from the frontcourt zone. They will alternate hitting one to deep target 3 and one to deep target 4.

Volley Scoring

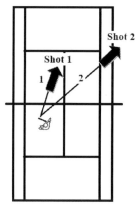

Diagram A-5

Outside Volley: An outside volley is hit off a down-the-line passing shot. The outside volley is aimed into the center of the diagonal short target box, i.e., 2-to-2 or 1-to-1. Angle is important.

- **Accuracy:**
  1-point for getting your shot in the court. *(Shot 1 in Diagram A-5)*
  2-points for getting your shot crosscourt and into the diagonal short target box. *(Shot 2 in Diagram A-5)*
- **Angle:**
  1-points if the second bounce is inside the doubles sideline.
  2-points if the second bounce is outside of the doubles sideline.

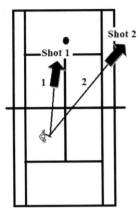

Diagram A-6

Inside-out Volley: An inside-out volley is hit off a crosscourt passing shot. Like the outside volley, it is aimed into the center of the diagonal short target box, i.e., 2-to-2 or 1-to-1. Angle is important.

- **Accuracy:**
  1-point for getting your shot in the court. *(Shot 1 in Diagram A-6)*
  2-points for getting your shot crosscourt and into the diagonal short target box. *(Shot 2 in Diagram A-6)*
- **Angle:**
  1-points if the second bounce is inside the doubles sideline.
  2-point if the second bounce is outside of the doubles sideline.

Overhead Scoring

Overhead: This is an overhead that is hit from the frontcourt zone. Players will alternate hitting one overhead to deep target 3 and one to deep target 4.

- **Accuracy:**
  1-point for getting your overhead in the court.
  2-points for hitting it into the correct deep target box *(Alternating targets 3 or 4)*
- **Angle:**
  0-points if the second bounce is inside the baseline or doubles sideline.
  1-point if the second bounce is outside the baseline or doubles sideline.
  2-points if the second bounce hits back fence.

Note: *Be aware that the distance to the back fence will vary from court to court. I suggest you put down a rope line at a distance of fifteen feet behind the baseline.*

Test Feeds: An essential part of the tennis skill test is a consistent feed. I have found that it works best if you use either a ball machine or a hand feed. Diagram A-1 illustrates the feed locations for each of the tests.

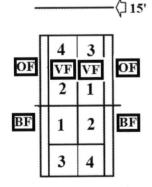

Diagram A-7

15': This is the rope line you would put down between the baseline and the back fence.

BF: This indicates the position for feeding the baseline test. The feed is an overhand toss into the deep diagonal target. Aim the feed for the center of the target, i.e., the number location. The player taking the baseline test would start behind the target square.

OF: This is the position for feeding the overhead test. The feed is an underhand lob toward the center of the court. The frontcourt feed should land near the middle of the frontcourt zone, i.e., the service T area. The midcourt feed should land near the center of the midcourt zone. The player taking the test would start on the service T for each test.

VF: This is the position for feeding the volley test. This feed is an underhand toss to the correct side of the player taking the test. The volleyer should be positioned on the opposite side of the net and in the middle of the service box. Thus the feed would be from 2-to-1 or 1-to-2.

Skill-Test Score Sheet for Right-handed Player

Player Name: _____ **Date:** _____

Directions: For each shot, record the total score for accuracy and depth or angle. Place a zero if the player did not score any points for a specific shot. Be as accurate as possible.

SERVE SCORING										
	Deuce-Court Serves			Total	Ad-Court Serves			Total		
Serve Score	1	2	3	Deuce	1	2	3	AD	S%	PT
Slice										
Topspin										
Power										

FOREHAND GROUNDSTROKE SCORING													
	TOPSPIN						SLICE						
Shot Score	1	2	3	Total	C%	PT	1	2	3	Total	C%	PT	
4 to 4													
4 to 3													
Inside-out													
Inside-in													

BACKHAND GROUNDSTROKE SCORING													
	TOPSPIN						SLICE						
Shot Score	1	2	3	Total	C%	PT	1	2	3	Total	C%	PT	
3 to 3													
3 to 4													

VOLLEY SCORING													
	Outside Volley						Inside Volley						
Volley Score	1	2	3	Total	C%	PT	1	2	3	Total	C%	PT	
Deuce Court													
Ad Court													

OVERHEAD SMASH SCORING											
Smash Score	1	2	3	4	5	6	7	8	Total	C%	PT
Alternating											

Key to Scoring Table

Total: Total Score – the sum of all shots.

C%: (Consistency) Percentage of good shots – divide made shots by number of shots.

PT: Average Score for each shot – the average score of each made shot. *(do not include errors)*

Note: A score of zero is equal to an error.

Skill-Test Score Sheet for Left-handed Player

Player Name: _____ **Date:** _____

Directions: For each shot, record the total score for accuracy and depth or angle. Place a zero if the player did not score any points for a specific shot. Be as accurate as possible.

SERVE SCORING										
	Deuce-Court Serves			**Total**	**Ad-Court Serves**			**Total**		
Serve Score	1	2	3	Deuce	1	2	3	AD	S%	PT
Slice										
Topspin										
Power										

FOREHAND GROUNDSTROKE SCORING												
	TOPSPIN						**SLICE**					
Shot Score	1	2	3	Total	C%	PT	1	2	3	Total	C%	PT
3 to 3												
3 to 4												
Inside-out												
Inside-in												

BACKHAND GROUNDSTROKE SCORING												
	TOPSPIN						**SLICE**					
Shot Score	1	2	3	Total	C%	PT	1	2	3	Total	C%	PT
4 to 4												
4 to 3												

VOLLEY SCORING												
	Outside Volley						**Inside Volley**					
Volley Score	1	2	3	Total	C%	PT	1	2	3	Total	C%	PT
Deuce Court												
Ad Court												

OVERHEAD SMASH SCORING											
Smash Score	1	2	3	4	5	6	7	8	Total	C%	PT
Alternating											

Key to Scoring Table

Total: Total Score – the sum of all shots.

C%: (Consistency) Percentage of good shots – divide made shots by number of shots.

PT: Average Score for each shot – the average score of each made shot. *(do not include errors)*

Note: A score of zero is equal to an error.

Appendix B
The Mental Game

The Point-Playing Mentality
Key Thought: *For as he thinks in his heart, so is he.* Proverbs 23:7 (NIV)

The ability to maintain your mental focus during the playing of a point is the difference between becoming a good player and becoming a champion. The champion can narrow their focus to the court and the ball. Whereas, the good player is often distracted. Having the proper point-playing mentality is divided into two parts: **1)** What you do between points that allows you to focus your attention on playing a tennis match one point at a time, and **2)** What you do during the point that will enable you to play the point one shot at a time. When you master both skills, you will advance from being merely a good player to becoming a champion.

STRESS AND ANXIETY EVALUATION FORM

NAME: _____ DATE: _____

Opponent: _____ Location: _____

**Use this form to evaluate your stress and anxiety level for today's match.
After the match, rate yourself in the following areas using this scale:**

3 = high level; 2 = moderate level; 1 low level; 0 = not at all

Physical Stress: I experienced physical stress such as shortness of breath, a pounding heart, sweating palms, or butterflies in my stomach. _____

Mental Stress: A voice inside my head continually criticized, second-guessed, or distracted me from my game. _____

Situational Stress: I perceived the match situation or my opponent as threatening. _____

Self-inflicted Stress: I was unprepared to compete. _____

Life Stress: My play was affected by outside concerns in my life *(school, social, family)* _____

0-5 = <u>Stress Free</u>; 5-10 = <u>Moderate Stress</u>; 11 plus = <u>High Stress</u>

POST-MATCH MENTAL EVALUATION FORM

NAME: _____ DATE: _____

OPPONENT: _____ LOCATION: _____

Evaluator: self or _____

Use this form to evaluate your mental performance between points.

Rate each of the following areas using this scale:
3 = almost always; 2 = sometimes; 1 = almost never

20-SECOND BETWEEN POINT RECOVERY

Eye Control: Eyes were on strings, ball, or ground. Eyes did not wander around the court or drift toward spectators. _____

Posture Control: Posture remained confident no matter the situations. Shoulders are back, head is up, after and before each point eye contact is made with opponent. _____

Gesture Control: Gestures remain positive. Stands with feet spread postures. Uses the hands-on-hips *(wonder woman stance)* to signal strength. Uses fist pumps to signal energy. Avoids the following: palm up or arms spread arm gestures; shoulder-shrugs and hanging arms; fidgeting, i.e., unnecessarily adjusting posture, or tugging on clothing. _____

Relaxed: arms hang freely, bends and stretches to remain loose, takes relaxation breaths, and allows sufficient time to recover from previous point. _____

Pauses Before Starting Point: Before each point to clearly decide on what tactic to use. _____

Emotional Release: Ends each point with a positive verbal and physical response. _____

High-Energy Walk: Walks on balls of feet, not heals. Movements project energy and confidence. _____

Serving Ritual: Follows well-defined ritual before serving. _____

Returning Ritual: Follows well-defined ritual before returning. _____

Momentum Pace: Establishes a winning pace between points. Slows down when behind and speeds up when ahead. Not rushed or rattled. Timing is appropriate to situation. _____

27-30 = <u>Poised</u>; 24-26 = <u>Confident</u>; 21-23 = <u>Competitive</u>; 18-20 = <u>Weak</u>; 17 or less = <u>Poor</u>

SELF-TALK ASSESSMENT

Name _____ Date _____

Opponent: _____ Location: _____

After the match, rate yourself in the following areas using this scale:
3 = Almost always; 2 = Sometimes; 1 = Almost never

Before the competition, my self-talk was focused on what to do and how to prepare. _____

Before the competition, my self-talk was focused on what I need to do, not on winning or losing. _____

During the match, I was my own best friend, i.e., supportive, encouraging, positive. _____

My self-talk remained positive after a mistake. _____

My self-talk helped me keep a high energy level throughout the match. _____

My self-talk helped me to perform at my very best. _____

My self-talk focused on my strengths, and not my weaknesses. _____

19-21 = <u>Poised</u>; 16-18 = <u>Confident</u>; 13-15 = <u>Competitive</u>; 11-13= <u>Weak</u>; 9 or less = <u>Poor</u>

About the Author

John Ruder has been coaching for thirty-four years. He has been a ranked player in both the Southwest and Texas divisions of the USTA. John is a United States Professional Tennis Association professional *(USPTA)* as well as a member of the Intercollegiate Tennis Association *(ITA)* and the Women's Tennis Coaching Association *(WTCA)*.

John attended Olivet Nazarene University where he was a starting shortstop and sometimes designated hitter on the Tiger baseball team. Upon graduation, he became an infantry officer in the United States Army rising to the rank of Captain. It was during his time in the military that John developed a love for the game of tennis.

After resigning his Army commission, John embarked on his second career as a teacher/coach. In his twenty-seven years as a high-school teacher, he was the head coach of five varsity sports: football, basketball *(both boys and girls)*, baseball, track *(both boys and girls)* and tennis *(both boys and girls)*.

John started the tennis program at Valley Union High School in Elfrida, Arizona. At that time, except for the court he built in his backyard, the closest tennis courts were twenty miles away. Not to be deterred, he raised enough money to buy two portable nets. Then after lining out two courts in the parking lot, they started practice. Within ten years, the program had produced four state finalists, one state champion, and six collegiate tennis players.

Next, John coached high school tennis at the 4A and 5A levels for seven years in Texas before moving on to coach at Tabor College, a member of the Kansas Collegiate Athletic Conference *(NAIA)*. In his seven years at Tabor College, his teams have shown consistent progress. His women's team rose from 7th in the KCAC to 5th, to 3rd, and then in 2018 became the KCAC conference champions. This was the first women's tennis conference championship in Tabor College history.

Not only did his Tabor College teams produce on the court, but they also won the KCAC Women's Tennis Champions of Character award in 2016, 2017, and 2018 as well as being the KCAC's Champions of Character Team for all sports in 2018.

In 2018, Coach Ruder was named the KCAC Women's Tennis Coach of the Year, the Central Region Women's Tennis ITA Wilson Coach of the Year and was awarded by Tabor College as the College's Champions of Character Coach of the Year for 2017 and 2018. In his seven years at the helm of the Tabor College tennis program, his teams have produced two NAIA All-Americans with two players ranked in the top twenty-five in the nation, one ranked as high as # 6. At the conference level there have been three KCAC Player of the Year recipients and numerous KCAC All Conference players.

Printed in the United States
By Bookmasters